MW01052758

Don Troiani's

SOLDIERS OF THE AMERICAN REVOLUTION

Art by Don Troiani
Text by James L. Kochan

Additional contributions by
Don Troiani, Erik Goldstein, and Bob McDonald

STACKPOLE
BOOKS

Published by
STACKPOLE BOOKS
5067 Ritter Road
Mechanicsburg, PA 17055
www.stackpolebooks.com

Printed in China

10 9 8 7 6 5 4 3

FIRST EDITION

For free information about the artwork and limited edition prints of Don Troiani, contact:

Historical Art Prints
P.O. Box 660
Southbury, CT 06488
203-262-6560
www.historicalartprints.com

For information on licensing images in this book, visit www.historicalimagebank.com

Library of Congress Cataloging-in-Publication Data

Troiani, Don.
Don Troiani's soldiers of the American Revolution / text by Don Troiani and James L. Kochan ; art by Don Troiani. — 1st ed.
p. cm.
Includes bibliographical references.
ISBN-13: 978-0-8117-3323-6
ISBN-10: 0-8117-3323-8
1. United States—History—Revolution, 1775–1783—American forces—Pictorial works. 2. United States—History—Revolution, 1775–1783—British forces—Pictorial works. 3. United States—History—Revolution, 1775–1783—Equipment and supplies—Pictorial works. 4. United States. Continental Army—Uniforms—Pictorial works. 5. Great Britain. Army—Uniforms—History—18th century—Pictorial works. 6. Soldiers—United States—History—18th century—Pictorial works. 7. Soldiers—Great Britain—History—18th century—Pictorial works.
I. Kochan, James, 1958– II. Title.

E251.T76 2006
973.3—dc22

2006008123

Dedicated to my father,
Technical Sergeant Dominick H. Troiani (1916–2005),
258th Field Artillery, HQ Company, 95th Infantry Division,
who served his country in France and Germany, 1944–45,

AND

to the heroes of the Revolution
who fought and died to forge this nation
and the gallant servicemen and women
who continue to defend our country.

CONTENTS

The Patriots and Their Allies

PREFACE

When *Soldiers in America* was first published in 1998, I was disappointed that, because of the broad span of time encompassed, we could not give the Revolution—my favorite era—more coverage. Browsing the shops at historic sites recently, I realized there were few affordable books on this important topic and even fewer with really clear color photographs of period artifacts. Stackpole Books agreed and decided to reprint the Revolutionary War chapter from *Soldiers in America* as a modestly expanded softbound volume. However, once the project got underway and the opportunity to include so many additional interesting items arose, it quickly became apparent that the book would have to be a larger hardbound. Fortunately, there was a deadline—or I'd still be adding more artifacts!

We have expanded the original Revolutionary War chapter from *Soldiers in America*, adding new artwork and photographs of relics, many of which have never been seen before. The original black-and-white photography has been completely redone in color, and the text has been updated to reflect new discoveries that have come to light since 1998. While this work is hardly meant to be the final word on any topic, I do hope it provides an overview of how a typical soldier in both armies appeared and illustrates some of the arms and equipage they used. Hopefully, this book will cultivate interest with young readers yet still offer fruitful information for serious students of the Revolution as well.

In this vein the reader will note there are no footnotes. Since the original volume did not have them and most of the artifacts speak for themselves, we have dispensed with them here and used the limited space to show more illustrations. Much of the documentation will be covered exhaustively by leading authority James L. Kochan in a forthcoming scholarly work on Revolutionary War uniforms and accoutrements. I'd like to thank Jim for generously contributing his immense knowledge, writing talent, and research to this new book. Special thanks, as well, to contributing authors Erik Goldstein and Bob McDonald, who, as always, were ready to help in every way. My old friend in collecting, Col. J. Craig Nannos, provided much invaluable support. To my charming wife, Donna, who had to hear about this project almost everyday but always remained cheerful, I give my most special thanks.

Don Troiani
Southbury, Connecticut

ACKNOWLEDGMENTS

For their generous assistance, I am grateful to Amy Northrup-Adamo, Lawrence E. Babbits, Herman Benninghoff, Richard Boyd, Christopher Bryant, Vincent Capone, Don Carroll, Rene Chartrand, Candee Cochran, Michael Comeau, Henry Cooke IV, Robin Feret, Scott Ferriss, Chris Fox, Fred Gaede, Pam Guthman, Penny Guthman, Scott Guthman, the late William H. Guthman, Bruce Herman, Steven Hill, Karen Hudson, Ed Hurley, Les Jensen, Timothy Jones, Dr. Rex Kessler, Ross Kimmel, Frank Kravic, Susan Greendyke-Lachevre, Bob McDonald, Michael J. McAfee, Richard C. Malley, Philip Mead, Mike O'Donnell, Dean Nelson, George C. Neumann, Kate Nittolo, Robert Nittolo, Donna O'Brien, Col. J. Craig Nannos, Steve Rogers, Bob Sadler, Charles Salerno, Eric Schnitzer, Dr. Susan P Schoelwer, Joseph Seymour, Anthony Wayne Tommel, Richard Ulbrich, Dan Umstead, and Stephen Wood.

I also owe thanks to the following institutions: American Revolution Center, Colonial Dames, Connecticut Historical Society Museum Hartford Connecticut, Connecticut Museum of History, First Troop of the Philadelphia City Cavalry, Fort Ticonderoga, Massachusetts State Archives, New Hampshire Historical Society, Fraunces Tavern ® Museum, Sons of the Revolution in the State of N.Y., New York Historical Society, Old Boston State House, Oneida Indian Nation, Pennsylvania Historical Society, Fort Stanwix National Monument, The West Point Museum at the United States Military Academy, Yorktown National Battlefield, The Military and Historical Image Bank, and National Museums of Scotland.

Don Troiani
Southbury, Connecticut

INTRODUCTION

The experience of both British and American troops in North America during the French and Indian War contributed significantly to changes in military tactics, weaponry, and military dress by the opening of the Revolutionary War. Earlier wilderness campaigning experience in the forests, waterways, and mountains of the Adirondack and Trans-Allegheny frontiers had made a significant impact on senior British military officers such as Sir Thomas Gage and Sir William Howe, who were now engaged in suppressing the rebellious thirteen colonies along the eastern seaboard. Light infantry companies had been reestablished in all British infantry regiments during 1771–72, and camps of instruction were established in England and Ireland to train the companies to work together on the battalion level in the conduct of irregular warfare. The value of light cavalry had been firmly established on the plains of Europe in the earlier conflict, and light dragoon regiments were now a standing feature of the British and Irish military establishments. Though the Board of Ordnance had been reticent about the adoption of rifled military arms, the stellar performance of Virginia, Maryland, and Pennsylvania rifle companies against the British during the first year of the rebellion soon brought about a change in thought, and by 1776, British gunmakers were producing both muzzleloading and breechloading (Ferguson) rifles for use by British and Loyalist corps in America.

Even before the outbreak of hostilities, volunteer companies were formed throughout the colonies, augmenting the handful of uniformed "ancient" corps already extant in the various colonies, such as the Ancient and Honorable Artillery Company of Boston or the Albany Grenadiers. Most of these new corps readily adopted the short coats or coatees characteristic of the light infantry and adopted names such as the Salem Rangers, Charleston Light Infantry, or the Philadelphia Associators (which boasted four uniformed battalions by 1774). The rage militaire spilled into the western counties of Virginia, Pennsylvania, and North Carolina, whose companies adopted cheap uniforms consisting of linen hunting shirts and trousers dyed a uniform color or trimmed with a contrasting fringe. Gen. George Washington would recommend these simple and economical hunting shirts and overalls as the stopgap uniform for the entire Continental Army during 1776 (although this was never fully achieved). Military arms, including muskets, bayonets, and swords, were imported from Europe while local gunsmiths began producing American copies of British muskets following Committee of Safety specifications.

Sir William Howe, who had assumed command of the British forces in North America by 1776, adopted a loose-order, two-rank formation for tactical deployment that had first been used in the forests of New York during the French and Indian War. Many officers set aside gorgets, sashes, and epaulettes to avoid the particular notice of American sharpshooters and even removed the metallic lace or embroidery from their coats to further lengthen their chances of survival. Similarly, British regiments began altering clothing and equipment to suit rough frontier conditions before they even landed on American shores. One good example was the Composite Brigade drawn from the three Guards regiments, who marched through the open farmlands of Long Island during the 1776 New York campaign looking very different from how they would have appeared on parade at St. James in London. Their cocked hats had been recut into round hats, their coats had been shortened, and all lace had been removed from their facings. Even accouterments were modified and lightened. Gaiter-trousers or overalls were readily adopted by both sides as a more practical and comfortable legwear than breeches and tight-fitting "spatterdashes."

As the war progressed, however, Washington and his senior officers were determined to make the Continental Army the equal of any European power, both in point of discipline and appearance. Under the supervision of Prussian-born Inspector General Wilhelm von Steuben, regiments perfected close-order drills, deploying from column into line with parade-ground precision. As supplies from France, the Netherlands, and Spain became more plentiful in the last years of the war and the frequency of combat declined, Continental Army officers vied with each other in keeping their respective regiments in martial splendor. Stoppages from whiskey rations paid for half-gaiters and feather plumes, as well as for black ball and whiting for accoutrements and uniforms. Loyalist corps similarly competed with British regiments to achieve martial perfection, both influenced by the ever-correct appearance and bearing of their German allies.

The British Army

BATTALION SOLDIER OF THE "VEIN-OPENERS," 1770

WILLIAM RODEN COLLECTION

Under the protective guns of Royal Navy warships, the British 14th and 29th Regiments of Foot were rowed ashore on October 1, 1768. Under a show of force, the 29th Foot marched through the town and encamped on Boston Common, where they quickly began erecting a military tent city on the public green. To enforce the collection of importation taxes imposed by the Stamp Act, Boston had been placed under military occupation, but this enforced peace would not last. While the troops settled into their military routines, the emboldened townspeople initiated their own sporadic campaign of opposition to the occupation by petition, verbal abuse, and, finally, random assault with fists, sticks, garbage, and cinders. Off-duty soldiers wisely began to visit shops, alehouses, and "pleasure gardens" in small groups for self-protection, as brawling between civilians and troops became a mounting problem. Tension escalated in 1770 as the "jetsam and floatsam" of the town faced

Cartridge Pouch

Although large, this older-fashioned British cartridge pouch held a narrow, wooden block drilled for only nineteen .75 caliber cartridges. Probably made in the early 1760s and fitted with three large brass-frame buckles with brass tines, the buff shoulder strap was later updated to conform to the 1768 Royal Warrant by removing the breast buckle, plugging the tine holes, and pipe-claying the leather white. Several examples of this exact pattern buckle have been recovered from Revolutionary sites in the Lake Champlain Valley.

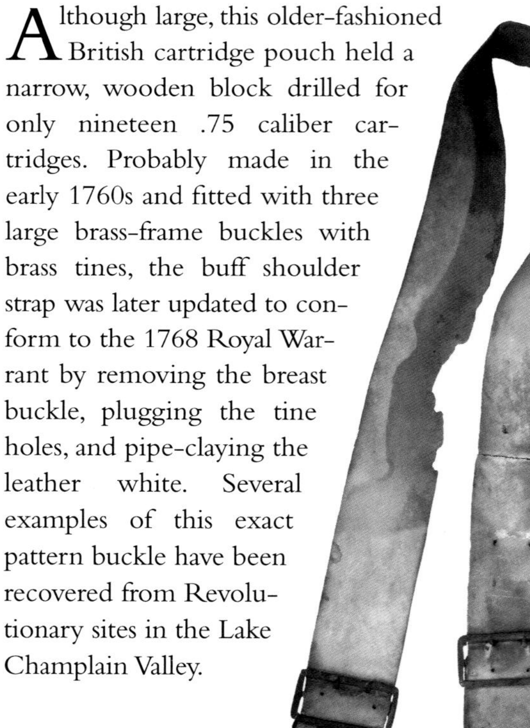

TROIANI COLLECTION

off against "lobsterbacks" of similar backgrounds. An off-duty soldier of the 29th was brutally beaten by a mob, leading to a series of fights that finally resulted in the "fatal fifth of March." On that day, seven soldiers from the 29th under Capt. William Preston fired into a large mob after provocation by insult and outright assault with ice balls, stones, and other objects, killing three and wounding others, two of whom later died. Following this "Boston Massacre," the 29th Foot was hereafter known to the townspeople as the "vein-openers."

As the 29th Foot was sailing to Boston, stylistic changes in military dress were officially sanctioned by the publication of a new royal warrant regulating the dress of the British Army. It was only shortly before the Boston Massacre that the 29th received its first issue of uniforms conforming to the 1768 specifications, and following traditional regimental economy, it would take even longer for the older articles of military clothing still in wearable condition to be cycled out of use. This reconstruction of a battalion private is based on both the published regulations and eyewitness artwork depicting the regiment in Boston (notably the Christian Remick watercolor of Boston Common and the Paul Revere engraving of the Boston Massacre). It consists of a pre–1768 warrant regimental coat, still lined with yellow and festooned with an older pattern lace first adopted by the regiment two decades earlier. It was common practice in many British regiments, including the 29th, to retain older coats for routine duties and off-duty wear, thereby preserving the new coats for dress parade and other formal duties. His white woolen waistcoat and breeches are of the new style, replacing the red "smallclothes" of earlier warrants. The hat is cocked in a form already outmoded in more fashionable British regiments. His accoutrement belts are of outmoded forms, but altered and whitened with pipe clay to conform to the new regulations.

British Grenadier Cap, 1768 Warrant

Following the French and Indian War, many British regiments began to request royal sanction to change the form of their grenadier and drummer caps from the traditional cloth miter form to fur caps copied from those worn by Austrian and French grenadiers. The popularity of this form led to its official sanction for all such troops, with the publication of the royal warrant of 1768, which specified: "The caps of the Grenadiers to be of black bear-skin. On the front, the King's crest, of silver plated metal, on a black ground with the motto, 'Nec aspera terrent.' A grenade on the back part, with the number of the regiment on it . . . the height of the cap (without the bear-skin which reaches beyond the top) to be twelve inches."

Drummers were to wear similar caps, but with metal front plates bearing the "King's crest . . . with trophies of Colours and drums" and instead of a grenade (unless a grenadier drummer), the "number of the Regiment on the back part," usually engraved on a small drum device cast of brass or white metal. Fusilier regiments were authorized similar bearskin caps, "but not so high; and not to have the grenade on the back part."

This grenadier cap conforms fully to the above 1768 specifications, although the small metal grenade device, originally sewn over the narrow fur edging at the rear bottom, is now missing. Also not visible in this photograph is a large oval of red cloth centered on the back of the cap; this is the vestigial remnant of the earlier miter cap's cloth "bag," or crown.

TROIANI COLLECTION

Neckstock Clasp

The 29th Regiment of Foot composed part of the garrison of Fort Ticonderoga in the summer and fall of 1777. This "male" half of copper-alloy neckstock clasp is inscribed to that regiment and was lost by an unfortunate soldier—the cost to replace it was almost certainly deducted from his meager pay.

FORT TICONDEROGA

British Eighteen-Hole Cartridge Box, Belt, and Frog, 1759–84

The design of this simple set of accoutrements had its origins in the early eighteenth century and continued in usage by the British Army for nearly a hundred years virtually unchanged in form. The cartridge box was a simple, curved block of black-painted poplar or beech wood drilled to hold eighteen rounds of musket or carbine cartridges. A royal cipher was embossed on the black leather flap, which was nailed to the back of the wooden block, and two leather belt keepers were similarly attached to the front. The cartridge box was worn on a narrow belt of blackened harness leather that closed with a simple square iron buckle. A sliding frog, made of two pieces of harness leather, crudely sewn together and reinforced with tinned iron rivets, held the bayonet of the soldier's firearm.

New recruits to British regiments were issued a "stand of arms" before joining their regiments. The box with frog and belt was part of this stand, in addition to the musket with its sling, bayonet, and scabbard. This specimen of the cartridge box is stamped with the GRIII cypher in false gold leaf, denoting its production during the reign of King George III (1760–1820). Nearly identical cartridge boxes survive in other collections with the cipher of King George II (1727–60). Simple and cheap to produce, tens of thousands of these sets were made under contract for the Board of Ordnance until replaced by the twenty-four-round tin "magazine" that was adopted in 1784.

TROIANI COLLECTION

Cartridge Box Badge

A detachment of forty-five officers and men of the 26th Regiment of Foot under Capt. William Delaplace composed the feeble garrison of Fort Ticonderoga when it was captured by Ethan Allen and Benedict Arnold on May 10, 1775. This brass cartridge box badge with "26" in open-work belonged to one of the enlisted men and was found in the ruins of the fort.

FORT TICONDEROGA

OFFICER OF THE ROYAL WELSH FUZILEERS, 1775

PRIVATE COLLECTION

Long before the Revolutionary War, the 23rd "Royal Welsh Fuzileers" had earned their reputation as one of Britain's finest infantry regiments. Known as "the heroes of Minden" for their pivotal role in that monumental 1759 battle, the 23rd disembarked in New York City in 1773 and sailed for Boston the following year. Early on the morning of April 19, 1775, the unit's flank companies marched to Lexington and Concord with Colonel Smith's expedition, with the battalion companies reinforcing them later in the day as part of Percy's relief column. The 23rd fought in more actions during the war than any other single-battalion unit, including Bunker Hill, Long Island, White Plains, Brandywine, Monmouth, Charleston, Camden, Guilford Courthouse, and, finally, Yorktown.

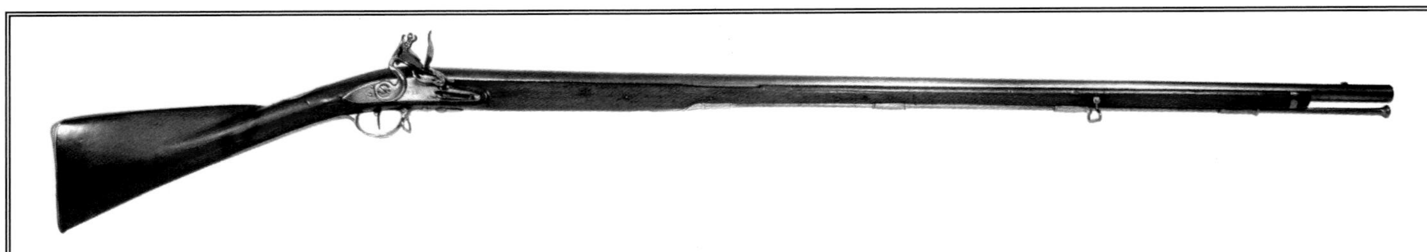

British Officer's Fusil, 1760–70

Although commissioned officers of foot troops were to be armed with spontoons, according to Royal warrant, by the early 1750s some regiments (such as the Royal artillery) were permitted to carry fusils in lieu of the proper polearm. The carrying of fusils was officially authorized for officers of fuzileer regiments in 1770, as well as for officers commanding grenadier and light infantry companies. By 1776 the approved use of this arm was extended to other corps, such as Highland and guard officers serving in America, and unofficially, it was probably carried by most foot officers on campaign.

This brass-mounted officer's fusil by Jover has a narrow-bore forty-two-inch barrel, and the front of the forestock is cut back four inches to allow for the mounting of a socket bayonet.

TROIANI COLLECTION

Sergeant's Sword, Royal Welsh Fuzileers

This small sword has a red-bronze hilt of very robust construction, with boat-shaped counter-guard and a double-edged blade of hexagonal section of "colichemarde" (broadening at the base) form. The underside of the counter-guard is engraved "XXIII REGt. B/2," indicating original issue to the second sergeant of the lieutenant colonel's company. Muster rolls for the 23rd taken in Boston in September 1775 list two sergeants for this company, John Dickenson and William Hillier.

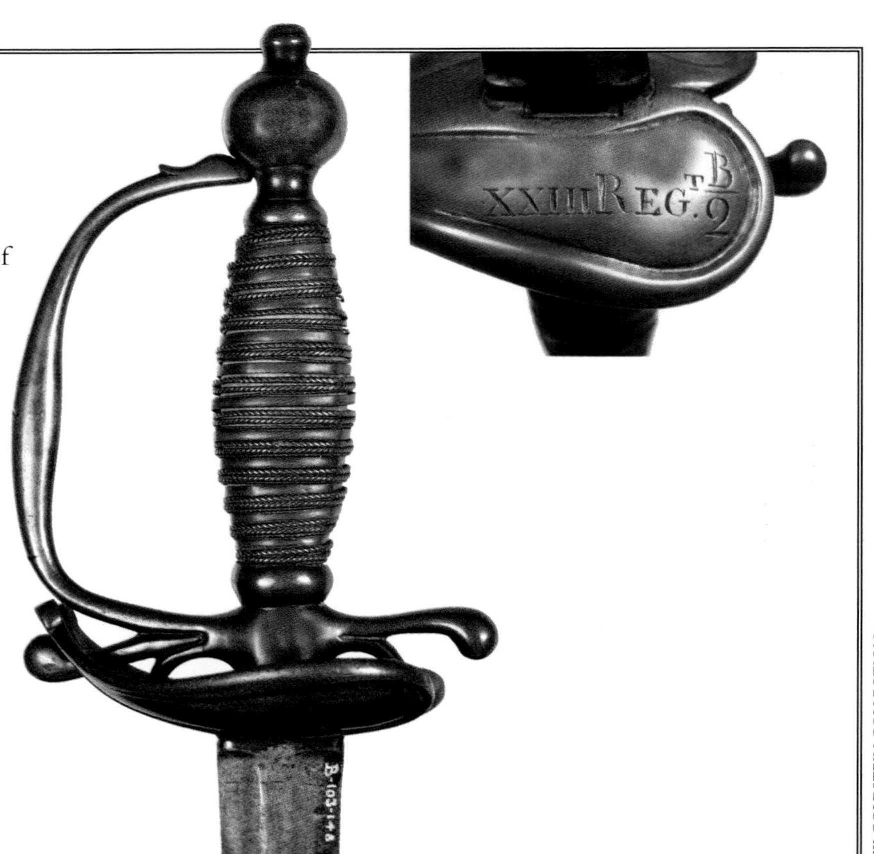

ERIK GOLDSTEIN COLLECTION

As one of the three fusilier regiments in the army, the battalion companies of the 23rd were most easily identified by their distinctive bearskin caps, similar in form but mandated in the 1768 Royal Clothing Warrant to be "not so high" as the foot-tall caps of the grenadiers. Additionally, all officers were to carry fusils instead of spontoons, while their sergeants carried carbines in lieu of the usual halberds. Being a Royal regiment, their coats were faced with dark blue and buttonholes bound with regimental lace of white worsted with red, blue, and yellow stripes. Officer's coats were of finer materials and had gold lace and gilt buttons and sported a pair of epaulettes—a distinction that fusilier officers shared with those of grenadiers. A number of different button forms were worn during the Revolution, all of which bore the numeral "23," the Prince of Wales' device, or a combination of the two.

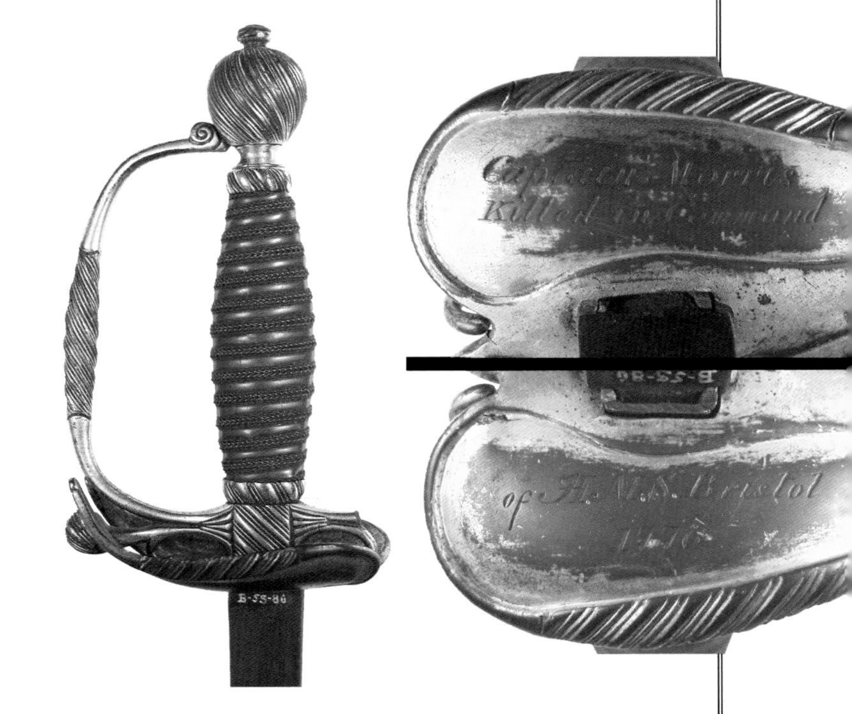

ERIK GOLDSTEIN COLLECTION

Sword of a Naval Officer

This gilt bronze spadroon with a boat-shaped guard, gadrooned decoration on all hilt elements, and single-edged, thirty-inch blade with a single fuller (c. 1750–70) belonged to Capt. John Morris of the Royal Navy.

Morris was captain of the newly built HMS *Bristol*, a fifty-gun frigate that served as the flagship of Adm. Sir Peter Parker during his disastrous attack on Fort Moultrie, outside of Charleston, South Carolina, on June 28, 1776. The *Bristol* was severely damaged with forty killed and seventy-one wounded, her hull shot through over seventy times and most of her rigging and mastwork shot away.

Captain Morris had one hand pierced by small-arms fire and the opposing arm blown off, dying several days later on July 2. His son, later Sir James Nicholl Morris, commanded the HMS *Colossus* at the Battle of Trafalgar and may have carried this sword during his long career in the Royal Navy.

Detail of an Officer's Coat

COLLECTION OF THE COLONIAL DAMES, PHOTOGRAPH BY HENRY COOKE

This floriated "herringbone form" skirt buttonhole is representative of the magnificent silver embroidery work found on the scarlet, yellow-faced coat of Lt. Ely Dagworthy of the 44th Foot. Dagworthy was still serving with the regiment in 1773 but resigned prior to 1774 and remained in America. While the coat still has some pre–1768 warrant elements in its cut and trimming (such as skirt trimmings, as opposed to the cross pockets stipulated by the warrant), the 44th and some other regiments continued to use embroidered holes even after the 1768 warrant was fully implemented. Also, officers in some regiments had "gala" or "court" uniforms made up that featured such embroidery, and it is possible that Dagworthy wore this coat on such special occasions.

British Tin Canteen

This British soldier's tin canteen, or water bottle, includes the original hemp shoulder cord. It is one of a number of styles utilized by both armies during the war. Specimens of this type have been excavated at Fort Ligonier in Pennsylvania, a site out of use well before the outbreak of the Revolution. The artist William Hogarth's painting "The March to Finchley" (1745) shows the foot guards with nearly identical canteens.

TROIANI COLLECTION

Officer's Spontoon

This spontoon (a long spear) was carried by officers as a badge of rank. It served not only as a weapon but also as a device to push men into formation. The blade is inscribed with the owner's initials, "IG," and the regimental designation, "XX REG." The crossguard is now missing. Found in New England years ago, it is most likely a relic of the Saratoga campaign where the 20th Regiment was nearly destroyed in battle, with the survivors becoming prisoners of the Americans.

TROIANI COLLECTION

Sergeant's Halberd

Carried by sergeants, the halberd served primarily as a badge of rank and a tool to keep men in formation, but it also could have been utilized as a weapon if necessary. By the time of the Revolution, they were mostly supplanted by fusils, but some did see service during the war. This example is engraved on the blade with "Cpt. Ewd Blacket," which indicates it belonged to a sergeant of his company. The blade is dated 1745.

TROIANI COLLECTION

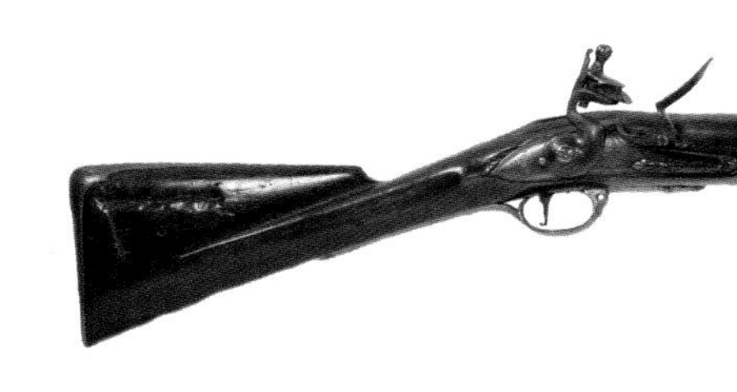

British Long Land Pattern Musket

The top of the barrel near the breech is engraved "47th Regt." The 47th Regiment of Foot arrived in Boston, October 23, 1774. Its flank companies fought at Lexington-Concord, and the entire regiment was engaged at Bunker Hill. In March 1776 the regiment moved to Canada and participated in operations on Lake Champlain. The unit was involved in the Burgoyne expedition, with several companies being captured at Saratoga. The butt of this musket is branded "United States" (partly effaced by a later user), indicating capture and subsequent Continental Army usage.

TROIANI COLLECTION

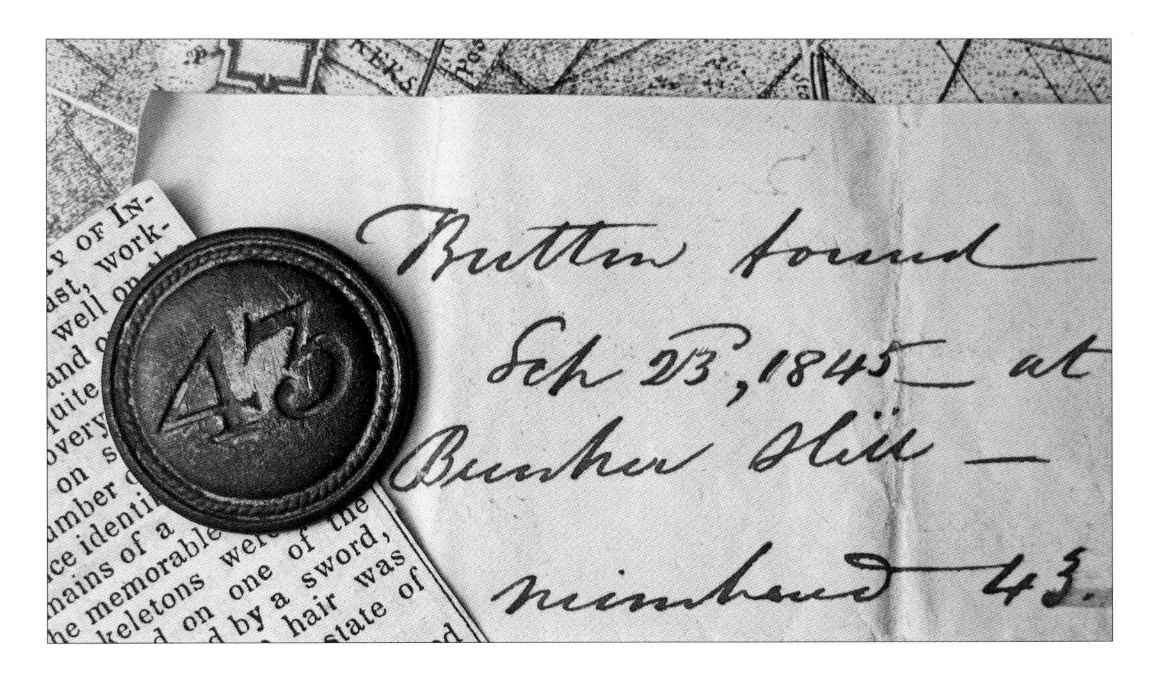

Button, 43rd Regiment of Foot

Exhumed among human remains during the excavation of a well on Breeds Hill in 1845, this pewter button of the 43rd Regiment of Foot was found on the precise position attacked by the British grenadier battalion. It is likely to have been from either the coat of Pvt. William Burrege or that of Pvt. Francis Vincent, the only 43rd grenadiers killed in action during the battle on June 17, 1775.

ERIK GOLDSTEIN COLLECTION

A Redcoat's Best Friend

TROIANI COLLECTION

Brass collar for a small dog engraved "Daniel Munroe, Soldier, 43rd Regt. 1773." Muster rolls confirm Munroe was with the British Army in Boston and died there in very late 1774. Family tradition testifies this item was captured at Bunker Hill by an American officer from Connecticut. A possible scenario might have been that, after Munroe's death, his little dog remained with his former comrades until it ran off towards the American lines during the battle and changed sides.

Award of Merit, 5th Regiment of Foot

ERIK GOLDSTEIN COLLECTION

Commencing in 1767, the 5th Regiment of Foot instituted an "Award of Merit" for soldiers with seven, fourteen, and twenty-one years of good conduct. They were worn suspended by a gosling green ribbon from a buttonhole on the coat lapel. So conspicuous were these awards that a Major Donkin of the 23rd Regiment discussed them in his collected essays, *Military Collections and Remarks*, published in New York City in 1778.

Cartridge Box Badge, 5th Regiment of Foot

St. George slaying the dragon was the ancient badge of the 5th Regiment of Foot, and the royal warrants specified its use on regimental colors, drums, and other items. In addition to the officers' gorgets, the device was also used as a cartridge box badge for the enlisted men. This is the only known complete example, although a fragment of another—with a different pattern and the regimental motto *"Quo fata vocant"* ("whither fate takes us")—was found in a midwar British camp in New Jersey.

OLD BOSTON STATE HOUSE COLLECTION, PHOTOGRAPH BY ERIK GOLDSTEIN

GRENADIER, 33RD REGIMENT OF FOOT, 1776

Arriving in the Carolinas in May 1776, the 33rd Regiment of Foot joined the expeditionary force besieging Charleston. Following that failed attempt, it sailed to join Maj. Gen. Sir William Howe's main army then preparing for the New York Campaign. The grenadier and light infantry companies were detached from the regiment and assigned to the provisional battalions of flank companies that had been organized. As part of the 1st Battalion of Grenadiers, the 33rd grenadier company was but lightly engaged until the Battle of Brandywine on September 11, 1777. There, despite heavy casualties received from a heavy fusillade of cannon shot and musketry, the grenadiers broke the American battle line and pursued them for two miles before halting. The 1st Battalion of Grenadiers again distinguished themselves during the hard-fought Battle of Monmouth, suffering heavy casualties from enemy fire and heat exhaustion. The 1st Battalion and the 33rd Foot both fought during the second and successful siege of Charleston in 1780. The grenadier company returned to New York afterward, not sharing in its parent regiment's impressive fighting record during the southern campaigns or in its subsequent captivity following Yorktown.

Each British regiment had distinctive, colored cuffs, lapels, and collars, collectively known as "facings"; those of the 33rd Foot were cut from the same red cloth as the coat body. Loopings or buttonholes on the facings and pocket flaps brightened this rather austere uniform. Each regiment had lace of a different pattern worn in a distinctive looping shape; that of the 33rd had a single red line running through the center, the buttonhole of "flower-pot" form. This grenadier of the 33rd Foot is in full marching order, consisting of goatskin-covered knapsack, linen haversack, and tin water flask, in addition to his accoutrements. He wears the impressive bearskin cap that proclaims his status as a member of that elite company, as well as other distinctive devices, such as shoulder wings and a brass match case on his pouch belt (used for lighting hand grenades in former days, but little more than a decorative vestige by the Revolution). His waistbelt, fixed with the brass regimental belt plate in front, bears two frogs on the left side—one for his bayonet, and the other for his brass-hilted hanger. After 1768 only sergeants, grenadiers, and drummers were permitted to carry swords in the "marching" English regiments.

PRIVATE COLLECTION

Regimental Gorgets

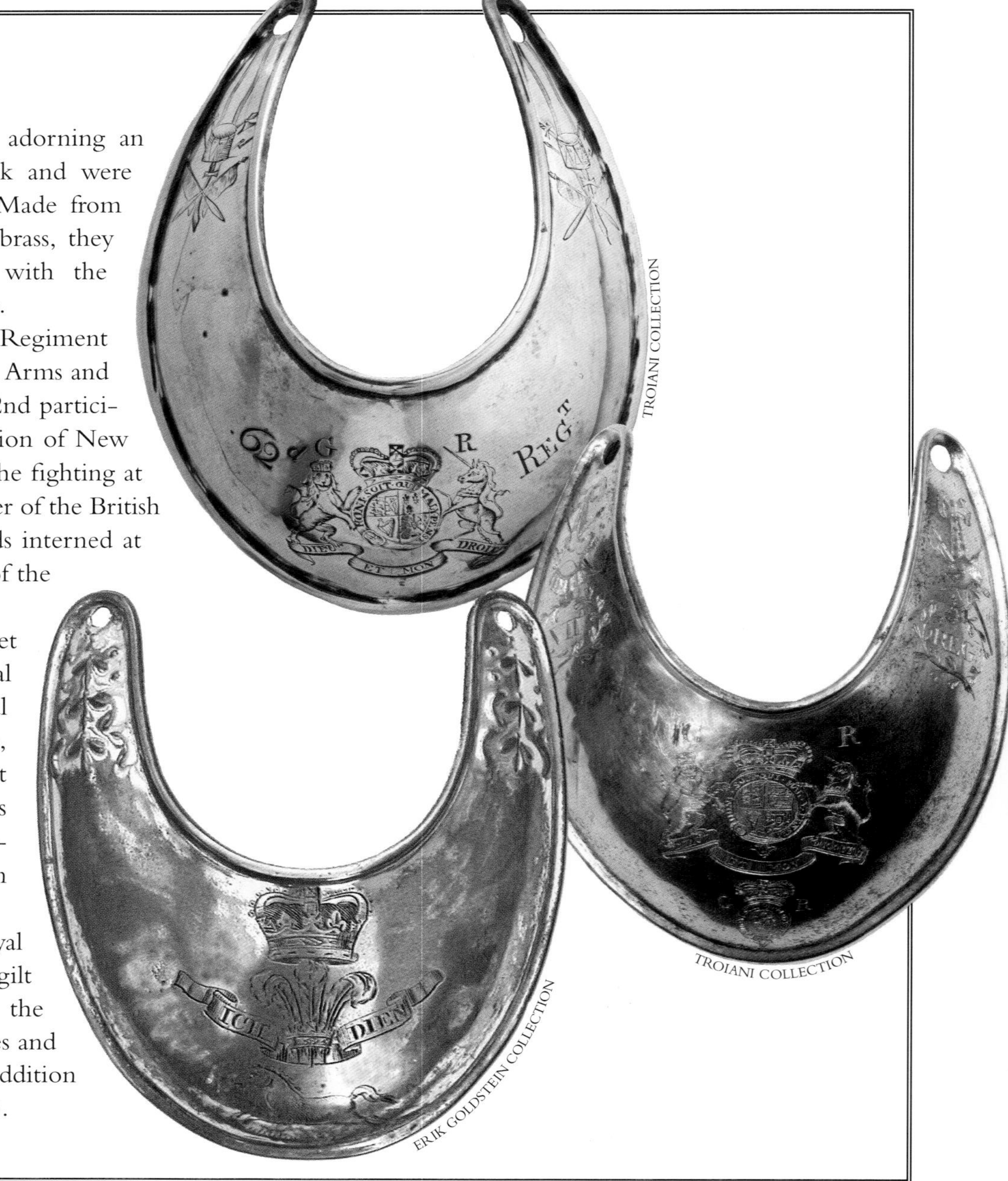
TROIANI COLLECTION

TROIANI COLLECTION

ERIK GOLDSTEIN COLLECTION

Gorgets were badges of rank adorning an officer's hung from the neck and were used as a visible badge of rank. Made from solid silver or gilded copper or brass, they were often highly ornamented with the Royal Arms and regimental devices.

The silver gorget of the 62nd Regiment of Foot is engraved with the Royal Arms and the regimental designation. The 62nd participated in the 1777 Burgoyne invasion of New York State and was decimated in the fighting at Freeman's Farm before the surrender of the British Army. The regiment was afterwards interned at Saratoga and spent the remainder of the war in American prison camps.

This fire gilt brass copper gorget of the 7th Regiment of Foot (Royal Fuzileers) bears the engraved Royal Arms surmounting the Tudor Rose, which is the authorized ancient badge of the regiment. The 7th was one of the two regular British regiments at the Battle of Cowpens in 1781.

An officer of the famed Royal Welsh Fuzileers wore this large gilt specimen, which is adorned with the three feathers of the Prince of Wales and the running horse of Hanover, in addition to the motto, "Ich Dien" ("I serve").

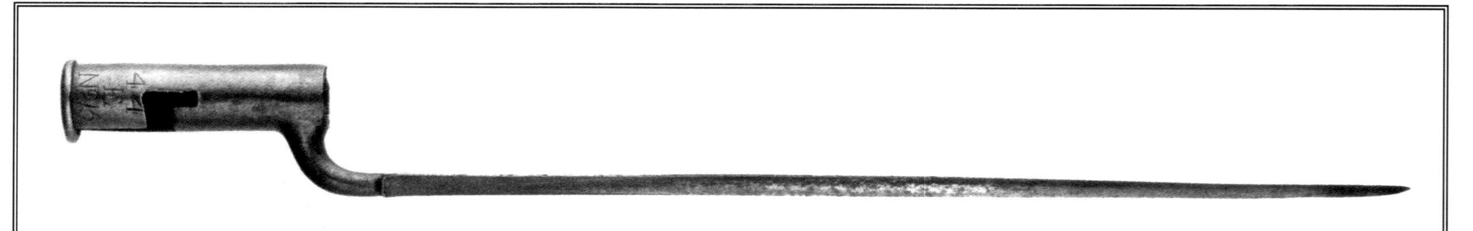

British Bayonet

British bayonet for a Land Pattern musket bearing the regimental markings of the 44th Regiment of Foot. While some bayonets bore full regiment, company, and issue number markings, many more had just the company designations or even nothing at all. The 44th served in America from June 1775 until August 1779 when they were transported to Canada.

ERIK GOLDSTEIN COLLECTION

A Grenadier Officer's Coat

This scarlet superfine coat with green facings belonged to a grenadier officer of a British regiment. Its specific identity is not known with certainty because of the loss of its distinctive buttons. Although the silver-laced "flank company" wings still survive, there are indications that epaulettes were additionally worn over the shoulders, their bullion-fringed ends partly draping over the wings. "Skirt ornaments" at the turnbacks of the coat are "flaming grenade" devices distinctive of these elite troops—in this case cut from the green facing cloth. Among the green-faced regiments of the British Army that served in American and whose officers had silver trimmings were the 5th, 24th, 45th, and 63rd Regiments of Foot.

ROBERT NITTOLO COLLECTION, DON TROIANI PHOTOGRAPH COURTESY OF VINCENT CAPONE

Light Infantry Cap

Superb officer's light infantry cap of an unknown Scottish regiment. The crown of the cap is jacked with leather encircled by three bands of defensive chain, while the leather front plate is covered with black velvet, as is the band or "turban" around the crown. The "GR" cipher and thistles—a traditional Scottish motif—are embroidered in silver.

NATIONAL MUSEUMS OF SCOTLAND, PHOTOGRAPH BY DON TROIANI

Embroidered Device

The king's color of the 7th Regiment of Foot, taken at Fort Chambly in 1775, was the first British regimental flag taken by the Continental Army during the war. The embroidered device from the center of the color bears the Tudor Rose, the traditional badge of the regiment, which can also be found on the officers' gorgets.

WEST POINT MUSEUM, PHOTOGRAPH BY DON TROIANI

Marine Officer's Button

Bearing the device of the British Marines, consisting of an anchor surrounded by a superbly detailed laurel wreath, this silver repousse button was worn by a commissioned officer of that corps.

TROIANI COLLECTION

British Bayonet Belt Plates, 1775–83

Frequently referred to as "clasps" in eighteenth-century British regimental accounts and correspondence, belt plates were used to secure the ends of the waistbelts and shoulderbelts that held the edged weapons of officers and soldiers. They were first adopted in British regiments shortly before the opening of the Revolutionary War, replacing the large buckles that had earlier been used for such purposes.

Nearly all known examples of the plates worn on the belts of the "other ranks," or enlisted men, in British regiments were of brass or copper alloy, while officers' plates were either gold plated or solid silver. The enlisted plates were usually cast brass, with the regimental number, device, or initials engraved or cast on the face of the plate. They were fastened to the thick leather belting on the underside, usually by means of a hook at one end and two studs at the other.

Clockwise from top: plate of the 80th Foot or Royal Edinburgh Volunteers, as denoted by the script "REV" engraving (raised in 1778 and surrendered at Yorktown in 1781, where this plate was found); plate of the 64th Regiment of Foot, dug in South Carolina, where the regiment served during 1779–82; Coldstream Guards (2nd Regiment of Foot Guards) openwork plate with letters "CG," excavated in South Carolina; 53rd Foot plate found near the site of Burgoyne's Convention Army encampment in Somerville, Massachusetts; and 33rd Foot plate, excavated near Saratoga, where a fifty-man detachment of the regiment surrendered with Burgoyne's Army in 1777. Center: oval plate of the famous (or infamous) Butler's Rangers, a Loyalist corps raised in 1778 that wreaked havoc on the New York frontier through most of the war.

Five of the six plates are rectangular and horizontal in form, denoting their original attachment to bayonet waistbelts. As shoulderbelts began to replace waistbelts in popularity in the late 1770s, there was a corresponding change to vertical marking (seen here on the Butler's Rangers plate), at which time the oval form also came into favor.

TROIANI COLLECTION

PRIVATE, BATTALION COMPANY, 15TH REGIMENT OF FOOT, 1777–81

PRIVATE COLLECTION

The British 15th Regiment of Foot, then serving in Ireland, was part of the reinforcement sent to Sir William Howe, commander in chief in North America in December 1775. It arrived in time to join in the unsuccessful expedition against Charleston, South Carolina, during summer 1776 and to fight in the battles of Long Island and Fort Washington later that year. During 1777 it took part in the Tryon's raid on Danbury, Connecticut, and fought brilliantly during the battles of Brandywine and Germantown. In the latter, its lieutenant colonel, John Bird, was killed while leading a counterattack at the head of the regiment. Following the evacuation of Philadelphia and the Battle of Monmouth in June 1778, the 15th sailed with Sir James Grant's expeditionary force to the West Indies, where it served for the remainder of the war.

Before being sent to North America, the regiment was furnished with a "slop" dress to save the full uniform from soilage during its Atlantic voyage and subsequent land-based fatigue duties. This consisted of a short red jacket with yellow facings, white ticking breeches, and "cap-hats"—a sort of hybrid between a hat and a cap made by cutting down the previous year's regimental hats. The cap-hats were trimmed with worsted tape and tassels, as well as a brass cap badge. By 1777 the breeches were replaced by the more practical linen gaiter-trousers or overalls favored by British and American troops alike. This private, seen here loading his Long Land Pattern musket, is dressed in the slop uniform of the regiment and stripped down to light combat order, consisting of pouch with belt and an issue waistbelt converted into a shoulderbelt. With the addition of small shoulder wings to his jacket and a change of belting from buff to black, this soldier could easily pass as a member of the light infantry, which wore similar dress on campaign in both North America and the Caribbean.

Long Land Musket, Infantry Hanger, and Shoulderbelt, 15th Regiment of Foot, c. 1777

The older, standing regiments sent out from the British Isles for active service during the Revolutionary War drew new stands of arms from the Tower of London or Dublin Castle before sailing, as their previous muskets had generally been in use since the close of the Seven Years' War and were too worn for active campaigning. The 15th drew a new issue of the Long Land Pattern musket, the standard arm of the British Army during most of the eighteenth century, its "old Set being worn out & rendered unserviceable." An improved pattern furnished with steel rammer, it was of the form commonly produced from the early 1760s onward, until slowly phased out by the introduction of the Short Land Pattern musket at the close of that decade. The 15th's light infantry company drew Short Land muskets, as did all light troops sent to North America. This Long Land, produced at the Tower of London, is regimentally marked on the barrel and with "XV/K/24" on the trigger guard.

The sword is the popular brass mastiff-head pommel hilt with imitation cast rope-wrapped grips. It is engraved on the guard to the 15th.

The 15th Foot also drew new accoutrements from regimental stores before sailing for America in December 1775. The 1768 Royal Warrant regulating the dress and accoutrements of the British Army called for two-inch-wide buff leather waistbelts bearing a single frog to contain the bayonet scabbard. This rare example of such a waistbelt conforms to the warrant but was carefully converted into a shoulderbelt, probably by a shoemaker or other leather worker in the ranks of the 15th Foot, sometime after its receipt by the regiment. The branches of the frog were separated and then carefully resewn to the belt closer together, thereby achieving a smoother fit against the left hip of the soldier than could be achieved by merely slinging the original waistbelt over the shoulder, a common practice in other corps.

The musket and the bayonet belt came from eighteenth-century homes in Connecticut and are probably "captured" objects from Tryon's April 1777 raid. The regimental belt plate is still attached to the belt.

TROIANI COLLECTION

TROOPER, THE QUEEN'S LIGHT DRAGOONS, DISMOUNTED DIVISION, 1777

WILLIAM RODEN COLLECTION

In anticipation of sending the "Queen's" or 16th Regiment of Light Dragoons to America, it was augmented by the addition of 9 mounted private men per each of 6 troops, plus an additional cornet, sergeant, 2 corporals, and 29 privates per troop to serve dismounted, bringing it to a full wartime authorization of 490, officers included. The dismounted dragoons were intended to act together as a light infantry "division" or detachment under the command of a captain and a lieutenant. Structured in this manner, the 16th Light Dragoons was also capable of acting as an independent legion, having its own combined-arms complement of horse and foot.

Arriving near New York in late September 1776, the 16th distinguished itself during minor actions in New Jersey, including the capture of Maj. Gen. Charles Lee, the second-ranking officer of the Continental Army. A detachment of the dismounted men were at the Battle of Princeton, and the entire regiment served with Howe's army during the 1777 Philadelphia campaign. The 16th fought its final battle on American soil on June 28, 1778, at Monmouth, New Jersey. Shortly afterward, the officers and noncommissioned officers were sent to England to recruit, while the men were drafted into the 17th Light Dragoons.

The regiment's lieutenant colonel, the Hon. William Harcourt, took great pains to properly prepare his men for American service, proudly writing to his father on May 23, 1776, about "the Dismounted part of the Regiment, which I have vanity enough to think are at least as well trained and much better armed and appointed than any Light Infantry in the army." The arms and appointments to which he referred included the Pattern 1776 short rifle, a billhook or hatchet in lieu of saber, and—according to a Hessian eyewitness—a pistol, probably worn in a simple holster or boot attached to a waist- or shoulderbelt. The men were issued haversacks and tin canteens, both with leather straps. Cloaks pro-

A Grenadier Officer's Fighting Sword, 1775–77

Prior to the Revolutionary War, colonels of certain British regiments had established "pattern" swords to be worn by their officers, along with such distinctive devices as gorgets and belt plates. Almost universally, the form was some variant of the small sword, either silver- or gilt-mounted, depending on the metal established for a particular corps. Various colonels, however, took this standardization to more precise levels, some describing in regimental orders the "pattern to be viewed" or purchased at a particular swordsmith's establishment, while others took it upon themselves to acquire an entire complement of swords for all their officers (usually debiting the cost of each sword against an individual officer's account in the regimental agent's books). Typically, a short, lightweight blade was preferred when on campaign, usually with a slight curve, allowing for both "cut and thrust."

The Hon. William Falconer of the 15th Regiment of Foot carried this well-made hunting sword during the Revolutionary War. This silver mounted sword has a shell guard with full knuckle bow, and the grip is black-dyed, fluted ivory. The reverse of the scabbard's throat bears the engraving "Willm. Falconer Lieut. Grenadiers."

During the Battle of Brandywine on September 11, 1777, while under a "heavy Fire of Artillery and Musquetry," the grenadiers "advanced fearlessly and very quickly; fired a volley, and then ran furiously at the rebels with fixed bayonets," driving them back two miles "without firing a shot, in spite of the fact the rebel fire was heavy." The 1st Battalion suffered heavily for their valor, with twelve killed and seventy wounded. Commissioned officers were particularly hard hit—seven wounded and three killed, among them the unfortunate Lieutenant Falconer. This sword, as well as Falconer's other personal effects, were sent to his family in England, and a postmortem memento engraving was placed on the scabbard throat: "The Honble Lieut. William Falconer of the 15th Regt. of Foot Commanded by Lieut. Colonel Bird was killed in the Action at Brandewine Sept. 11th 1777 in the 19th year of his Age."

TROIANI COLLECTION

vided for inclement weather were carried rolled on top of the knapsacks. Belting was of whitened buff leather.

The dismounted division's uniforms were similar to those furnished to the mounted men, although probably cut shorter in the skirts. As appropriate to a royal regiment, the madder red coats had blue facings, with buttons and holes placed "two and two." Epaulette straps of blue cloth, edged with narrow white lace and trimmed with worsted fringe, were fastened to each shoulder. Instead of the boots worn by mounted troopers, the dismounted men were supplied with brown gaiters and shoes. Leather caps of "an entire new construction" were purchased in 1776, trimmed with imitation leopard-skin turbans and "three rows of iron chains around the crown," and surmounted with bearskin crests.

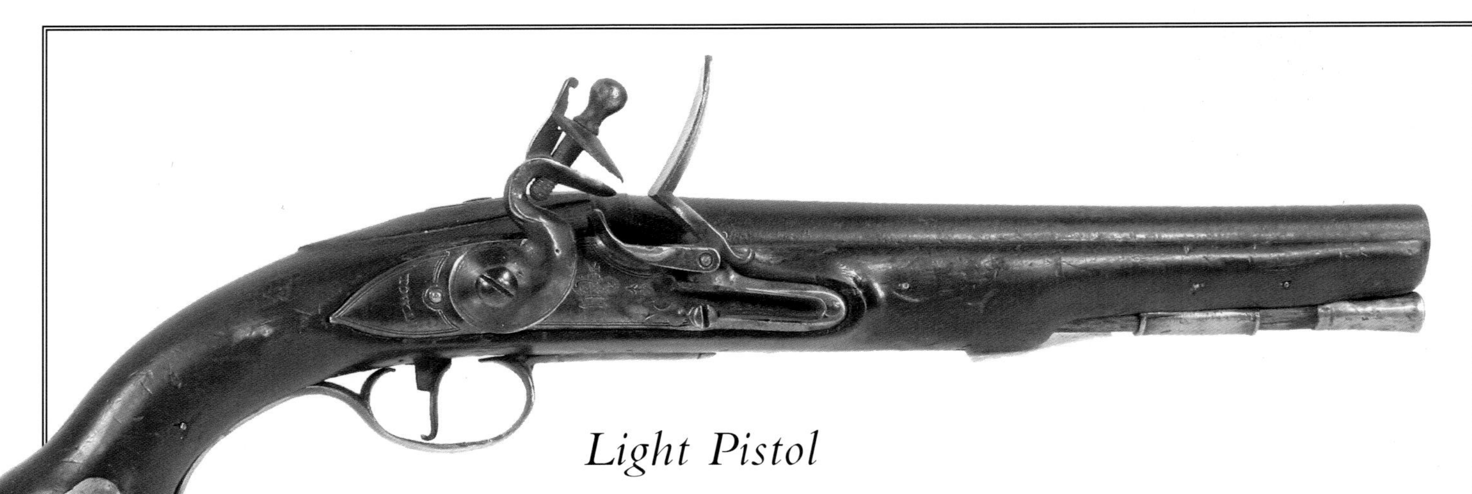

Light Pistol

With the official creation of light dragoon regiments in 1759, the British Army adopted a lighter pistol with a nine-inch barrel. Well-made and popular, it remained the official pattern through the Revolutionary War period and was carried by British light dragoons and Loyalist cavalry, as well as their American opponents, during that conflict. This example is marked on the lock plate with "Tower" and on the barrel with "Q.L.D." for the 16th (Queen's) Light Dragoons, one of the two British dragoon regiments serving in America.

TROIANI COLLECTION

Germantown Medal

Introduced into the 40th Regiment of Foot by its new colonel in 1785, this medal was presented to commemorate its gallant defense of Cliveden (the Chew Mansion) during the Battle of Germantown in 1777. Silver ones were given to the officers, and bronze ones were also struck and presented to enlisted men as an award of merit for faithful service. As such, this is the only general award produced for heroism at a specific Revolutionary War battle.

ERIK GOLDSTEIN COLLECTION

Dragoon Stirrup

Large English-style iron dragoon stirrup excavated on the site of Fort Stanwix. It features a swiveling strap loop at the top and a slotted oval tread. A similar specimen was found in the British campsites of upper Manhattan in the 1920s.

NATIONAL PARK SERVICE, PHOTOGRAPH BY DON TROIANI

MATROSS, 4TH BATTALION OF ROYAL ARTILLERY, 1778–81

MICHAEL FLANAGAN COLLECTION

Grapeshot

COL. J. CRAIG NANNOS COLLECTION

"Grapeshot" consisted of large iron shot placed in a bag of coarse canvas and mounted to a wooden base, with the shot quilted into position with twine to keep it from shifting. It thereby formed a canister equal in diameter to the ball fitted to a particular cannon—in this case, likely a 3- or 4-pounder. This example is painted with red oxide paint to preserve the shot inside from rust. An anti-personnel shot or charge, it was deadly when fired at close range.

In 1773, the 4th Battalion of Royal Artillery was sent to North America, arriving in New York that July. Although small detachments were scattered at various posts and one company had previously been left in Newfoundland, the better part of the regiment re-embarked for Boston and served with great merit during its occupation and subsequent siege in 1775. From that point onward, the 4th Battalion's battle record in the Revolutionary War is unparalleled, as detachments from it fought with distinction in nearly every major action fought by Generals Gage, Howe, Clinton, Cornwallis, and their key subordinates—from the first shots of April 19, 1775, until the close of the war. Perhaps their steadfast and stellar service throughout the conflict is best described by Lord Cornwallis's tribute to a detachment that served under Tarleton at the 1781 Battle of Cowpens: "In justice to the Royal Artillery, I must here

British Twenty-Nine-Hole Cartridge Pouch, 1768–84

TROIANI COLLECTION

Before 1784 there was no established pattern or model for cartridge pouches in the British Army. Procurement of uniforms and accoutrements, such as pouches and bayonet belts, was the responsibility of the proprietary or colonel in chief of a regiment, usually a general officer, who would turn over the actual responsibilities to a regimental agent, usually a merchant or financier, who would then be reimbursed for his troubles by a commission (typically 2 percent above actual purchase costs). The colonel, in turn, would be reimbursed by the Crown at a set allowance for clothing and equipage.

This well-made cartridge pouch is one of perhaps three patterns in widespread use among the infantry regiments of the British Army during the Revolutionary War, yet only five examples of this type are known to survive today. Made of thick, substantial blackened leather, it contained a wooden block (usually beech) drilled to accommodate twenty-nine cartridges. Below the block, there was space for an additional eleven rounds or so, plus musket tools and spare flints, accessed by a pull-down flap cut into the front of the pouch under the large covering flap. The flap of the pouch was heavily polished with "blackball," a substance somewhat like shoe polish, made of beeswax, tallow, and lampblack. When well rubbed in, it made the pouch nearly impervious to water. The width of the buff shoulder belt is 2 3/4 inches, as governed by specifications in the 1768 Royal Warrant, which was not superseded until 1784.

observe that no terror could induce them to quit their guns, and they were all killed or wounded in defence of them."

Since its establishment in 1716, the Royal Regiment of Artillery had worn a uniform consisting of blue coats with scarlet facings and yellow metal buttons. White waistcoats and breeches were introduced in 1772, along with whitened buff accoutrement belts. Campaign conditions in the embattled colonies led to further modifications. By 1777 cap-hats or felt caps with distinctive front devices and bearskin crests were adopted in the battalion. The following year, the battalion's commander approved minor changes, which included replacing the bearskin with raccoon tails on the matrosses' caps—the fronts to be edged with narrow, black binding—while those of non-commissioned officers and gunners were trimmed with gold lace edging and upright, black plumes. By 1778 the practice of wearing two bound shoulderstraps ending in rose knots was established for other ranks' coats, non-commissioned officers' having a pair of gold epaulettes similar in form but fringed. This matross wears the distinctive artillery pouch of buff leather, bearing priming horn and wires, hammer, and vent spike on the strap. After 1779 it was little worn in the field to prevent encumbrance to the men while manning guns; instead, twelve rounds of carbine cartridges were carried in their coat pockets.

Royal Artillery Carbine

This pattern 1756 Royal Artillery carbine has a .65-caliber bore and a thirty-nine-inch barrel with a lock plate marked "Grice 1762." Lighter weight than an infantry musket, its role was to give artillerymen a means of defending their guns and trains without the encumbrance of the heavier arm. This specimen is regimentally marked to the 1st Battalion, elements of which served with Burgoyne's Army at Saratoga.

TROIANI COLLECTION

Royal Artillery Pistol

The Henshaws were a well-established family of London gunsmiths during much of the eighteenth century. One of them made and signed this brass-framed, cannon-style-barrel pistol. The officer who owned this weapon had his initials and "Royl. Artillery" engraved along the side of the barrel.

WILLIAM H. GUTHMAN COLLECTION

Light Infantry 3-Pounder

Produced by the Verbruggen family at the Royal British Foundry at Woolwich, this bronze light infantry 3-pounder was one of seventy-seven of this pattern of cannon cast and ready for delivery in August 1776. Thirty-six inches long, it was light, easily carried by only a few men, and ideally suited for the rough terrain of North America. Dated 1776, it was one of twenty shipped to Canada for use by Gen. John Burgoyne in his 1777 invasion of New York. Note that the government "broad arrow" normally found on the top of the barrel between the trunnions has been effaced, possibly after capture by American forces. The bore and touchhole are enlarged from extensive firing.

COL. J. CRAIG NANNOS COLLECTION

British Infantry Hangers

Hangers, or short swords, were carried by the enlisted ranks of the British Army until they were abolished for all but sergeants, grenadiers, and musicians, by decree of the Warrant of 1768.

The example on the far left has a cast-brass hilt and a dished, heart-shaped counterguard that is engraved to the 59th Regiment of Foot, which served in North America from 1765 to 1775.

The next example (second from left) was carried by a grenadier sergeant of the 16th Regiment of Foot, which served in the colonies from 1767 to 1782. It also is made of cast brass but has a "dog's head" pommel and a grip imitating spiral cord binding. The massive counterguard is composed of two shell guards connected to the knucklebow by a series of branches and is engraved "XVI. Rt. Gr. No. 39." This pommel style is believed to have been the most commonly carried infantry hanger during the American Revolutionary War era.

Second from the right and somewhat similar to the first, this brass-hilted specimen is engraved to the 54th Regiment of Foot.

On the far right is a light-weight, iron-hilted hunting or short sword with a horn grip. It was probably used by an officer or sergeant. The top of the pommel cap is inscribed to the 46th Regiment of Foot.

TROIANI COLLECTION

British Copper Halfpenny

This deeply patinated British copper halfpenny, dated 1775, was recovered from a Revolutionary War campsite. It comprised part of the pay for both armies during the war and was the most common coin in North America. Examples from earlier military occupations show it was typical for these coins to circulate until they were so worn as to be unreadable.

TROIANI COLLECTION

Pewter Spoon

British soldier's pewter spoon found near the site of Fort Haldimand, Carleton Island. Soldiers often marked the soft metal with their initials to identify their personal eating implements.

TROIANI COLLECTION

UNITED MUSEUMS OF SCOTLAND, PHOTOGRAPH BY DON TROIANI

Front Plate of a British Cap

Detail of the front plate of a British pioneer's fur cap—conforming to the Warrant of 1768—decorated with stands of tools on a red lacquered background.

Broad Arrow Cannonball and Axe Head

The British government property mark, a "broad arrow," was applied to nearly every conceivable item, even cannonballs. This twelve-pound British cast-iron ball was found on a colonial campsite in Pennsylvania and bears the deeply struck mark prominently.

This axe head, found near Fort Haldimand, is stamped with four "broad arrow" markings on one side (in addition to a large letter "E") and two on the other, leaving no doubt that this is British government property. Part of the original haft still remains.

TROIANI COLLECTION

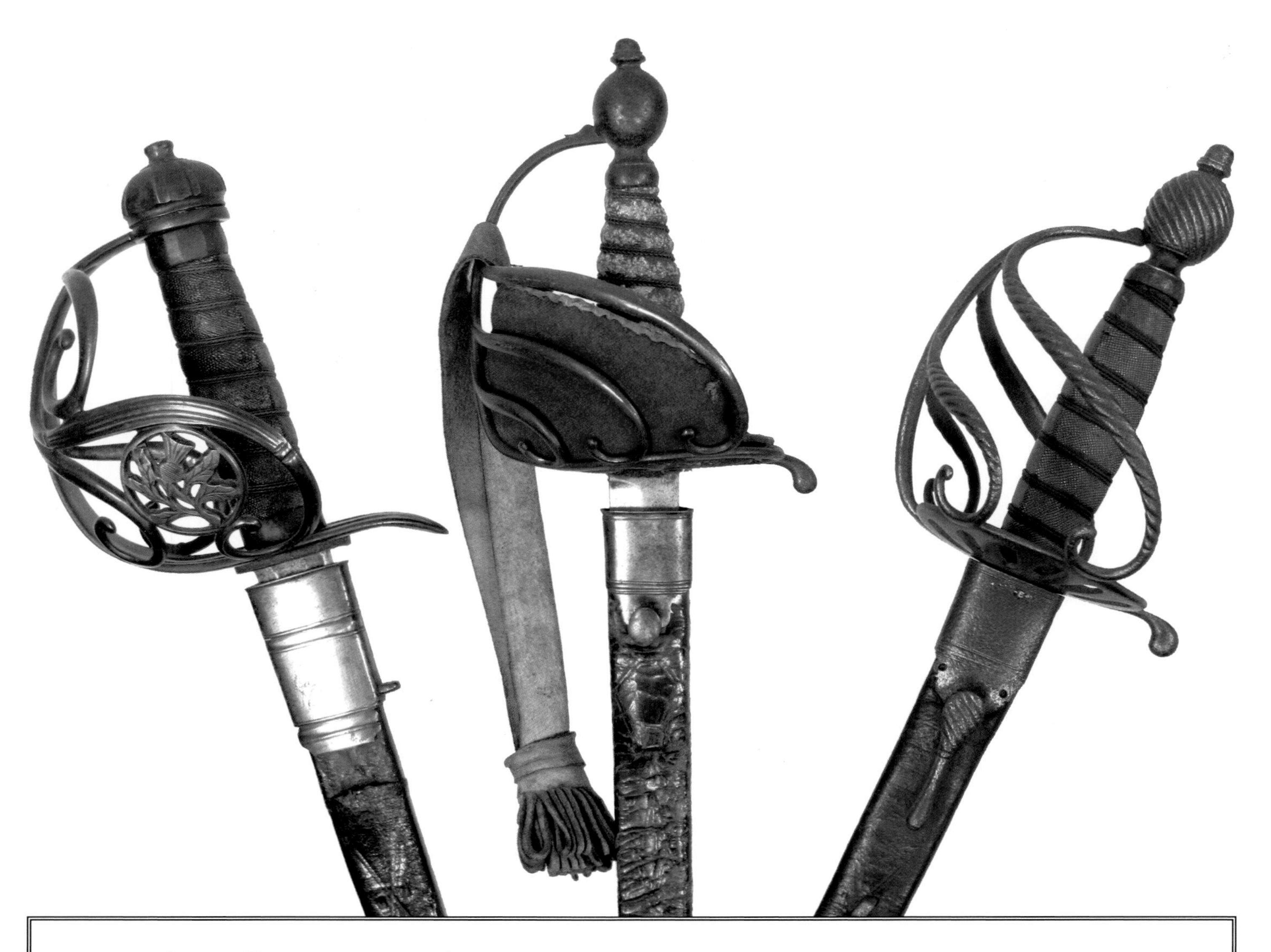

British Officers' Swords, c. 1770–80

While enlisted men in the British Army were issued with plain utilitarian swords, officers were responsible for arming themselves and were somewhat free to choose whatever style weapon they saw fit. The only regulation pertaining to their swords was the Warrant of 1768, which dictated that the color of the hilt's metal match the color of the lace on the coat.

The splendid sword on the left is an iron-hilted, "half-basket" hilt known as a "spadroon" because of its straight, fullered, single-edged blade. An open-work highland thistle device adorns the guard. It is typical of the type of sword Highland officers preferred to use when actually in the field, as opposed to the heavy and unwieldy "full-basket" hilted broadsword. This sword has an attribution of use by an officer of the 71st Regiment of Foot, Frazier's Highlanders.

On the fine infantry officer's sword in the center, the iron hilt is composed of an olive-shaped pommel; wire-bound, white-sharkskin-covered grip; and a pierced heart-shaped counterguard supporting three scrolling outboard branches. The ricasso of the blade is marked "S&G Harvey," a father-and-son partnership that worked together until 1778. In addition, the sword is complete with a rarely encountered buff-leather sword knot and red-cloth, leather-hilt liner.

The basket-hilted saber on the right was intended for use by a mounted officer, evidenced by its large hilt meant to accommodate a gloved hand. Its olive-shaped pommel and its four branches are covered with finely executed fluting known as gadrooning. Its straight, single-edged blade has two fullers, one wide and one narrow, with a false edge. The reverse of the scabbard locket is rocker-engraved "Bibb Newport Street," a London cutler listed at this address from 1758 to 1775.

TROIANI COLLECTION

PRIVATE, BATTALION COMPANY, THE ROYAL NORTH BRITISH FUZILEERS, SPRING–FALL 1777

The 21st Regiment of Foot was first raised in 1678 as the Scots Fuzileers Regiment, although it was redesignated the Royal North British Fuzileers Regiment of Foot in 1712. The Fuzileers was one of the "ancient" and royal regiments of the British Army and therefore entitled to display its traditional badge or device on colors, drums, caps, gorgets, and certain other regimental appointments. In the case of the 21st, the Scottish thistle had long been accepted as the regiment's distinctive device—an appropriate selection for a Scottish corps. Arriving for the relief of Canada in May 1776 and participating in the southward thrust down the Lake Champlain corridor later that year, the 21st wintered in Canada with the rest of Maj. Gen. John Burgoyne's army. It was assigned to the 2nd Brigade during the 1777 campaign, fighting at the two battles of Freeman's Farm before being interned as part of the Convention Army following capitulation at Saratoga on October 17, 1777.

PAUL SCHIERL COLLECTION

The uniform worn by the 21st Foot followed the 1768 regulations, which specified dark blue facings as the facing color worn by all "royal" regiments. The regimental buttonholes were applied "singly" or equidistant on the facings and were made of white lace with a single dark blue stripe along the outside edge. The 1777 uniforms shipped for the use of Burgoyne's army had been captured at sea; thus, while preparing for the expedition southward, orders were given to Burgoyne's regiments in April to cut down the skirts of their coats and use the excess fabric to patch their threadbare coats of 1776 issue. To replace the worn, woolen breeches for the warm-weather campaign, linen gaiter-trousers or overalls were made locally by the regimental tailors. Hats were similarly ordered to be cut down into caps or cap-hats, with a vertical front plate and a crest made from cow tails, dyed a particular color for each regiment. With such field alterations, Burgoyne's British regiments all resembled light infantry troops, and clearly this was the intent, as the men were also trained to march and fight in the loose tactical order necessary for forest warfare.

The 21st, as a fusilier regiment, was authorized bearskin caps by the 1768 warrant, but there is little evidence to suggest that the regiment brought such caps with them to North America. According to a watercolor by a German eyewitness, the 21st Foot wore felt cap-hats during 1777, trimmed with a white crest and featuring a thistle device of cast pewter affixed to the front plate. The fusiliers' coats were altered to closely imitate light infantry jackets by removing the horizontal, or "cross," pocket flaps and reattaching them "long," or vertically. Bayonet waistbelts were slung over the shoulder to alleviate constraint on the abdomen. This soldier of the 21st, who carries a Long Land Pattern musket, with which the battalion companies were still armed, has slung his linen haversack reversed to prevent the flap from catching on brush.

Sergeant's Fusil, Royal North British "Fuzileers," c. 1770

During the French and Indian War, British sergeants frequently left their halberds in store and carried "firelocks" in their place when serving in the field. On March 12, 1770, orders were circulated authorizing ordnance to produce and issue a new "particular Pattern" fusil that had been selected for the use of grenadier sergeants of infantry regiments. This authorization was also extended to light infantry sergeants upon the reestablishment of such companies later that year, the battalion company sergeants retaining their traditional halberds.

This fusil is regimentally marked on the top of the barrel, "ROYL. N[orth] B[ritish] FUZILEERS"—the 21st Regiment of Foot. It is of the pattern authorized for flank company sergeants in 1770, essentially a scaled-down version of the Short Land Pattern musket, with a 39-inch barrel and .65-caliber bore.

TROIANI COLLECTION

"GR" Badge

This diminutive open-work brass "GR" badge was discovered near Fort Ticonderoga. Several other examples have been found on campsites of Burgoyne's army among artifacts and buttons of the 29th Regiment. It may have been worn on a cartridge box flap or even a cap.

FORT TICONDEROGA

Cap Badge, 62nd Regiment of Foot

When the men of Burgoyne's army cut down their hats into caps in Canada prior to the start of the 1777 campaign, at least two regiments (the 21st and 62nd Foot) locally produced small, rudimentary pewter badges for the fronts. This specimen from the 62nd was recovered on the Saratoga battlefield.

SARATOGA NATIONAL PARK

British Haversack and Strap

British Army haversack of natural brown linen of the form used in the Revolutionary War and afterward. Found in New England, it is one of a few examples of this utilitarian ration bag extant today. Each British soldier would be annually issued one of these for carrying his rations, usually up to three days' worth, while on campaign. On the reverse it bears the broad arrow over "GR" device—signifying Crown ownership—stamped in black paint or ink.

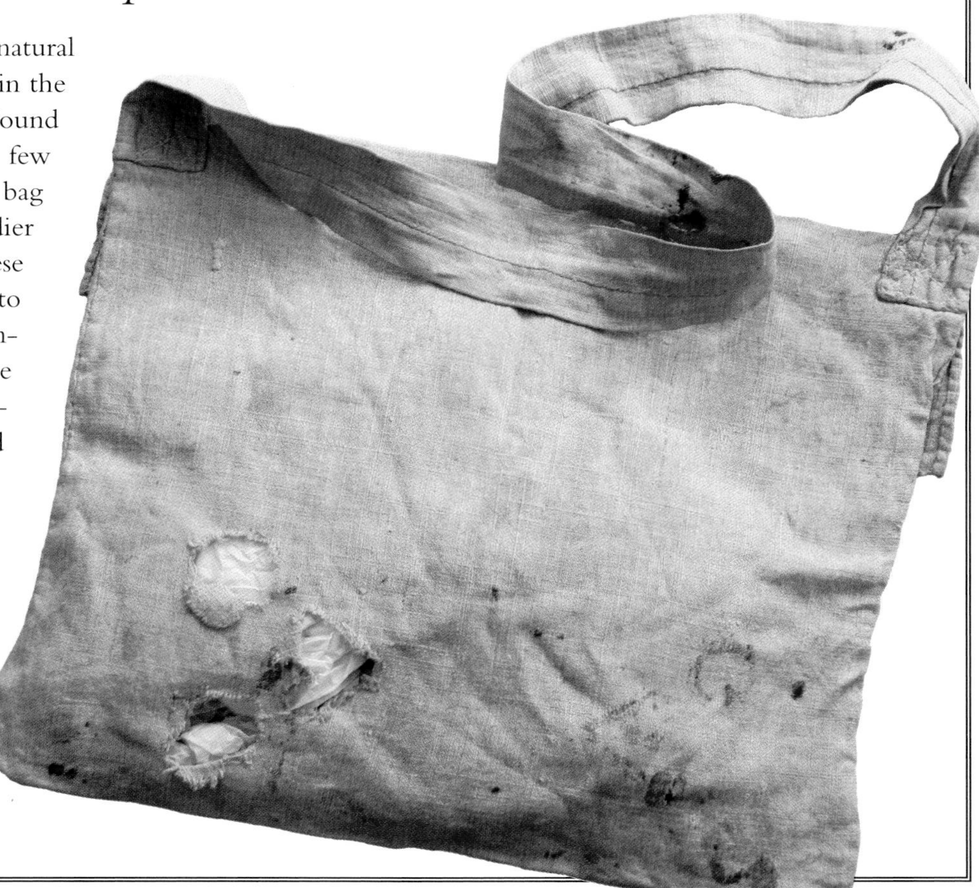

COL. J. CRAIG NANNOS COLLECTION

Short Land Pattern Musket, 20th Regiment of Foot, 1770–77

On March 15, 1776, the 20th Regiment of Foot, then serving in Ireland, was transferred to the British Establishment and ordered to North America. Before sailing, the regiment drew a new set of arms from stores at Dublin Castle. Apparently, as can be seen in this regimentally marked survivor from the Saratoga Campaign, the 20th Foot received the Short Land Pattern musket, as did many other regiments departing from Ireland. Approved in 1768 as "more convenient" than the heavier Long Land muskets, the forty-two-inch-barreled Short Land Pattern muskets were first issued to the light infantry companies reestablished in British regiments between 1770 and 1771. However, it was not until the Revolutionary War that their usage became widespread in the British Army, the bulk of Short Lands having remained in store until the outbreak of hostilities.

Short Land muskets were used widely and with great success as the war progressed, although it was not until 1790 that they fully replaced the Long Land, with a final halt in production of the longer barrels. The various Land Pattern muskets are commonly called "Brown Bess" muskets today, a late-eighteenth-century nickname probably inspired by the natural brown walnut stock of such arms, earlier pattern muskets and marine muskets frequently having been painted black or red ocher.

TROIANI COLLECTION

Musket Balls and Tool

Typical .75-caliber lead musket balls excavated from British campsites.

A soldier of the 9th Regiment of Foot lost this excavated British "turnscrew" or musket tool during the skirmish near Hubbardton, Vermont, in 1777. Its triangular form allowed for good torque, and it featured two screwdriver blades and one punch.

TROIANI COLLECTION

Cartridge Pouches, 62nd Regiment of Foot

This cartridge "pouch" features a wooden "box" or block with holes drilled to accommodate .75-caliber cartridges, eighteen on top and the same number underneath. When the upper cartridges were expended, a soldier could remove the block, flip it over, and access the remaining rounds. This specimen is marked to the 62nd Regiment of Foot and, according to the accompanying nineteenth-century note, was found in the eaves of a home in Boston. Two other identically marked 62nd pouches are known, possibly from the same house, neither of which ever had badges attached to their flaps.

The second pouch, also bearing 62nd Foot markings, was also found in Boston during the nineteenth century and is probably the pattern carried by the light infantry company and/or the non-commissioned officers. Despite bearing a period label claiming it was a relic of Bunker Hill, it is more likely a trophy of the Burgoyne expedition, brought to Boston following the surrender at Saratoga. In addition to the regimental markings, this box also has a regimental button of the 62nd sewn on to replace the original leather button that secured the leather flap closure.

TROIANI COLLECTION

COL. J. CRAIG NANNOS COLLECTION

TROIANI COLLECTION

British Cartridge Pouch Badges, 1775–83

This representative sampling of British cartridge pouch badges reflects the diversity of forms used by British infantry regiments during the Revolutionary War. Cast from heavy brass, they helped weigh down the leather flaps of cartridge pouches when in use, thereby preventing the accidental spillage of cartridges. At the same time, they served to show unit affiliation. Generic "GR" types were popular from the late 1750s through the early 1770s when regiment specific plates appeared, but their use—except by the three regiments of Foot Guards—was officially prohibited after 1784.

These badges were all excavated from Revolutionary War sites. Clockwise from top left: 43rd Foot light company badge, recovered from an American 1780–82 winter cantonment in the Hudson Highlands, probably cast off from a pouch captured at Yorktown; 9th Regiment of Foot grenadier company badge, found on the 1777 route of Burgoyne's army along Lake Champlain; 60th Foot grenadier's badge, found near St. Augustine, Florida; large generic "GR" openwork badge found in New York City; a 3rd Foot ("the Buffs") dragon device, found on a battlefield in South Carolina; and a badge of the 4th King's Own Regiment. Grenadier companies typically favored a flaming grenade device, whereas light infantry badges were smaller to suit the lighter pouches carried by these companies. "Ancient" regiments of the British Army were permitted to place their distinctive regimental devices—or in the case of the Buffs, a stylized dragon or griffin motif in use prior to 1742—on their accoutrements and caps. Badges cast with open work were handsomely backed with red cloth for additional effect.

English Officer's Horse Pistol, c. 1770

Made by Hadley of Charing Cross, this officer's brass-mounted horse pistol is marked "Henry Harnage/Major/62nd Regt./1770" on the wrist escutcheon plate.

Harnage served with his regiment during the northern campaigns of 1776 and 1777 and until the surrender of Burgoyne's army at Saratoga. Paroled to New York City, Harnage was permitted to keep his arms and personal belongings with him. The butt of the pistol was later engraved with the name of his son, Sir George Harnage, baronet and last of the family line, and is dated "Belswardyne 1845." As a mounted field-grade officer, Major Harnage likely carried this pistol, and probably an identical mate, in his saddle holsters.

TROIANI COLLECTION

Scissor and Thimbles

This small iron scissor and grouping of brass thimbles were excavated at Fort Ticonderoga and are representative of the ongoing activities required in the alteration and repair of military clothing.

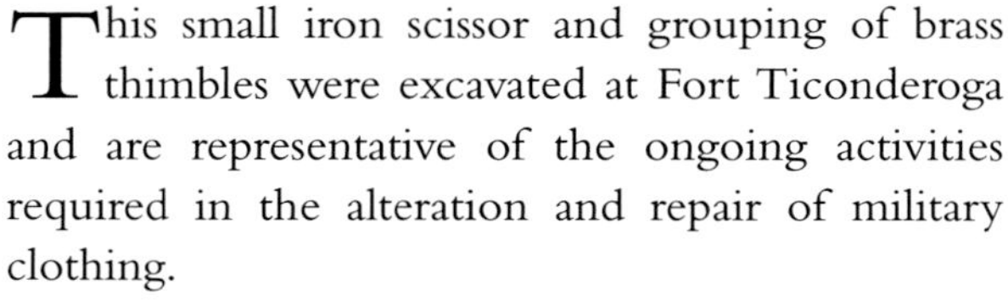

FORT TICONDEROGA

A GRENADIER OF THE BLACK WATCH, WINTER 1779–80

The 42nd, or "Royal Highland Regiment," first served in America during the French and Indian War and the subsequent 1763-64 Indian campaigns. However, "The Black Watch" (as it was also known) returned to North America once again in 1776, fighting at the Battle of Long Island. The 42nd Grenadier Company, along with its parent battalion, joined in the fierce fighting that raged around British-occupied western New Jersey during spring 1777 and in the Philadelphia Campaign later that year, where it fought with great distinction at the Battle of Brandywine.

As part of the 1st Battalion of Grenadiers, the 42nd's grenadier company played a key role in the hotly contested Battle of Monmouth on June 28, 1778—the last pitched battle fought in the North between the Continental and British armies. Throughout that long, hot day—fought under a blazing sun with temperatures in the nineties—the British grenadiers (wearing their heavy woolen uniforms and fully-loaded packs) pushed back superior forces of attacking Americans, until coming upon the main American battle line. There, following a seesaw struggle for control of high ground that exposed them to heavy artillery fire, and suffering heavy casualties from both the fighting and heat exhaustion, they finally withdrew under cover of darkness. The 42nd grenadiers continued to serve with the 1st Battalion for the remainder of the war; they would fight together in only one final campaign—during the 1780 Siege of Charleston.

The Highland grenadiers wore coats similar to those in other regiments, although made with short skirts to allow for wearing the belted plaid in lieu of breeches. The grenadiers' uniforms—in wear since April 1779 and described as "very ragged" the following April—remained on the men's backs until September 1780, when new ones were issued upon their return to New York. Just prior to boarding transports for the Carolinas, the 42nd grenadiers were issued gaiter-trousers of brown wool, which were worn during the Siege of Charleston until replaced with ones of Russia (hemp) linen for hot weather service in May 1780. In lieu of lofty bearskin caps, they wore the same Highland bonnets as the rest of the 42nd Foot on campaign—blue, with diced bands of red, white, and green, trimmed with a silk ribbon cockade and surmounted by black ostrich plumes.

CHARLES HILL COLLECTION

Before departure for America, 392 new "Cartridge Boxes, with Straps and Frogs . . . to replace a like number worn out and rendered unserviceable" were issued by the Board of Ordnance, and every soldier was furnished with a Short Land Pattern musket and bayonet. Their broadswords and pistols were left in store, in keeping with their commander's 1775 declaration that during the previous war, "the Highlanders on several occasions declined using broadswords in America, that they all prefer bayonets." Capt. John Peebles of the grenadier company proclaimed the cheaply produced accoutrements "bad," and "got a Set of tin Cartridge boxes for the Co[mpan]y from N[ew] York" during May 1777. Using the new tin cartridge boxes with the old "belly" boxes, the grenadiers were able to carry the full "50 rounds of Ammunition" per man required on field service during the 1780 Charleston Campaign.

TROOPER, 17TH LIGHT DRAGOONS, 1775–83

PRIVATE COLLECTION

Perhaps no other regiment saw as varied and arduous service in both the Northern and Southern theaters of war as the 17th Regiment of Light Dragoons, one of the two British regular regiments of light horse sent to America. Arriving in Boston on May 24, 1775, elements of the regiment fought in nearly every major battle and in numerous skirmishes in New York , New Jersey, and Pennsylvania. One troop of the 17th was attached to Tarleton's British Legion in 1779 to bolster its cavalry and fought with it through the Southern campaigns of 1780–81. Although once offered the new, green jackets of the Legion, these proud Britons declined, preferring instead to fight in their worn and faded red coats.

British Revolutionary War Buttons

The Warrant of 1768 prescribed numbered buttons for the line regiments of the British Army. This proved popular, and many regiments added special devices as well as numbers and other ornaments. Buttons of the enlisted men were generally cast of pewter, with a large iron shank that was pushed through the fabric of the uniform and held with a leather or cloth thong. This allowed the soldier to remove the buttons quickly for cleaning and prevented soiling of the uniform. Officers' buttons were usually of stamped sheet silver or gilded copper with bone back. These were sewn directly onto the uniform. Often they were of different designs than those of the enlisted men of the same regiment.

The excavated enlisted buttons shown here are all made of cast pewter. Top row, left to right: the 8th (or King's) Regiment of Foot, which served along the Canadian and western frontiers throughout the war; the 9th Regiment of Foot, which used a simple motif of a broken circle and Roman numerals; the 10th Regiment of Foot, which participated in the first engagements of the war at Lexington and Concord Bridge and afterward in Howe's Philadelphia Campaign, before returning to England in late 1778; and the 21st Regiment of Foot, or Royal North British Fuzileers, which formed part of the expedition under Gen. John Burgoyne during his invasion of New York State.

Bottom row, left to right: the 27th (or Inniskilling) Regiment of Foot, whose button bears the turreted castle that was the ancient badge of the regiment and which served in the major campaigns of 1776–77 in New York and Pennsylvania; the 42nd Regiment of Foot, also known as the Royal Highland Regiment or The Black Watch, which served in many of the major engagements in the north and south; the 47th Regiment of Foot, which fought in the early engagements around Boston in 1775 and, with the exception of the flank companies, avoided capture at Saratoga; and the 44th, which served in most of the major campaigns from 1775 until 1779 when they were sent to Canada.

TROIANI COLLECTION

These coats, with paired buttonholes on white facings, set them clearly apart from their green-clad, Loyalist compatriots. More distinctive still were their stiff leather helmets with brass trimmings and red horsehair crests. The helmets' metal front-plates bore a white metal skull over crossbones on a black background, edged with brown-fleeced goatskin. This sinister device represented the regiment's motto, "Death or Glory," a phrase the troopers upheld during their many actions. Unlike the Legion light horse, the 17th was intended to serve on both horse and foot and carried, in addition to sabers and pistols, carbines with bayonets.

A Highlander's Toiletry Set

This toiletry set, bound in red "Turkey" leather, was taken as a trophy by acting Maj. Henry Champion, who commanded the four Connecticut Light Infantry companies in the South column during the night assault at Stony Point, July 16, 1779. The ink inscription inside relates: "Taken in Stoney Point Fort, 16 July 1779 at 1'O'Clock A.M. by Henry Champion from Lieut. Duncanson 71st Highlanders." Champion, who died in 1836, remained justly proud of his part in the epic engagement and, every July 16, celebrated "Stony Point Day." The original owner of the set was Lt. Robertson Duncanson of the Grenadier Company of the 71st Regiment of Foot (Frazier's Highlanders), 2nd Battalion. Duncanson had the misfortune of being captured twice by the Americans—the first when his transport ship *Lord Howe* sailed mistakenly into American occupied Boston Harbor in 1776. Exchanged, he was captured once again defending the outer works with his grenadiers.

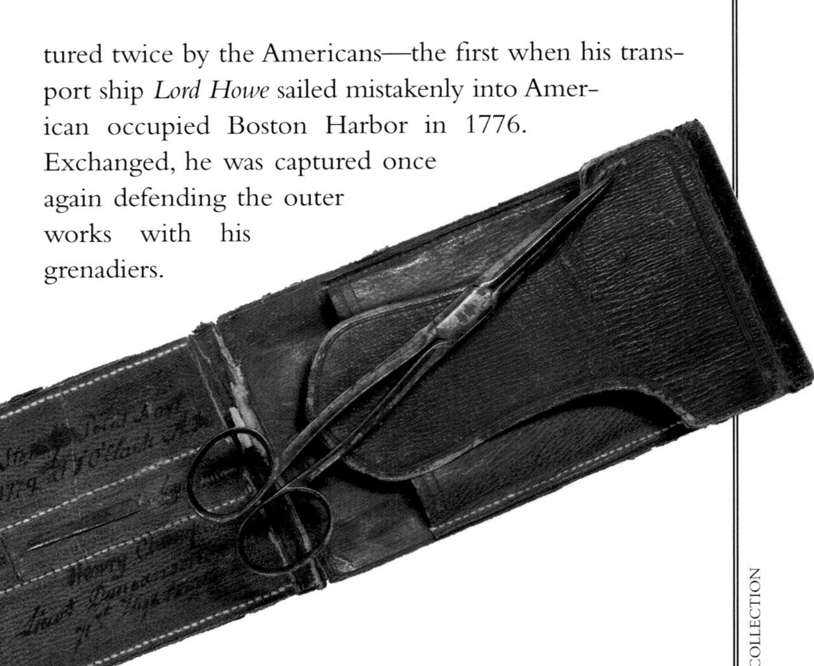

TROIANI COLLECTION

"Flesh" Fork from Stony Point

Among the items supplied by the British Quartermaster General for the barracks of enlisted men were simple kitchen utensils, including large "flesh" or meat forks used for preparing the soldiers' rations. This 18½-inch long "cooking fork taken from stores captured from the British at Stony Pt., July 1779," per its nineteenth-century label, is the only documented example from the Revolution. It bears on its underside a partially obliterated makers' stamp and the engraved ownership mark of the 17th Regiment of Foot, which composed the main part of the garrison when Wayne's Light Infantry took Stony Point.

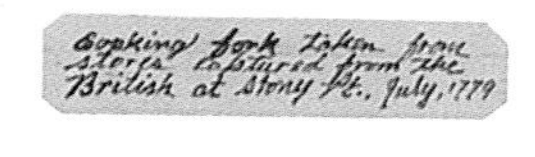

JAMES L. KOCHAN COLLECTION, PHOTOGRAPH BY JAMES L. KOCHAN

Buckles, 37th Regiment of Foot

Brass frames for a soldier's shoe and knee buckles, both regimentally marked to the 37th Regiment of Foot. Few regiments were this meticulous about marking small items, although examples also exist from the 22nd and 29th Regiments, as well as the Guards. These were found at a British campsite in the New York City area.

CHARLES SALERNO COLLECTION

Light Dragoon Officer's Sword

This steel-hilted saber with a lion's head pommel is a type shown in portraits of light dragoon officers and similar to that shown in the monument to Cornet Francis Geary of the 16th Light Dragoons, killed December 13, 1776, while leading a scouting party in New Jersey. Examples with silver and steel hilts are known, the substantial steel probably for use on active campaign. This robust saber has a curved, double-fuller blade and sharkskin-wrapped grips.

TROIANI COLLECTION

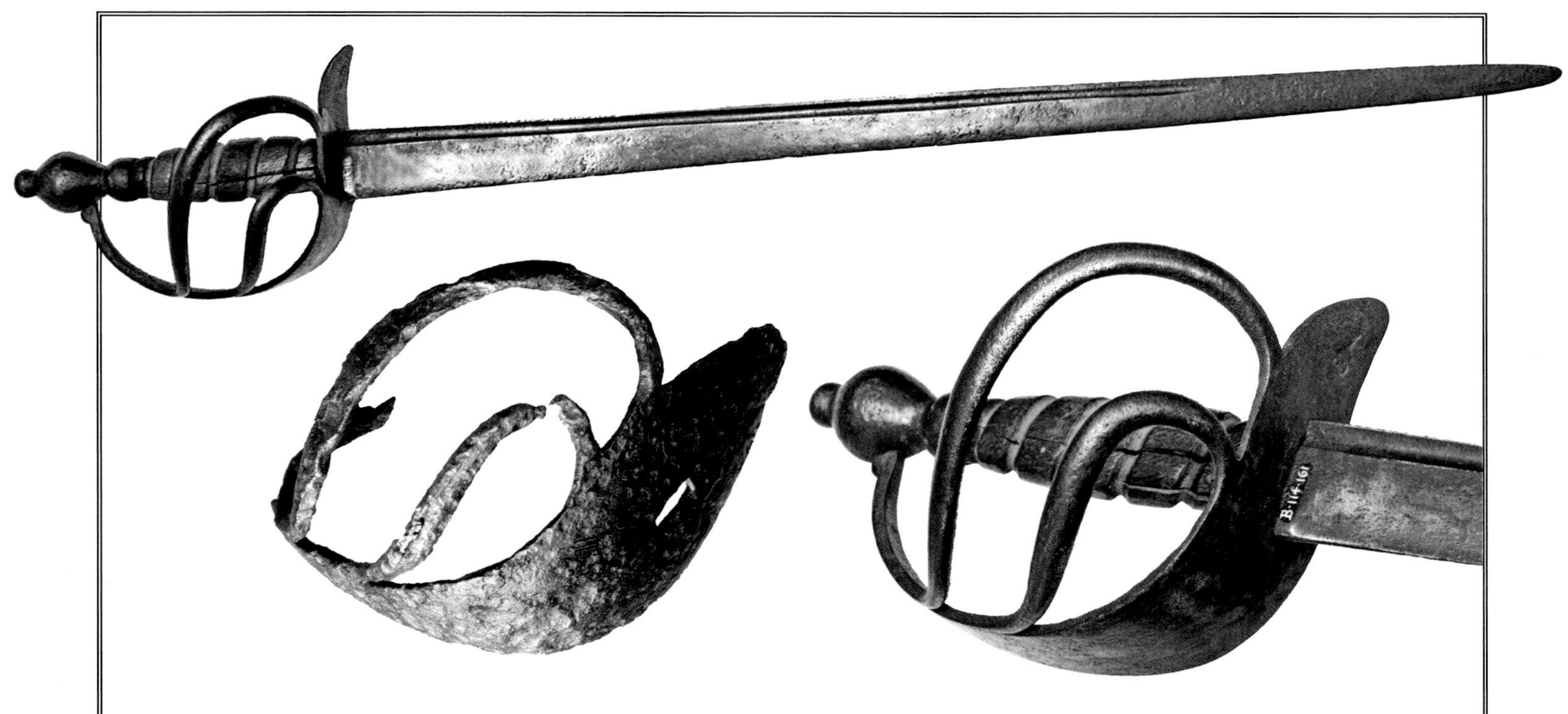

Iron Sword Guards

Unearthed in the 1920s at the campsite of the British 17th Regiment of Foot on Dykeman Street in upper Manhattan, this is one of two identical iron sword hilts found at that location. Illustrated with it is an example of the same sword in an unexcavated state. It is likely that this was a regimental pattern for the non-commissioned officers of the 17th Regiment and conceivably of other regiments as well.

EXCAVATED GUARD COURTESY OF THE COLLECTION OF THE NEW-YORK HISTORICAL SOCIETY (1947.594.); SWORD COURTESY OF THE ERIK GOLDSTEIN COLLECTION

"LIGHT BOB" PRIVATE, 16TH REGIMENT OF FOOT, 1777–81

NATIONAL PARK SERVICE

First formed during the French and Indian War to deal with the French irregulars and their Indian allies, the provisional light infantry formations of the British Army were disbanded with the advent of peace. The importance of light-armed troops was finally officially recognized during 1770–71 with the establishment of a permanent light infantry company in each of the "Marching Regiments of Foot." In selecting men for such service, officers were advised to take into account that as "the Attack may frequently become personal between Man and man, It is therefore necessary to be particular in selecting Men for this Service not only of Activity and Bodyly Strength but also some Experience and approved Spirit." Light infantrymen were expected to be equally proficient in both loose, skirmish order and in the closed ranks of battalion formations, with special attention given to their skills as marksmen.

Clothing and equipage were selected appropriate to the service expected of these new troops. Short coats or "jackets" were adopted, with "squared-front" waistcoats of red wool underneath. Leather caps and lightweight accoutrements of tanned leather replaced the felt hats and heavy buff belting worn by battalion troops. Tomahawks or hatchets supplemented muskets and bayonets of the new Short Land Pattern, the light infantry companies being the first recipients of these new arms. Although broadly governed by the 1771 guidelines, great variety existed in the form of both equipage and dress between different regiments' light companies.

This light infantryman, nicknamed a "light bob" because of his shortened clothing, belongs to the 16th Regiment of Foot. With the exception of the brown, woolen gaiter-trousers issued for winter campaign wear in North America, he is dressed very much in accordance with the prewar specifications for light infantry troops. He wears crossbelts of

British Light Infantry Cap, 1776–98

The standard headgear issued to many British troops during the Revolutionary War proved poorly suited to active campaign service. Particularly unpopular was the light infantry cap, a form selected by the board of general officers that had established the dress and accoutrements of the light infantry in 1771. Essentially a skull cap of hard, "jacked" leather, it had a vertical front plate decorated with the king's device surmounted by the British crown, with the regimental number below. It was trimmed with three rings of light chain around the crown, ostensibly to render the cap saber-proof. The pattern cap was heavy and hot, failing to adequately fulfill the need for which it was adopted—providing functional, comfortable headgear for these fast-moving, lightly equipped infantrymen. On campaign it was often discarded or left behind, replaced by a "cap-hat" made from a cut-down felt hat or by a simple "round hat" with narrow brim. These felt caps and hats were less durable than leather, and frequent replacement ultimately made them more expensive.

A simplified leather cap capable of collapsing flat was introduced during the Revolutionary War. It was considerably lighter and was made of thinner leather, with a soft, easily folded center or crown, as can be seen on this fine original that came from a British collection. This form of cap seems to have first made a midwar appearance among Loyalist "Provincial" corps, notably the Queen's Rangers. Its commandant, Lt. Col. John Graves Simcoe, purchased similar but visorless "light and commodious" caps for his men in 1780. By 1782 the Royal Artillery had adopted such "forage caps" for fatigue duty, folded and stowed in the knapsack when the regimental hat was worn for full dress. They often had a regimental badge affixed to the upright front panel, although this particular example never carried such a device.

TROIANI COLLECTION

TROIANI COLLECTION

Marine Bayonet Belt Clasp

A British Marine lost this handsome brass bayonet "belt clasp" during the siege of Yorktown, Virginia. The raised-anchor motif was also used on the pewter buttons and other insignia of the Marines. The Marines adopted shoulderbelts for carrying bayonets in 1772 and had such belt plates made for them shortly thereafter. Other examples of this pattern have been recovered in Pensacola, Florida, and from shipwrecks at Yorktown and New York City.

blackened leather; a powder horn suspended by a cord is attached to that of his cartridge pouch. The horn was to be used for "loose loading" with powder and ball, saving the fixed cartridges of the cartridge box or pouch for fast firing at close range. It was frequently left in store during the Revolutionary War by seasoned light troops, being viewed as an inconvenience, and its issue was rescinded in 1784.

His parent regiment served in the South during most of the war, fighting with great credit during the successful 1779 defense of Savannah, only to surrender two years later following siege of Pensacola. The light infantry company, however, had previously been detached for active field service in a provisional light infantry battalion consisting of itself; the light infantry companies of the 1st and 2nd Battalions, 71st Foot; and that of the Prince of Wales's Volunteers (a provincial regiment). This battalion "signalized themselves on many occasions" but were captured during the fierce fighting at the Battle of Cowpens on January 17, 1781.

Sea Service Pistol and Sword

With an "iron rib" or belt hook attached to the side plate on the reverse side, the Patter 1756/1777 Sea Service Pistol could be worn on a British sailor's cutlass or cartridge box belt or thrust into a trouser waistband when boarding a ship or working the ship's cannon in battle.

Officially known as a sea service sword, the iron-hilted cutlass with its distinctive double-disk or "figure-eight" guard was in use through the second half of the eighteenth century. A shortage of cavalry sabers led to some of these being issued to Loyalist mounted troops as a military expedient during the Southern Campaign. Fragments have also been recovered from Continental Army campsites.

TROIANI COLLECTION

Death from Above

Iron hand grenades (similar to this one) hurled from the "fighting tops" of the *Bon Homme Richard* onto the deck of the HMS *Serapis* helped give American Capt. John Paul Jones his victory in the hard fought battle off Ushant. This superb specimen was recovered from the 1758 wreck of the HMS *Invincible*, a seventy-four-gun ship, and still has its paper-covered, wooden fuse plug intact.

ERIK GOLDSTEIN COLLECTION

LORD CHARLES CORNWALLIS AT YORKTOWN, SEPTEMBER 1781

In January 1776, Lord Charles Cornwallis arrived in America bearing the "local" rank of major general and commanding a 2,500-troop reinforcement for General Sir William Howe. After distinguishing himself in the battles of Long Island, Brandywine, Germantown, Monmouth, and other actions, he sailed for England in late 1778 because his wife was dying. He returned a year later as second-in-command in America under Sir Henry Clinton and, following the surrender of Charleston in May 1780, was left to hold the South for the Crown. Mounting an aggressive campaign to subdue the interior of the Carolinas and Georgia, he destroyed the Americans' Southern Army under Horatio Gates at the Battle of Camden in August, concluding a brilliant campaign. However, in his attempts to invade North Carolina and Virginia the following year, he came against the rebuilt Southern Army under Nathaniel Greene. Although defeating the latter at Guilford Courthouse, he made a series of strategic errors that left the Americans in control of much of the interior. Cornwallis then invaded Virginia and attempted to trap and destroy the American forces under the Marquis de Lafayette, but he missed his opportunity at the Battle of Green Spring on July 6, 1781. Cornwallis established his main post at Yorktown in late August, fortifying both it and Gloucester Point during September while he waited for reinforcements and supplies by sea.

HERMAN BENNINGHOFF COLLECTION

Cartridge Box Badge, 7th Regiment of Foot

This small brass cartridge box badge from the light infantry company of the 7th Regiment of Foot bears an intertwined, open-work "RF" cipher for the "Royal Fuzileers," the regiment's title. This was one of two found in a late-war Continental Army cantonment in the Hudson Highlands and was undoubtedly a trophy of Yorktown.

CHARLES SALERNO COLLECTION

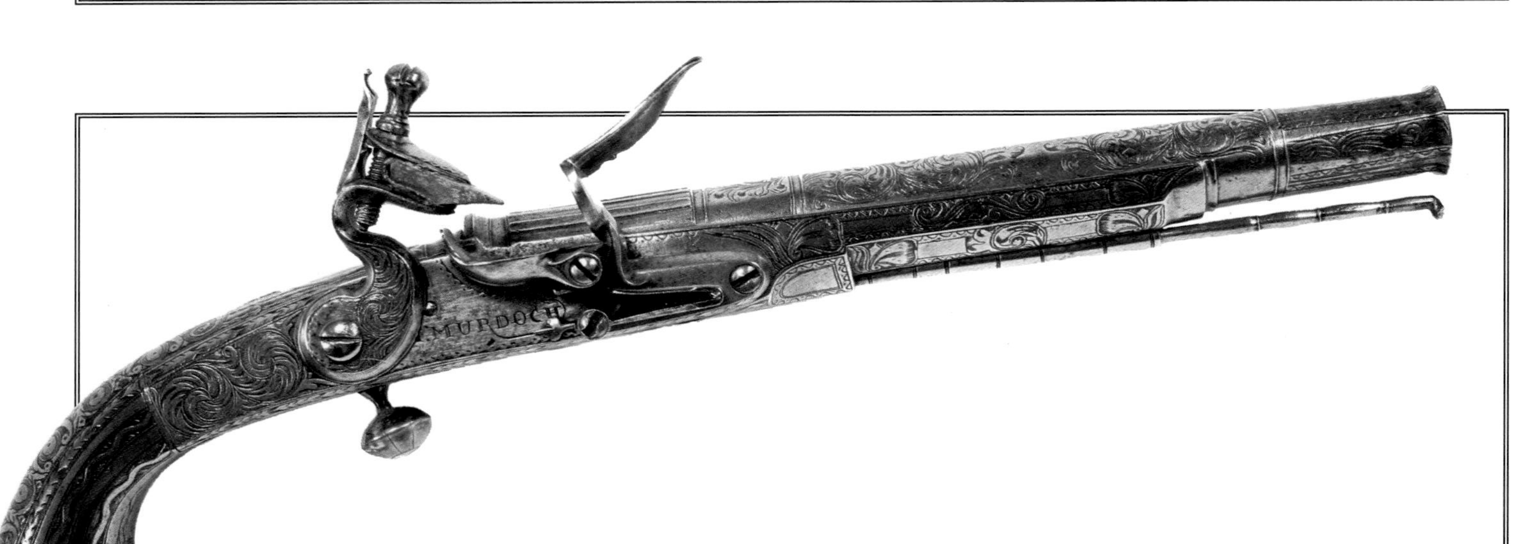

Highland Pistol

This Highland officer's pistol is nearly identical to a pair reputedly taken from Major Pitcairn of the British Marines on the retreat from Lexington, April 19, 1775. Made by the famed John Murdoch and lavishly embellished with the finest engraving and silver inlays overall, it is the epitome of Scottish craftmanship. Resplendent as they were, such sidearms were considered a useless nuisance on campaign, and most were likely reserved only for full-dress occasions.

TROIANI COLLECTION

Cornwallis occupied the home of Thomas Nelson, the patriot governor of Virginia, which served as his headquarters until he was forced to abandon it for safer accommodations during the subsequent siege. Here, he is shown before it in the full dress uniform of a major general, scarlet-faced blue, with gold-laced buttonholes set on the coat in pairs. For daily duties, a similar uniform—unlaced—was worn. Saluting his commander with presented arms is a private of the 43rd Regiment of Foot, serving on guard duty. Upon their arrival in Virginia from New York in May, soldiers of the 43rd Foot prepared themselves for service in the hot southern climate as best they could. Coats were ordered to be shortened in the skirts, and their woolen waistcoats were carried in the baggage wagons, rather than worn in the field. Now in garrison, this soldier is turned out in as smart a fashion as possible: coat, waistcoat (restored for guard mount), and hat are well brushed; his hair is carefully powdered, and the accoutrement belts well whitened; and linen gaiter-trousers are freshly laundered. Once the siege got underway, Cornwallis—never one for such formalities in any event—ordered that "the Guards are not to turn out or the Sentries take Notice of Lord Cornwallis as he passes," presumably because such honors also attracted enemy fire.

Highland Accoutrement Badges, 1776–83

The traditional Scottish thistle appears as a motif in the buttons and other distinctive devices of Highland corps from the eighteenth century to this day. The circular device on the center left badge is the "cartridge box ornament" produced for the 71st Regiment of Foot (Fraser's Highlanders), as can be seen from the "71" engraved below the thistle. This example was found near Savannah, Georgia. On the center-right object is a nearly identical, but unnumbered example worn by the "Royal Highland Emigrants" (later the 84th Regiment of Foot). Others like it have been found in their campsites in Canada and Georgia. This cartridge box badge has previously been misidentified as a "bonnet badge" among collectors.

The heart was another popular form among the Scots, and heart-shaped devices were frequently used to trim the tips of their broadsword belts. This brass belt tip (upper center) of the 42nd Regiment of Foot (Black Watch or Royal Highland Regiment) was excavated in Pennsylvania, and an additional specimen was recovered in the fort at Stony Point, New York. These belt tips have been formerly erroneously identified as "turnback hearts" that decorated the skirts of officers' coats.

The lower cast-brass example has a thistle engraved on it and is a tip from a sergeant's swordbelt of the 84th; numerous plain examples, of slightly smaller dimension, are believed to be those issued to the "other ranks" of the same regiment. Both types have been found at Fort Haldimand, which was occupied by elements of the 1st Battalion, 84th Foot, during 1779–83.

TROIANI COLLECTION

ERIK GOLDSTEIN COLLECTION

An Officer's Button

More than two hundred years of ground action have not dulled all the gilt of this one-piece button of the 23rd Regiment of Foot (Royal Welsh Fuzileers), which was found in Aylett, Virginia, near the site of tobacco warehouses burned by the British in May–June 1781.

PRIVATE, "FRASER'S HIGHLANDERS," 71ST REGIMENT OF FOOT, WINTER 1780–81

Raised and recruited in the Scottish Highlands during winter 1775–76, the two-battalion 71st Regiment of Foot sailed with a fleet bound for America on April 21, 1776. According to one of its officers, the men "were excellent, nothing, indeed, could be superior, for the recruits, having been collected chiefly from the lands of their chief [the Honorable Simon Fraser], were, with few exceptions, young, able-bodied and full of attachment to their superiors, whom for the most part, they followed from motives of hereditary affection." During the dreary two-month voyage, the fleet was scattered by an Atlantic storm, and three transports, containing some of the companies with their arms and equipage, were captured by American privateers and brought to Boston as prizes.

Most of the regiment, however, safely joined Howe's army on Staten Island in time to fight during the New York Campaign of 1776. Elements of the two battalions fought in the Philadelphia Campaign of 1777, while a smaller contingent remained in New York and participated in the taking of Fort Clinton and Fort Montgomery. The regiment was later sent to Georgia, fighting at Briar Creek, Stone Creek, Augusta, and the Siege of Savannah in 1779. Marching overland from Savannah in December 1779, they joined Clinton's army for the taking of Charleston, then fought at Camden and other actions in the Carolinas during 1780. The 1st Battalion was captured at the Battle of Cowpens, while the men of the 2nd continued their exemplary fighting record in Lord Cornwallis's army, fighting at Wetzell's Mills, Guilford Courthouse, and Green Spring, until they were interned following the capitulation at Yorktown in October 1781.

As with the 42nd Foot, the 71st was clothed and armed in the Highland fashion, which included "Highland jackets" of red faced with white. Buttons were placed in pairs on the facings, and the buttonholes were "White with a Red Worm." Instead of the breeches worn in English regiments, "belted plaids" of "government sett" tartan were issued, serving as garments by day and blankets at night. All enlisted men carried Short Land Pattern muskets, and initially, each man also carried a Highland broadsword and steel-mounted pistol. Unlike the 42nd, the 71st resolutely clung to their Highland plaids and side arms, however impractical, until at least 1779, long after the senior regiment had discarded its own. This can be partly explained as a matter of stubborn pride, as Fraser's men were almost entirely Highland-born, while the 42nd had many Lowland Scots in its ranks.

This soldier of Capt. Aenas McIntosh's company in the 2nd Battalion is dressed as he would have appeared during the winter campaign of 1780–81 in North Carolina. His uniform coat is worn and patched, though his white waistcoat is in slightly better condition, redone with new woolen fronts that autumn. He wears tartan gaiter-trousers or "trews" made from his old plaid, although new brown trousers of wool had also been issued to his company. Spare clothing is rolled in his blanket, which is worn slung over the left shoulder in lieu of the red-painted knapsack usually worn for such purpose. Arms and accoutrements have been minimized to the belly-mounted cartridge box bearing its regimental "ornament" of cast brass. On the opposite shoulder from the blanket roll is carried the haversack and tin water flask. His bonnet is trimmed according to regimental practice, with the two black ostrich plumes above his cockade denoting his status as a battalion company private.

The Loyalist, German, and Native American Allies

"PICKED MAN," NORTH CAROLINA HIGHLAND LOYALISTS

PRIVATE COLLECTION

In 1775 a large proportion of North Carolina's population remained loyal to the Crown, many of them Highland Scots who arrived in the colony relatively recently. Recognizing this, Gen. Thomas Gage had already dispatched officers to recruit a Highland corps from among these loyal subjects. With a planned British expedition to the Carolinas in the offing in early 1776, the royal governor made plans for a coordinated uprising of Loyalists to act in concert. The Loyalist leaders called for a rendezvous of their forces, however, before any tangible British support had materialized. Nearly 1,500 Loyalists, mostly Scots Highlanders and some ex-Regulators, gathered and marched toward the coast. Patriot regulars and militia, including artillery, set out to intercept them at Moore's Creek Bridge, just above Wilmington. Setting up earthworks and placing their cannon to dominate the crossing point, they also removed about half of the bridge planking and greased the two stringers. The Loyalists reached Moore's Creek at dawn on February 27.

A group of approximately eighty "picked men" from the Highlanders was to serve as the initial assault force. Lightly armed only with broadswords and the occasional side pistol, their role was to dash across the stringers and secure a bridgehead on the other bank. Shouting "King George and Broadswords," they charged onto the bridge and attempted to make their way across. Their commanders and a few of the Highlanders made it across and were killed before the "rebel" works, but many were killed on the bridge or fell into the creek after losing their balance, where some drowned. Thirty Highlanders were killed and more than 850 Loyalists surrendered following a patriot counterattack; the rest fled, although many were subsequently captured. This charging Scot is representative of the brave "forlorn hope" that attempted the bridge assault. He wears his civilian clothing, which includes Scots bonnet, tartan breeches, and stockings—the wearing of traditional Highland belted plaids having been outlawed following the Rising of '45. He is armed with a basket-hilt broadsword, and an iron-stocked Highland pistol is slung under his arm.

Highland Swords

These three Highland basket-hilted swords of the mid-eighteenth century represent the typical forms Scottish immigrants to the Carolinas and Georgia might have brought with them from their homeland or acquired from prior military service. The upper specimen is a regimental pattern and is marked to the Royal Highland or 42nd Regiment of Foot, also known as "The Black Watch."

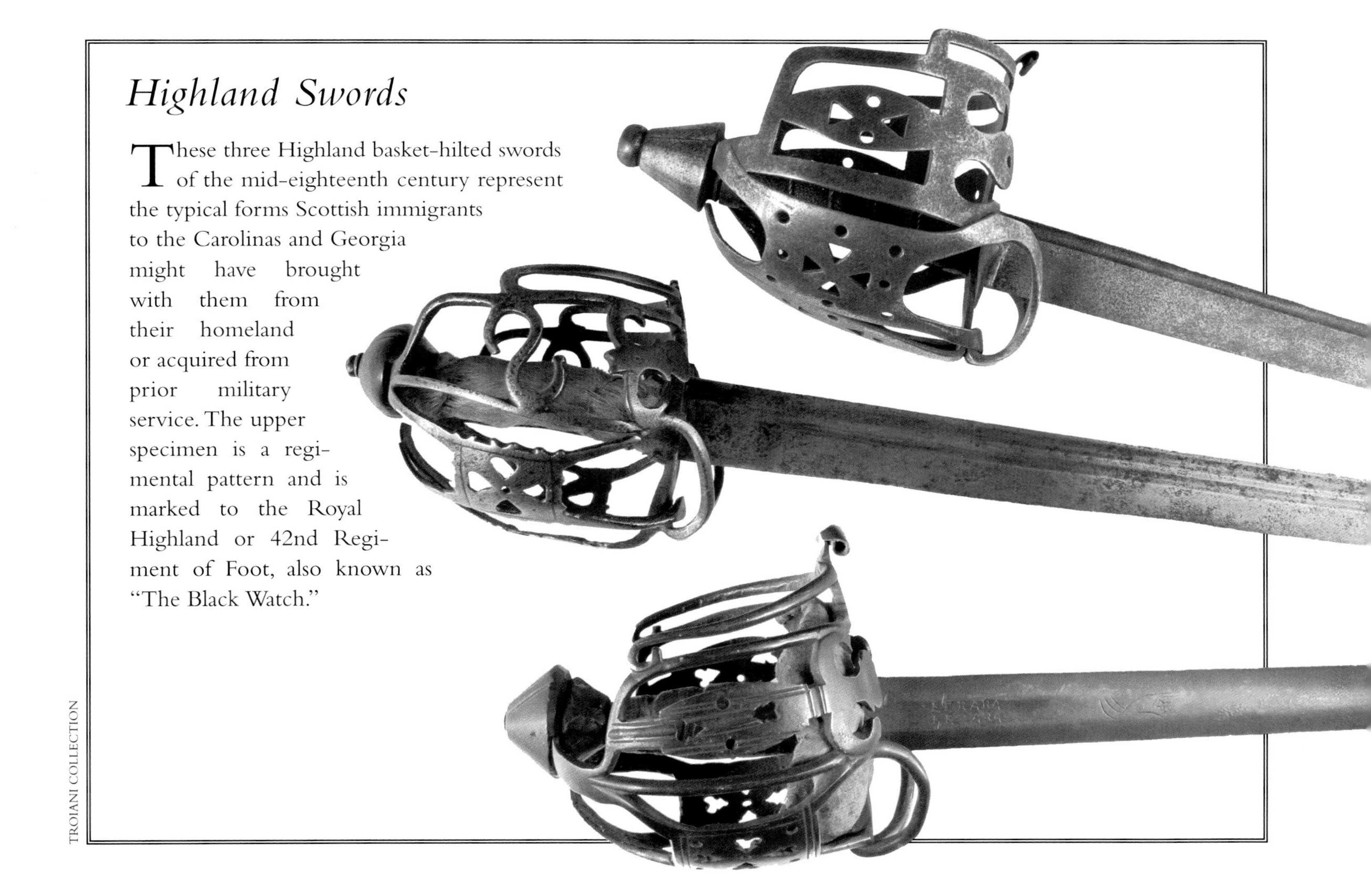

TROIANI COLLECTION

THE ONEIDA AT THE BATTLE OF ORISKANY, AUGUST 6, 1777

The ambush was perfectly placed: four miles from Fort Schuyler, the dirt road through the mature forest snaked down to a ravine (over which a "corduroy," or log-bed, causeway had been laid in the past to make it passable by wagons during wet weather) before rising again and then coming to yet another ravine. Between the two ravines, the road was closely hemmed in by standing hemlock and other trees—broken at one point by a large deadfall created from a prior tornado. On the heights above the second ravine, the light infantry company of Sir John Johnson's Royal Regiment of New York was placed to block the advance guard of the coming "patriot" militia. Supporting the green-coated Loyalists (or "Tories," as they were known to their former Tryon County neighbors) was a small detachment of German riflemen from the Hesse-Hanau Jaegers, also dressed in green. On the high ground commanding one side of the road between the two ravines, their Native American allies—composed principally of warriors from the Seneca, Onondaga, and Cayuga nations, as well as Canada and Lake Indians and some Tory rangers—had carefully concealed themselves in anticipation of the pending assault on the main body of the "rebel" column of Americans. Closing the trap in the rear would be Capt. John Brant and his band of Mohawks. Now it was just a matter of quietly and patiently waiting for their prey during the rising heat and humidity of this August morning.

The approximately 800 men of the Tryon County militia were strung out in a column extending for approximately one mile, hampered by the narrow track and a slow-moving baggage train of ox-drawn wagons and carts near its rear. They had set out from their rendezvous at Fort Dayton two days earlier to relieve the beleaguered garrison of Continental regulars at Fort Stanwix (which had recently been renamed "Fort Schuyler") before it was fully encircled. This strategic post was the gateway to the Mohawk Valley, and if it fell to the invading force of British and Loyalist troops and their native allies, the entire valley would be at their mercy. Setting out early this morning and now reinforced by sixty warriors from the Oneida nation under war captains Honyery Tewahangaraghkan and Henry Cornelius Haunnagwasuke, they were now only four miles from their ultimate goal, and it was not quite 10 A.M.

Suddenly, before the supply train had fully crossed the first ravine, a shot rang out from near the center. The trap had been sprung, but too soon—either an inexperienced, young ambusher's gun discharged prematurely or perhaps it was a discovery-warning shot fired by an alert flanker. In a matter of seconds, the scattered barks of squirrels were replaced by the pops of hundreds of muskets, fowlers, and rifles. The forest was soon enveloped with clouds of acrid, black-powder smoke. Gen. Nicholas Herkimer, the fifty-year-old militia commander, was near the head of the column when a ball went through his horse and exited—shattering his leg and

ONEIDA INDIAN NATION COLLECTION

wedging it beneath the collapsed and dying horse. Dragged free and carried back to a safer position, he continued to direct his men as the battle soon developed into hand-to-hand combat.

After the initial shock dissipated, the militia fought back valiantly, later taking advantage of the tree cover in the same fashion as their enemy had earlier, often fighting in teams of two—one firing while the other reloaded. Resolute Oneida

A Butler's Rangers Silver-hilted Officer's Saber

Carried by Ralph Clench, an officer of Butler's Rangers, the famous Loyalist corps that fought on the New York frontier, this silver-hilted officer's saber is either of colonial American or Canadian manufacture. It has an unusual lion's head pommel, a plain stirrup guard, and a spiral ivory grip stained to the same dark green worn by the regiment. Silver tape winds down the channel of the grip, and a brown leather scabbard protects its double-fullered blade.

After first serving as a volunteer in the 8th and 42nd Regiments earlier in the war, Clench was commissioned as a second lieutenant in Butler's Rangers in January 1780. Later that year, he was in command at Detroit and saw action at the battles of Sandusky (Ohio) and Blue Licks (Kentucky) in 1782. At the close of the war, Clench, along with most of his corps, was stationed at Fort Niagara.

According to a manuscript preserved in the family papers, his wife and daughter hid this sword from the Americans who raided Niagara-on-the-Lake in October 1812. It remained with his descendants until 1901.

ERIK GOLDSTEIN COLLECTION

warriors such as Blatcop moved quickly into the woods, the best defense being offensive hit-and-run tactics. In the ensuing struggle, he broke the arm of one attacker with his tomahawk before dispatching him with a mortal blow; other Oneida were not as fortunate, and the blood of those killed, including the resolute Spencer brothers, comingled on the ground with that spilled by their patriot allies and enemies alike. The powerful Tewahangaraghkan fought bravely—according to one account, killing at least nine warriors before taking a ball in his wrist. He battled on at close quarters, wielding his tomahawk while his wife, Senagena, who had accompanied him with the column, reloaded his fusil for him.

The fighting continued obstinately on both sides, and with the opening surprise advantage now squandered, the tide began to shift as the patriots tightened their defense cordon and fought back with effect. To counter this, the Royal Yorker "light bobs" and the Jaegers mounted a valiant, but ultimately futile, bayonet charge against the militia, suffering numerous casualties. Unobserved during the heat of battle, the sky darkened, and suddenly, a torrential downpour of rain was unleashed, providing nearly an hour's respite from the fierce fighting. Once it passed, the conflict was renewed in a major onslaught against the American positions, which soon boiled down into a series of small, bloody, localized skirmishes. Both sides suffered heavy casualties; ammunition was running low; and the participants were exhausted. Finally, almost as if by mutual consent, the day-long battle ended with the attackers withdrawing back to their camps. While the ambush successfully prevented the relief of the besieged fort, ultimately the events of the day contributed to the abandonment of the siege by St. Leger's army and its subsequent retreat from the Mohawk Valley.

SHAWNEE WARRIOR

Skillful and resourceful warriors, the Shawnee excelled in raiding and ambush tactics. During this period, the Shawnee, like most Eastern Woodland Indians, used a mixture of traditional Indian articles of dress (though often made of trade goods) and European garments, such as shirts, coats, and blankets, which they wore as "matchcoats," a traditional Indian garment of togalike form. As related by an eyewitness who served against them in 1764:

> *Their dress consists of the skins of some wild beast, or a blanket, a shirt either of linen, or of dressed skins, a beech clout, leggins, reaching halfway up the thigh, and fastened to a belt, with mokawsons on their feet. . . . They shave their head, reserving only a small tuft of hair on the top; and slit the outer part of their ears, to which, by weights, they give a circular form, extending it down to their shoulder.*
>
> *They adorn themselves with ear and nose rings, bracelets of silver and wampum, and paint their faces with various colors. When they prepare for an engagement they paint themselves black, and fight naked.*
>
> *Their arms are a fusil, or rifle, a powder horn, a shot pouch, a tomahawk, and a scalping knife hanging to their neck.*
>
> *When they are in want of firearms, they supply them by a bow, a spear, or a death hammer, which is a short club made of hard wood.*

The warrior shown here typifies the appearance of Eastern Woodland warriors of most tribes during the Revolutionary War period.

SCOTT FERRIS COLLECTION

Camp Color, Royal Highland Emigrants

Raised from Scottish settlers in Canada, the Royal Highland Emigrants were uniformed and equipped in the manner of the 42nd or Black Watch and sometimes called the "Young Royal Highlanders." Consisting of two battalions, they wore red uniforms with blue facings and had Highland appointments, including tartans and knit bonnets. In 1779 they were placed on the British regular establishment and numbered the 84th Foot. This camp color is made in the regimental facing color but from twilled blue serge rather than the regulation silk, probably made to replace the original ones once they wore out.

FORT TICONDEROGA

Spike Tomahawk

Meant strictly for business on either end, the curved spike was capable of putting a neat, square puncture in the thickest skull. There are accounts of these being thrown so that the spike was the principal weapon. Other versions existed with an additional blade placed vertically at the top to form a halberd-type head. This object was found near the site of Fort Miller, New York.

TROIANI COLLECTION

TROIANI COLLECTION

Scalping Knife, c. 1779

Found near Fort Haldimand, a British-built fortification constructed on Carleton Island during the Revolutionary War, this is an outstanding example of what was commonly called a "scalping knife" during the eighteenth century. Although the tip of the corroded blade is now missing, the knife is in excellent condition, considering that it was submerged for two hundred years, and it retains its original wooden handle or grip. Similar blades have been excavated at numerous forts, trading posts, and Indian villages throughout eastern North America, and they figure prominently in period artwork depicting warriors of the Eastern Woodland tribes. Bone- and wood-handled scalping knifes are listed among the supplies furnished to the British Indian Department, as well as among the stores of most frontier trading establishments.

Iron Pipe Tomahawk Head

This dainty iron pipe tomahawk head was recovered during excavations at Fort Stanwix near Rome, New York. Whether it belonged to an Indian, a soldier, or trader will never be known, but it provides an excellent example of this once everyday frontier necessity.

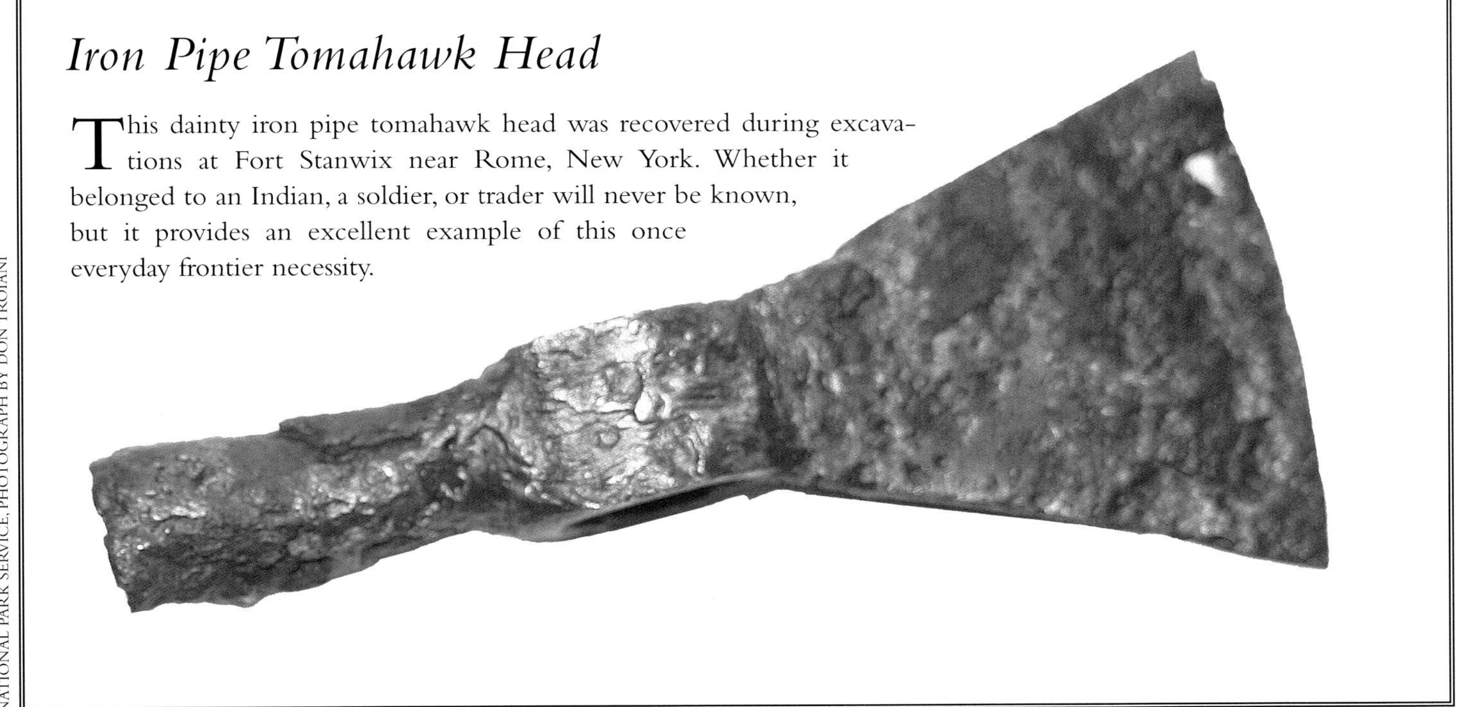

NATIONAL PARK SERVICE, PHOTOGRAPH BY DON TROIANI

PRIVATE, BATTALION COMPANY, KING'S AMERICAN REGIMENT, SUMMER 1777

PAUL SCHIERL COLLECTION

The King's American Regiment was raised by Edmund Fanning in New York in early 1777. Recruits initially attracted to the regiment included both Loyalist refugees seeking revenge for the wrongs inflicted on them and captured patriot soldiers seeking refuge from possible death aboard the disease-filled British prison ships anchored in Jamaica Bay. Under strict discipline, the regiment soon became known as one of the best provincial corps and was one of five such units accepted on the American Establishment of the British Army and redesignated the 4th American Regiment on March 7, 1781. It served during the capture of Forts Montgomery and Clinton in 1777 and distinguished itself in numerous actions in the South before being disbanded in Canada with the cessation of hostilities in 1783.

Responding to a requisition from Sir William Howe, the Crown furnished 5,000 uniforms to clothe provincial corps to be raised from the Loyalist population in the colonies.

Loyalist Officer's Shoulder Belt Plate

MILITARY AND HISTORICAL IMAGE BANK

A marvelously engraved solid silver Loyalist officer's shoulderbelt plate of the South Carolina Royalists, this item is of the unusually small size favored by some British horse regiments. The sapling loblolly pine tree motif bears a Latin motto that translates "Under the King I Flourish." The unit was originally raised in East Florida in 1778 and later sent to Charleston, South Carolina, in 1780. They were engaged at Ninety-Six and Eutaw Springs and then were converted into cavalry in 1781. In addition to being superb soldiers, many of the Loyalist regiments were the equals of their British counterparts in quality of dress and appointments.

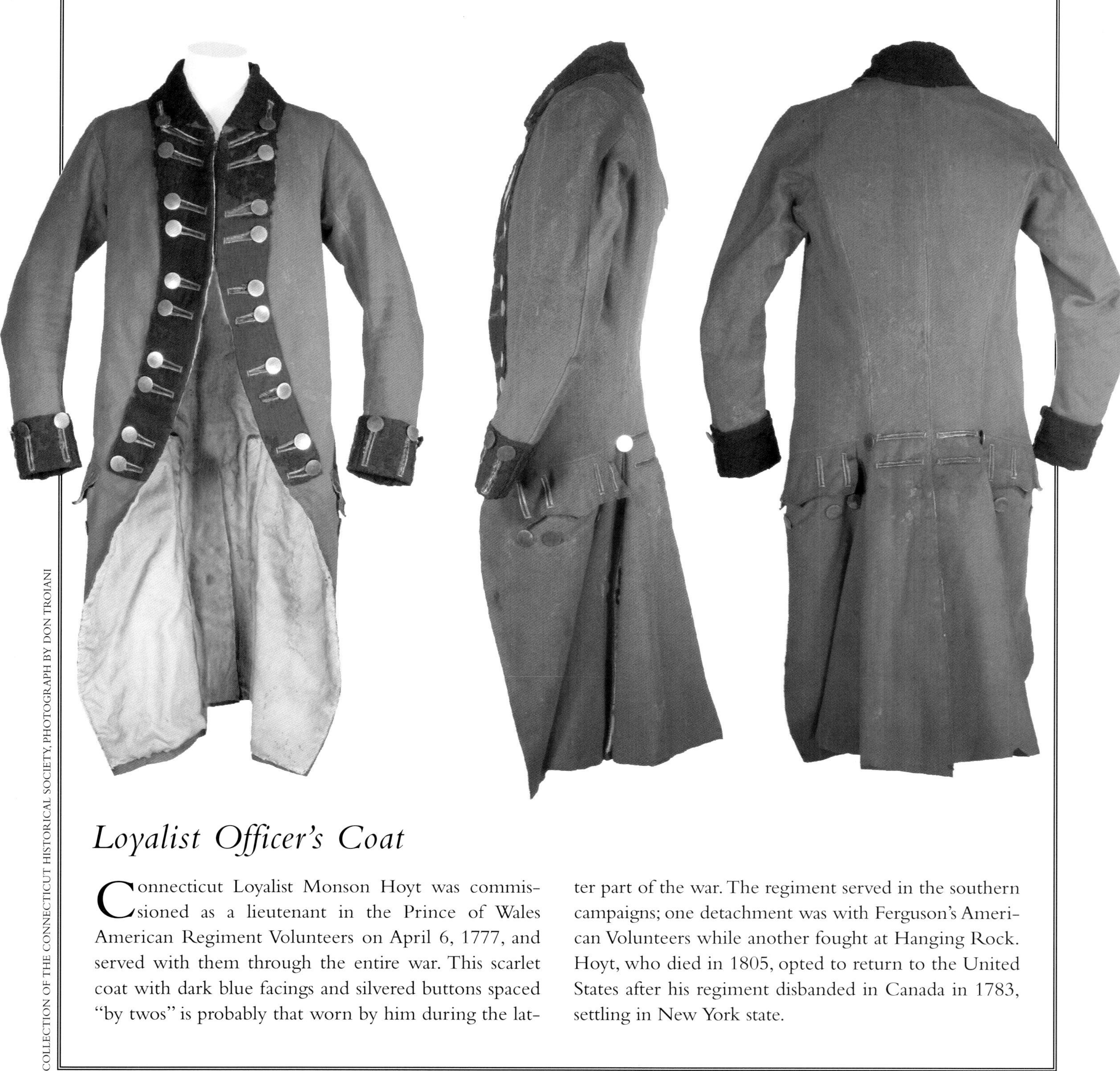

COLLECTION OF THE CONNECTICUT HISTORICAL SOCIETY, PHOTOGRAPH BY DON TROIANI

Loyalist Officer's Coat

Connecticut Loyalist Monson Hoyt was commissioned as a lieutenant in the Prince of Wales American Regiment Volunteers on April 6, 1777, and served with them through the entire war. This scarlet coat with dark blue facings and silvered buttons spaced "by twos" is probably that worn by him during the latter part of the war. The regiment served in the southern campaigns; one detachment was with Ferguson's American Volunteers while another fought at Hanging Rock. Hoyt, who died in 1805, opted to return to the United States after his regiment disbanded in Canada in 1783, settling in New York state.

Shipped to North America in September 1776, the suits consisted of "Coats Green & Lined with White baize, Waistcoat & Breeches White & White Buttons" and felt "round hats." Two months later, the *New York Gazette* was proud to report that Fanning's and other Provincial regiments were "mostly clothed, and make a very handsome Appearance" in uniforms of "Green, faced with White, and made of the best Materials." Fanning was a stickler for details and in August 1777 reminded his men in strong terms that "in every Part of dress" they were to maintain "the most exact Uniformity." In preparation for field service that autumn, the men of the King's American Regiment were ordered to affix their cartridge boxes to the straps of their cartridge pouches, the intent being to convert the waist-mounted, supplemental ammunition containers to a more effective shoulder arrangement. They were likewise ordered to sling their narrow waistbelts, with bayonet frogs, over the opposite, or right, shoulder. The regiment was also furnished with linen gaiter-trousers, paid for by "stoppages" from the men's pay and made by the regimental tailors.

Officer's Shoulder Belt Plate, King's County Militia, c. 1780

This silver belt plate was worn by Lt. Hendrick Wyckoff of the King's County Militia, a Loyalist unit raised to patrol Brooklyn, New York. It has been suggested that the empty space within the oval below the "KCM" may have been reserved for the engraved initials or cipher of the wearer, since other known Loyalist officers' belt plates have this feature. This plate was found in the Toronto, Canada, area in the 1960s and survives with Wyckoff's 1777 lieutenant's commission, his 1776 loyalty oath, and two pieces of colonial paper money.

ERIK GOLDSTEIN COLLECTION

Loyalist Regimental Buttons

Left to right: 1.) Gilt one-piece button of the King's (4th) American Regiment. 2.) 1st American Regiment (Queen's Rangers). 3.) Butler's Rangers. 4.) 3rd American (New York Volunteers). 5.) Royal Highland Emigrants. 6.) Royal Provincials, used by units without their own distinctive button, adopted in 1780. Specimens two through six are pewter.

TROIANI COLLECTION

PRIVATE, BATTALION COMPANY, QUEEN'S RANGERS, 1780–83

HERMAN BENNINGHOFF COLLECTION

The Queen's Rangers were probably the most famous, and certainly the most effective, of all the Loyalist corps that fought for the Crown during the Revolutionary War. Robert Rogers—of "Roger's Rangers" fame—originally raised the unit in 1776 but his questionable loyalty led to Rogers's replacement by a string of competent British officers, the third and final commandant being Capt. John Graves Simcoe, 40th Foot grenadier captain, who succeeded to that post on October 15, 1777, with the provincial rank of major. This was the first provincial regiment to take the field in Sir William Howe's army, having bloodied itself earlier at the battles of Brandywine and Germantown.

Originally, the Queen's Rangers was organized as a standard infantry regiment, but Simcoe began to remodel it into a legionary corps, operating with a mixed force of horse and foot. The infantry consisted of grenadier, light infantry, rifle,

Brass Bridle Rosette

Brass bridle rosette of the King's American Dragoons, a Loyalist cavalry corps that was formed in New York during 1781. This corps, later expanded to include "flying artillery" and light infantry, mainly served in and around New York until the close of the war, although a detachment fought with great merit in the minor actions around Charleston, South Carolina, during late 1781–82. The button of the regiment (slightly smaller) is nearly identical in shape and motif to this rosette, giving some indication of the high quality appointments procured for this short-lived but fine regiment.

TROIANI COLLECTION

Oval Cartridge Pouch Plate

Brass oval cartridge pouch plate with "GR" on the face and inscribed on the reverse with "Albany, Geo Haines." Haines enlisted in Van Der Burgh's Company of Emmerick's Chasseurs on May 19, 1778. He was later transferred to the New York Volunteer Rifle Company when the chasseurs were disbanded and served in the South where this was excavated years ago. Other plates of this Loyalist stock pattern were excavated in New York City and at Saratoga battlefield.

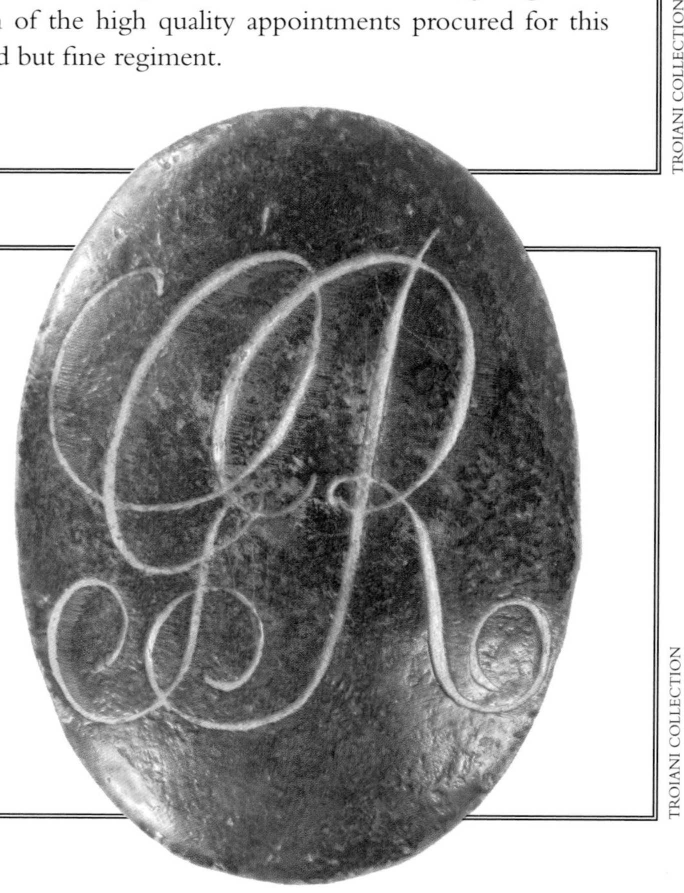

TROIANI COLLECTION

and battalion companies—although all were trained and equipped to function as light infantry—while the horse included hussars and light dragoons. Simcoe was an expert in partisan warfare, and under his tutelage, few excelled the Rangers. At the Battle of Monmouth, the unit covered the retreat of the British light infantry and recovered their abandoned "grasshopper" gun, which was presented to them by Sir Henry Clinton, thereby adding an artillery section to the corps. In the Virginia campaigns of 1780–81, they covered themselves with further glory, executing brilliant maneuvers in such actions as Point of Fork, Richmond, and Spencer's Ordinary. Simcoe, now a lieutenant colonel, and most of the regiment went into captivity after defending the works at Gloucester Point as part of Cornwallis's surrender at Yorktown.

Simcoe fought to preserve the original green uniforms issued to the Queen's Rangers at the same time that most provincial corps were being clothed in red, noting that "green is without comparison the best colour for light troops." He had green waistcoats made in the British light infantry form, to which the sleeves of the coats were sewn. These jackets were worn in hot weather; then in winter sleeves were added to the coat shell again, the waistcoat worn underneath. The coats themselves were modified by shortening them, and instead of colored facings, plain green collar, cuffs, and half lapels were worn. Originally, the Rangers wore the "miserable contract" round hats provided by the Crown for all provincial troops, but Simcoe replaced these in early 1780 with light caps of leather "neat and commodious." This battalion private is dressed in his full (cool weather) uniform, consisting of short coat, waistcoat, woolen breeches, and half-gaiters. He is armed with a Short Land Pattern and its bayonet, a menacing weapon in the hands of such a skilled practitioner of its use.

CAVALRY TROOPER, THE BRITISH LEGION, 1780–81

NATIONAL PARK SERVICE

The British Legion was a mixed command of provincial horse and foot raised in 1778 by Lord William Cathcart, who commanded with the rank of colonel. When Cathcart returned to England in late 1779, his second in command, a daring young English cavalry officer by the name of Banastre Tarleton, was named lieutenant-colonel-commandant of the corps. By 1780 the British Legion consisted of six cavalry troops and four light infantry companies

An Infantry Officer's Sword

Of typical Germanic form, this brass-hilted officer's sword bears the coat of arms of Brunswick on its straight blade.

Officer's Gilt Repousse Button

Dating from the latter part of the war, this officer's gilt repousse button with a bone back of the King's Royal Regiment of New York is of the highest quality. Raised by Sir Guy Johnson, elements of this celebrated unit fought in many actions on the New York frontier over the course of the war.

TROIANI COLLECTION

and soon established its reputation as an effective fighting force. It was part of the British expeditionary force that encircled Charleston in 1780. Tarleton, leading his own British Legion and other detachments, successfully surprised and defeated the patriot horse posted at Monck's Corner on April 14, establishing the Tory corps as a particularly ruthless and savage opponent and earning its commander the epithet of "Blood Ban" and the implacable hatred of the Patriot foe. When defeated at Cowpens, revenge would be inflicted on the Legion and its commander with the capture of its infantry, most of its cavalry fleeing the field after being but little engaged. Tarleton and a remnant of his legion, now mostly cavalry, continued to fight as part of Cornwallis's army until its surrender following the siege of Yorktown on October 19, 1781.

Lord Cathcart felt that "the Provincial clothing was too gaudy and the accoutrements too slight," and arranged to have the men outfitted according to his own notions of what was most appropriate for a partisan corps. In 1780 the British Legion cavalry was described by a London newspaper as follows:

The cavalry that Coll. Tarleton commands is a provincial corps, and makes rather a singular figure; for as service has been consulted more than show, their horses are all manner of colours and sizes. Their uniforms are a light green waistcoat, without skirts, with black cuffs and capes, and nothing more. Their arms consist of a sabre and one pistol. The spare holster contains their bread and cheese. Thus lightly accoutred, and mounted on the swiftest horses the country produces, it is impossible for the enemy to have any notice of their approach till they actually receive the shock of their charge.

Officers wore jackets edged with narrow gilt lace and trimmed with gilt buttons, and troopers wore a plainer jacket trimmed with pewter buttons. Bearskin-crested helmets were adopted, with green turbans or sashes round the crown and black plumes. Breeches of white cloth and whitened buckskin were both worn as legwear, along with boots. Both the horse and cavalry accoutrements were of black, tanned leather, and the saddle-mounted pistol holsters had "caps," or covers, of bearskin.

FUSILIER, HESSE-CASSEL REGIMENT ERBPRINZ, 1776

BRUCE HERMAN COLLECTION

Upon the outbreak of the war in the Colonies, the British Army was clearly not large enough to defend its homeland and colonial possessions while also putting put down the rebellion. On January 15, 1776, the British government contracted with Langraf Frederich II of Hesse-Cassel for fifteen regiments of infantry to serve in North America. Hiring foreign troops was a regular practice of many nations and, for the rulers of smaller principalities, a way to supplement their often impoverished treasuries. Germans, Irish, Scots, and others also served in the employ of foreign rulers, sometimes for nationalist reasons, other times for pay.

The fusiliers of the Erbprinz Regiment arrived in New York on August 12, 1776, and were active in the defeat of the rebel army during that campaign. For most of the war, they composed part of the garrison of that city and saw little action. In 1781 the regiment was sent to join Cornwallis's army in Virginia and participated in the siege of Yorktown, where they surrendered 484 men to the Americans. After Yorktown more than 100 men of the regiment deserted to begin new lives in America. After stints in various prisons, the remainder of the Erbprinz returned to Hesse-Cassel in 1783.

The first uniform of the regiment as shown here consisted of a dark blue coat faced rose-red, which was changed in 1780 to carmoisin-red (deep red) when the regiment became musketeers and exchanged their metal caps for cocked hats. The fusilier caps were of polished white metal with a cloth-covered felt body reinforced with decorative metal strips and a flaming-grenade device on the top. There is some conjecture as to the exact motif on the cap, and the most likely one has been chosen for this figure. Arms consisted of a brass-hilted hanger or short sword and a Prussian-style musket with short six-sided bayonet.

Hessian Fusilier's Cap

This rare fusilier cap of the Hessian Regiment von Knyphausen was, by family tradition, taken by a Pennsylvania soldier named Morrow at the Battle of Trenton in December 1776. Three regiments—Rall, von Lossberg, and von Knyphausen—surrendered to Washington's army that Christmas morning. The Knyphausen Regiment was the only unit whose caps had a buff, cloth-covered body. These caps were cleverly constructed with the metal parts wired to the crown or body, thereby allowing for effortless disassembling of the embossed brass front plate and crown edging for polishing and repairs.

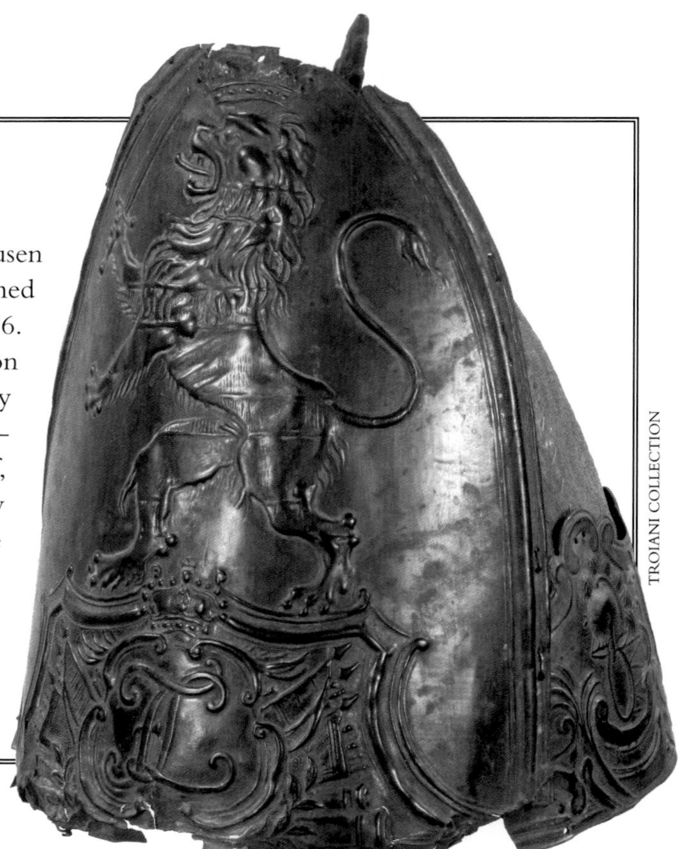

TROIANI COLLECTION

Hessian Officer's Sword

While British officers had a certain degree of latitude in the selection of arms and equipage, the dress, weapons, and accoutrements of Hessian officers were strictly regulated by Frederick II, ruler of Hesse-Cassel. When he was informed in 1776 that his officers, following the lead of their red-coated brethren, had removed the metallic lace from their hats and coats to minimize their becoming targets for American riflemen, he furiously ordered the lace restored and insisted on strict adherence to regulation dress in the future. As such, it is doubtful that a Hessian infantry officer would dare to carry any blade other than the type pictured here with the inscription of his prince on it, a design borrowed from the Prussian Army. Although classified as a small sword by its form, the heavy cast-brass hilt and substantial, double-edged blade rendered it an effective fighting weapon.

TROIANI COLLECTION

Brunswick Dragoon, Regiment Prinz Ludwig, 1777

Although originally raised in 1698, this regiment was first designated a dragoon regiment in 1772. Its commandant was Col. Friedrich A. Riedesel, who had been promoted to major general and assigned overall command of the Brunswick Corps in America in 1776. During the reorganization of the Brunswick troops for the expedition to Canada in 1776, it was renamed the Dragoon Regiment "Prinz Ludwig" in honor of its chief, the younger brother of Duke Carl I. Under its field commander, Lt. Col. Friedrich Baum, the four-squadron regiment arrived in Quebec without horses, but with full horse equipage for mounted service. They were paid as infantry (heavy dragoons such as these were essentially mounted infantry) and largely served in this capacity on the 1777 Saratoga campaign, although the intent was to mount them when, and if, horses became available. Baum and approximately 120 dismounted dragoons fought bravely, but against overwhelming odds, at the Battle of Bennington on August 16, 1777, most being captured or killed. The survivors rejoined the main body with Burgoyne, where they were interned with the rest of the Brunswick corps following the surrender at Saratoga. The regiment was reconstituted in Canada from the small cadre of dragoons that had remained there in 1777, supplemented by recruits from Europe and dragoons who had escaped their confinement and made their way back to the regiment via New York. The understrength regiment remained in garrison duty there until 1783, when it returned to Brunswick.

PRIVATE COLLECTION

The Brunswick Dragoons wore a striking uniform coat of light blue, with yellow facings and lining. The white metal buttons were placed single-paired then single on the half-lapels in the fashion of all Brunswick regiments, with two buttons on the Swedish or boot cuffs. Underneath was worn a yellow waistcoat and buff-colored leather breeches, over which were worn

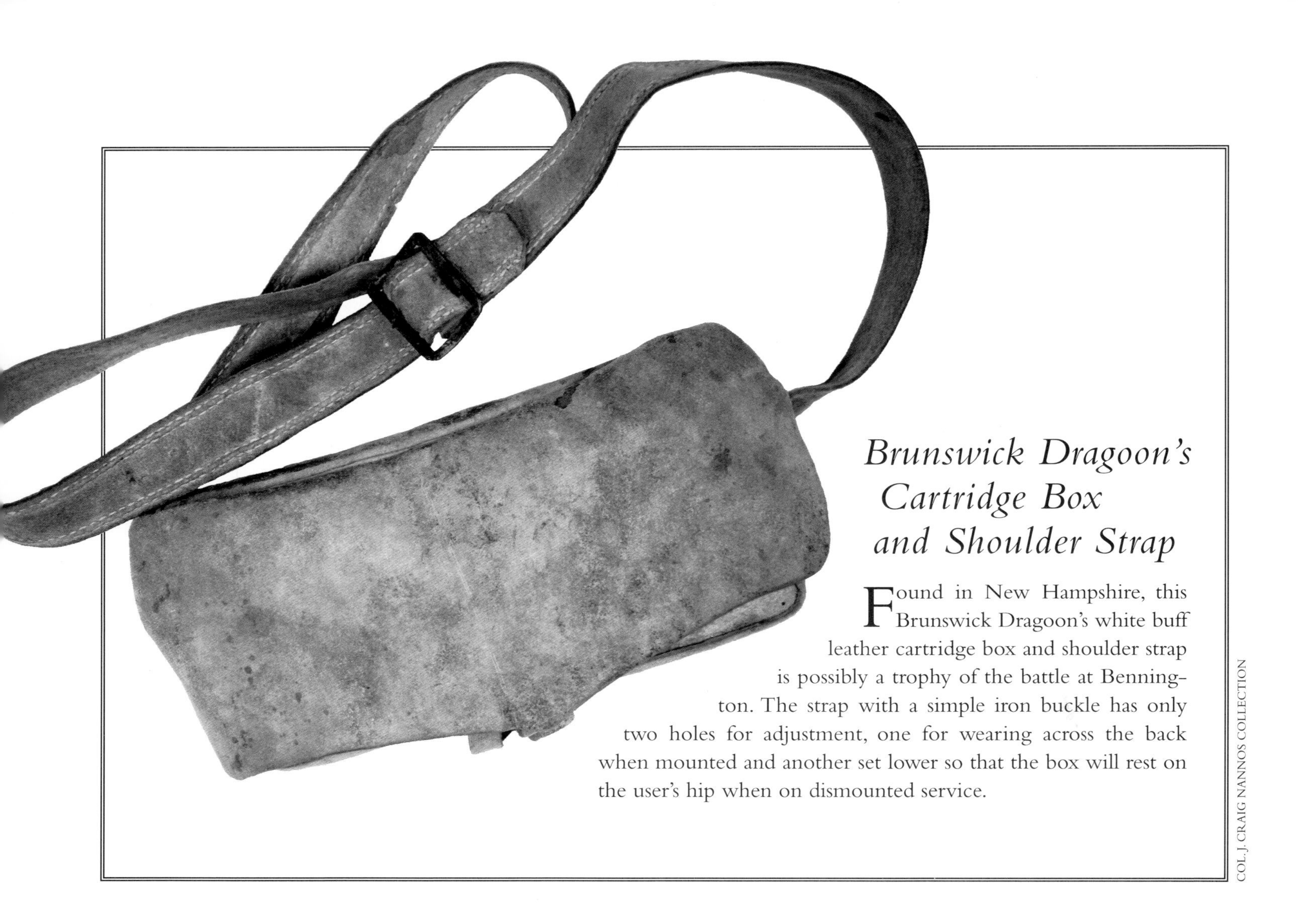

Brunswick Dragoon's Cartridge Box and Shoulder Strap

Found in New Hampshire, this Brunswick Dragoon's white buff leather cartridge box and shoulder strap is possibly a trophy of the battle at Bennington. The strap with a simple iron buckle has only two holes for adjustment, one for wearing across the back when mounted and another set lower so that the box will rest on the user's hip when on dismounted service.

COL. J. CRAIG NANNOS COLLECTION

Brass Dragoon Drum

This impressive brass drum bearing the monogram of the Duke of Brunswick in relief was captured by the Americans at the Battle of Bennington. Mounted with brass rims instead of the usual wood ones used by infantry regiments, it is believed this drum belonged to the contingent of dragoons from the Regiment Prinz Ernst Ludwig.

PHOTOGRAPH COURTESY OF THE NEW HAMPSHIRE HISTORICAL SOCIETY

Brunswick Dragoon Sword

An other-ranks Brunswick Dragoon Pallash, complete with its iron-mounted, leather-covered wooden scabbard and white buff waistbelt. This specimen was captured at Bennington.

MASSACHUSETTS STATE ARCHIVES, PHOTOGRAPH BY DON TROIANI

Dragoon Broadswords

Among the arms captured by the Americans at Bennington and Saratoga were the heavy dragoon broadswords that were carried by the Prinz Ludwig Dragoons. One hundred and forty-nine of these swords were shipped south for the use of the 2nd Continental Light Dragoons, and their receipt in February 1778 was acknowledged by Maj. Benjamin Tallmadge, who wrote, "They are very strong & heavy having steel Scabbards."

Few of these Brunswick swords, known as a "Pallash," are extant today. The other-ranks pattern (bottom) has a heavy, double-edged blade and basket hilt with a domed pommel of brass. Cast into the sword's guard is a "C," the cipher of Charles I, Duke of Brunswick (1735–80), surmounted by a crown. The officer's pattern (top) has an openwork guard with doubled "Cs" under a crown. Some parts of the crown were purposely removed at the time of use, possibly to lighten the hilt. Both were originally carried in a leather-covered wooden scabbard reinforced with steel that was buckled to a broad, buff-leather waistbelt.

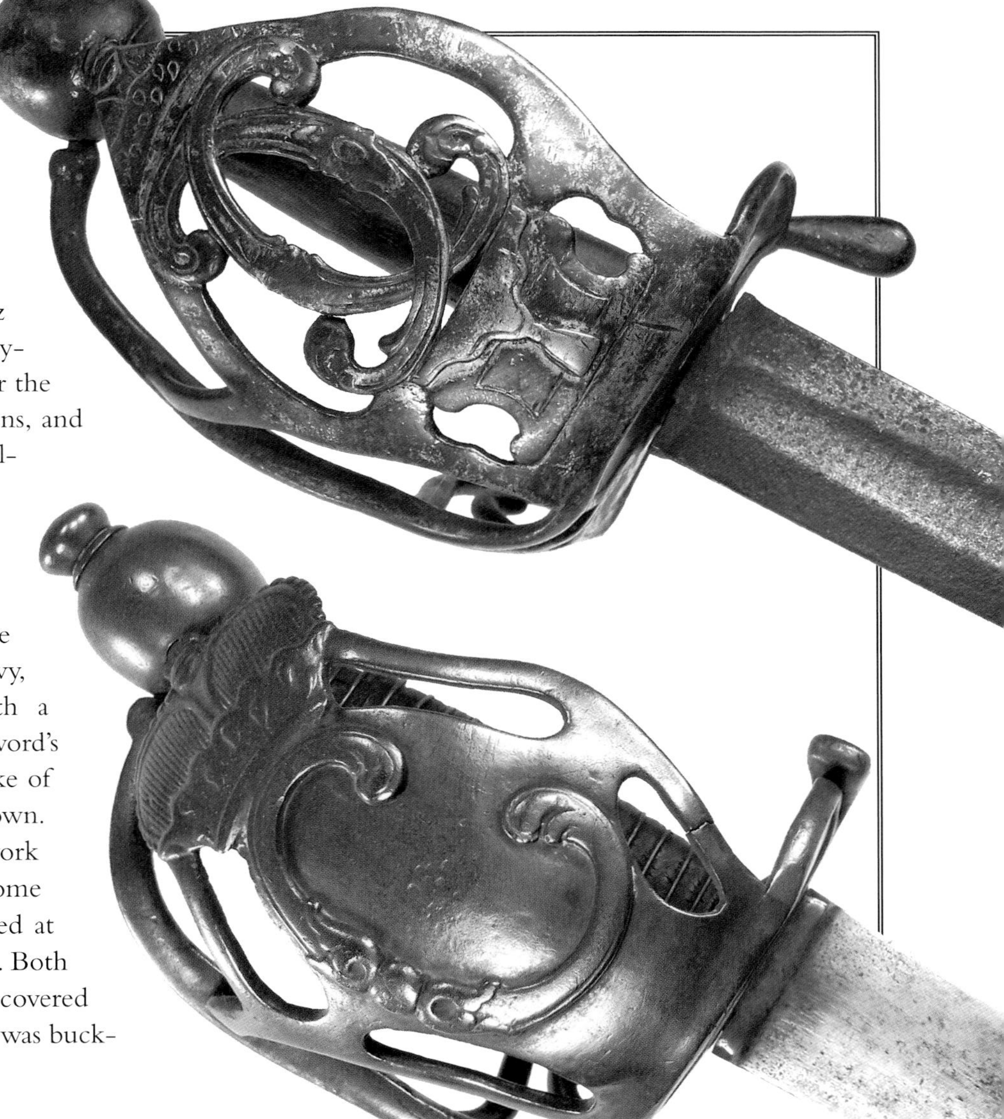

TROIANI COLLECTION

high, black gaiters. Headgear consisted of a large cocked hat with white plume. Here, a buff cartridge pouch is slung on a narrow belt across the right shoulder of the dragoon, while the broad carbine sling is suspended across the opposite shoulder. His waistbelt supports a heavy, straight-bladed broadsword—still carried on campaign with pride (and perhaps some curses) by the dismounted dragoons as they negotiated the forests and meadows of North America.

JAEGER, 2ND COMPANY, HESSE-CASSEL FIELD JAEGER CORPS, 1776–77

HERMAN BENNINGHOFF COLLECTION

The Field Jaegers were the elite troops of the Hesse-Cassel forces serving with the British Army during the Revolutionary War. Recruited from hunters, gamekeepers, and other marksmen, they were famous for their skills as riflemen and skirmishers, as well as for discipline and bravery under arms in the most trying of circumstances. Mustered into British service during March 1776 in Hesse-Cassel, the jaegers were described as "a stout, active Body of Men, armed with Rifle-Barrel Guns, to the Use of which They are thoroughly inured . . . commanded by skillful, experienced Officers. They cannot fail of being very serviceable." In June 1776 two companies of foot jaegers accompanied the second contingent of Hessian units sent to North America. They were augmented in 1777 with three additional compa-

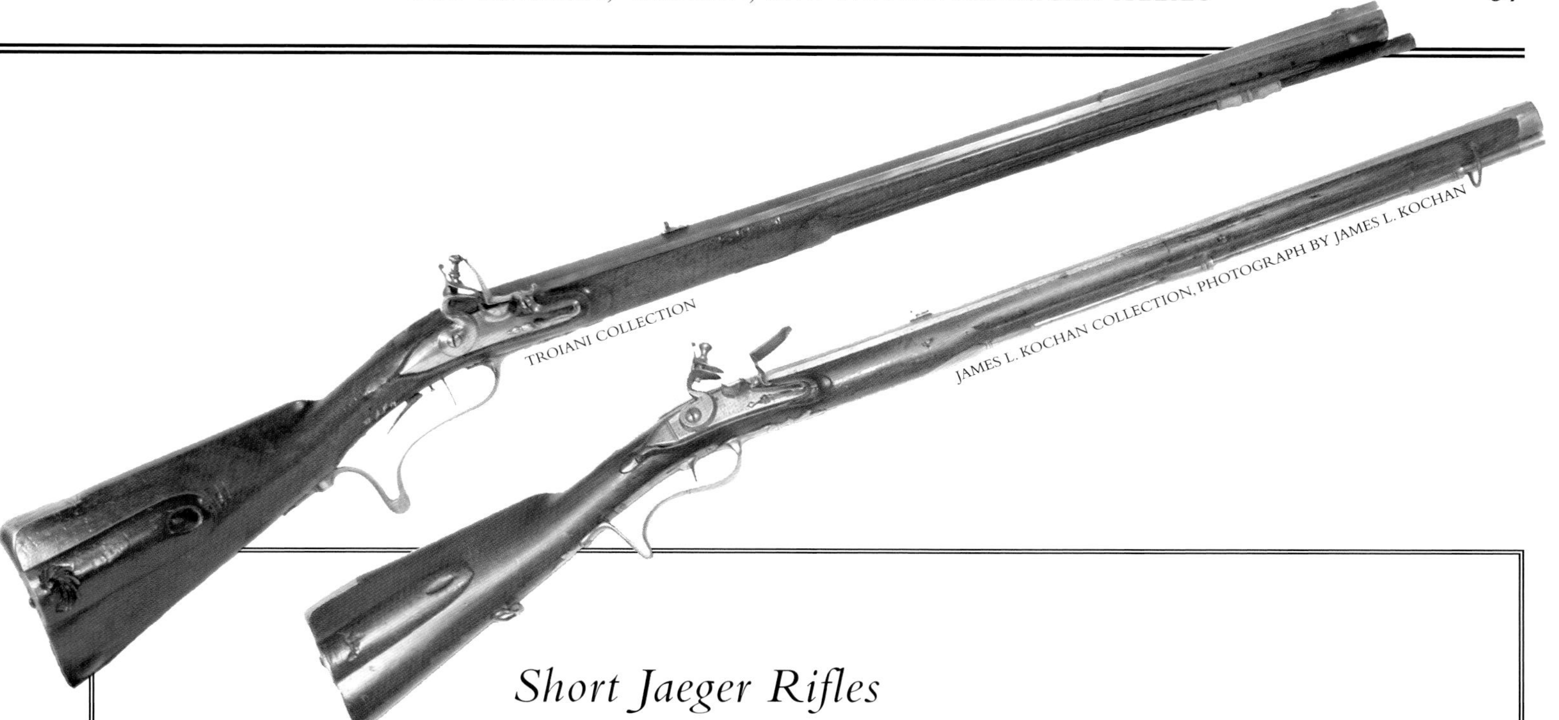

Short Jaeger Rifles

The short jaeger rifle at the top was made by Bernard Pistor and is signed and dated 1769 on the barrel. Not an issue weapon but of military form, this beautifully crafted weapon was probably used by an officer or sergeant in the Hesse-Cassel Jaeger Corps. It is similar in form to an enlisted pattern rifle of this corps, also made by Pistor, now in the collection of the West Point Museum.

Short, light, accurate, and well-balanced, the Hanau-made military rifle at the bottom is the pattern carried by the Hesse Hanau Corps of Jaegers. It was a dangerous weapon in the hands of a skilled German marksman. This specimenis engraved "No. 79" on the barrel, just behind the front sight.

nies of foot and one mounted company, forming a provisional Field Jaeger Corps of nearly 500 officers and enlisted men. Usually serving in company-size or smaller detachments, the jaegers could be found in the van of advancing British columns or covering the rear of those withdrawing. Widely deployed and serving on campaigns that ranged from New York to the Carolinas, the jaeger corps was able to amass an almost unexcelled battle record during the war.

The Hesse-Cassel Field Jaegers wore uniforms coats of grass green, faced and lined with crimson red. Almost identical to those worn by the Prussian jaegers, on which they were modeled, the coats had six brass buttons arranged in pairs on each half-lapel, and their round Prussian-style cuffs had a slit on the underside. Grass-green waistcoats (changed to buff in 1782) were worn underneath. Legwear consisted of buff-colored leather or cloth breeches, substituted by ones of linen during hot weather. Foot jaegers wore gray leggings trimmed with brass buttons to protect their lower legs from brush and damp. All companies wore large cocked hats, nearly bicorne in form. The hat was trimmed with a red and green feather, a green cockade with yellow loop and button, and round, white worsted tufts with crimson centers at the hat's corners. The coarse clothing of the jaegers suffered from the hard and prolonged field service to which it was subjected and wore out long before the annual replacement suits were sent from Hesse-Cassel each year. While inspecting the jaeger advanced posts outside of New Brunswick, New Jersey, on January 9, 1777, Lord Cornwallis was impressed that they "were very cheerful despite their ragged clothing and hard duty."

The principal arm of a Hessian jaeger was his short rifle, produced at the Pistor Manufactory in Schmalkalden. The rifle had a near 29-inch, swamped, octagonal barrel of .65-caliber bore, a wooden patch box, and brass fittings. His accoutrement belts and cartridge pouch were of brown leather, and the rifle sling was dyed a reddish color. A short, brass-hilted hunting sword was carried by each jaeger, with the exception of those in the mounted company, who differed in dress and equipment only by "wearing Sabres instead of Swords; and having Spurs fix'd to the Heels of their Boots." Their musicians also carried "Trumpets instead of French Horns," which they used for signaling commands to dismounted companies. The waistbelt was occasionally fitted with a cartridge box and supplemental ammunition and, notwithstanding in-garrison orders to the contrary, was frequently worn slung over the shoulder in the field.

SERGEANT, GRENADIER REGIMENT RALL, 1776

BRUCE HERMAN COLLECTION

Despite being a regiment of grenadiers, the Hessian Regiment Rall was composed of men of average, or even below average, height. During the New York campaign, the regiment and its commander, Col. Johann Gottlieb Rall, a veteran of the Russian Army, distinguished themselves at the battles of White Plains and Fort Washington. On the fateful night of Trenton, December 26, 1776, the regiment along with two others was defeated and surrendered with its colors to Washington's forces after being surprised in a dawn attack. Colonel Rall was mortally wounded during the fighting and died the next day. Reconstituted after Trenton, the regiment was renamed Von Wollwarth, then Von Trumbach, and finally Marquis d'Angelli by war's end.

This sergeant is armed with a partizan with a steel crossguard and flat leaf-style blade engraved with the large "FL" cipher of Frederick II and a brass-mounted short sword. The uniform included brass grenadier caps and dark blue regimental coats with red linings but no facings. Unlike other Hessian grenadiers, contemporary illustrations show the enlisted men of the regiment as clean shaven without the traditional black waxed mustaches.

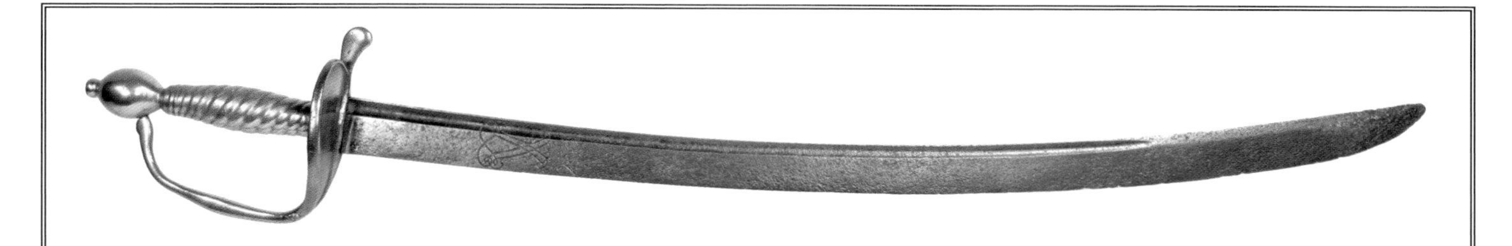

TROIANI COLLECTION

Hessian Infantry Hanger

A brass-hilted infantry hanger whose blade is emblazoned with the doubled "FL" cipher of the ruler of Hesse-Cassel. Coinage of this principality during the reign of Frederick II bears the identical device. All Hessian infantry, with the exception of jaegers, and artillery would have carried swords of this type.

TROIANI COLLECTION

"Hard Currency"

When available, "hard currency"—such as these 1752 one- and eight-reales minted in Mexico and this 1746 Brazilian gold "quarter Joe"—was the preferred method of payment in lieu of Continental or colonial script notes, both for army contracts and military pay.

Officer's Spontoon

Officer's spontoon bearing the "FL" cypher of Frederick Landgraf II of Hesse-Cassel. Finely made of steel, it was principally intended as a badge of rank for officers but could certainly have been used as a weapon if required.

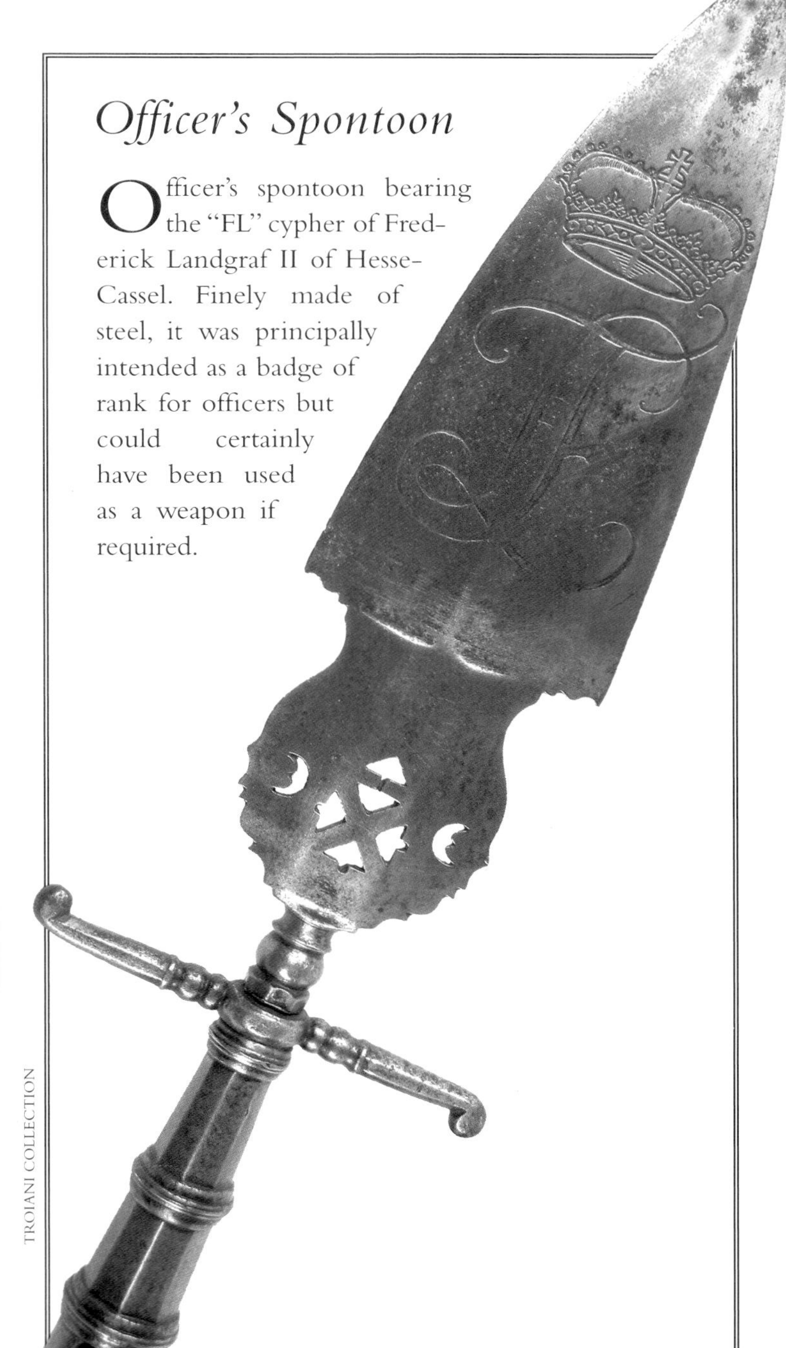

TROIANI COLLECTION

TROIANI COLLECTION

German Musket

The muskets carried by German troops during the Revolutionary War are poorly documented, and few examples of such firearms are extant. Despite the surrender of significant numbers of German troops with their arms, only a few hundred were listed in postwar American inventories. However, in the collection of the Massachusetts State Archives is a musket like this one captured at Bennington and presented by Gen. John Stark to the state as a memento of his victory over the Brunswickers. Although unmarked, this trophy weapon is nearly identical to the Prussian model 1740 musket, manufactured at Potsdam. Musket parts have been excavated from the Brunswick camp at Saratoga that identically match this musket, leaving little doubt that at least some of that principality's muskets were of the Prussian pattern.

The heavily faceted brass mountings, large lock plate with rear point, and high comb and pronounced relief carving around the lock plate, breech, and lower ramrod pipe on the walnut stock are characteristic of German military arms of this period and are found on muskets produced not only at Potsdam but also at other arms manufactories such as Herzberg, Schmalkalden, and Suhl. The barrel is forty-one inches long and the bore is .72 caliber, allowing the use of standard British musket cartridges as issued from ordnance stores.

Brunswick Bayonet and Musket

This Brunswick bayonet taken at Bennington was copied from the Prussian pattern in use since the 1730s.

Below is detail of the side plate of a Brunswick musket taken at Bennington. The musket differs from the Prussian form more commonly associated with the Brunswickers, known from other captured muskets of the battle and fragments excavated on the battlefield.

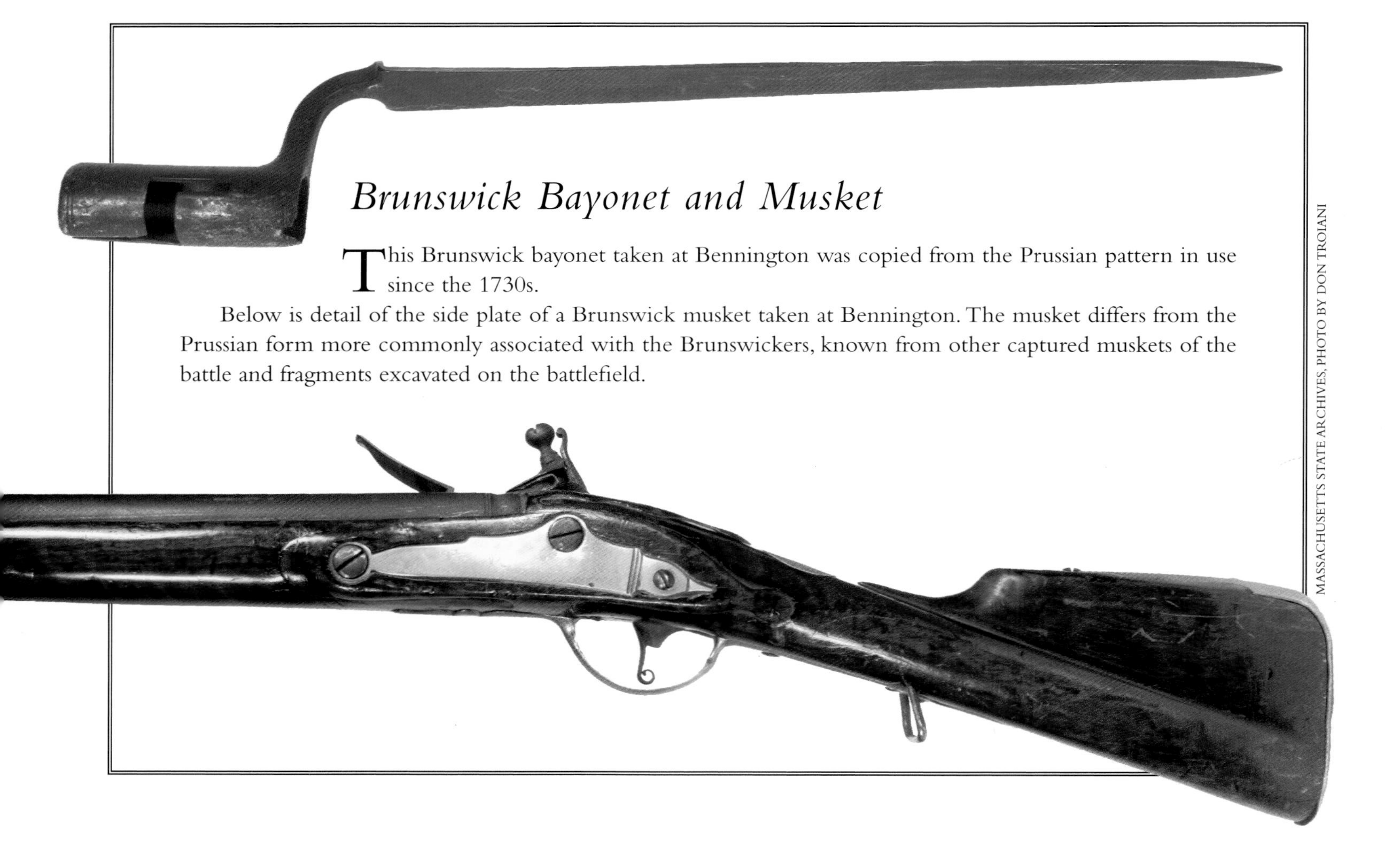

MASSACHUSETTS STATE ARCHIVES, PHOTO BY DON TROIANI

Hessian Finial, Flag, and Tassel

Of gilded iron, this finial for the staff of a color of a Hessian regiment bears the "FL" cipher of the Frederick II (near right).

Portions of the central cartouche and white field of what is probably the *Leibfahne* of the Hessian Regiment von Rall (above) are all that now remain of this proud regiment's silk standards. This flag was among those captured at Trenton on Christmas Day 1776 and later hung as a trophy in the Continental Congress's meeting room. It is undoubtedly the Hessian color with white ground shown in Charles Wilson Peale's famous 1779 portrait of Washington at Princeton.

Woven of scarlet and metallic gold, this handsome tassel at far right was removed from a Hessian flag taken at Trenton.

FINIAL: TROIANI COLLECTION; FLAG: PENNSYLVANIA HISTORICAL SOCIETY COLLECTION, PHOTOGRAPH BY STEVEN HILL; TASSEL: COLLECTION OF THE FIRST TROOP OF THE PHILADELPHIA CITY CAVALRY

PRIVATE, FUSILIER REGIMENT VON LOSSBERG, 1776

SCOTT FERRIS COLLECTION

The Fusilier Regiment von Lossberg was part of the 1st Division of Hessian troops sent to North America from Hesse-Cassel. Fighting with distinction at Long Island, Fort Washington, and White Plains, the regiment enjoyed a fine reputation until it, along with the rest of the Hessian garrison at Trenton, was captured in a surprise attack on Christmas morning, 1776. The regiment was eventually reraised in 1778 from survivors, escaped prisoners, and new recruits and served at New York until 1780, when it was sent to Quebec, where it remained until the close of the war.

Frederick II was heavily influenced by the military system of nearby Prussia, as were many other rulers. As a result, the uniforms, equipage, and organization of Hessian regiments closely resembled those of corresponding Prussian corps. The Fusilier Regiment von Lossberg wore a short, blue coat of Prussian cut, with orange facings and red linings. The half lapels had six buttons set in pairs, a standard feature on all Hessian coats that were also borrowed from Prussia. The collarless coats were heavy and made of coarse materials that by the winter of 1776 had already begun to wear thin from the active campaigning. Neckstocks of stiff, black leather were worn by the regiment. "Smallclothes"—waistcoat and breeches—were of white cloth, and the lower legs were encased in snug-fitting gaiters of black cloth. Caps of miter shape, with stamped brass fittings over a stiffened cloth crown, were worn by all Hessian fusilier companies. The troops were armed with a musket and bayonets of the "Potsdam" pattern and a brass-hilted hanger. Cartridges were carried in a large cartridge pouch, its flap embellished with stamped brass devices and slung by a broad, whitened buff leather belt. The waistbelt was of the same construction, and the musket sling was of red-dyed leather.

TROIANI COLLECTION

Barrel and Bayonet of a Hessian Musket

This barrel of a Hessian musket, complete with six-sided bayonet, was recovered near the site of Fort Mercer at Red Bank, New Jersey. A relic of the stunning October 22, 1777, defeat of Hessian forces under Col. Carl Emil Kurt von Dunop, it appears to have been cut in two by an artillery projectile during the battle. The wood has long since rotted away, but the brass ramrod pipes still remain.

Hessian Buttons

This group of assorted plain brass and tin alloy buttons was excavated on the site of a Hessian outpost in Westchester County, New York. The regiments of these principalities usually did not have numbers assigned to them, the unit name being typically after the *Chef* or commandant of the regiment or after the ruling prince or other members of the royal family.

TROIANI COLLECTION

BREYMANN'S REDOUBT

In the late spring of 1777, with the American Revolution still in the balance, Gen. John Burgoyne began his march south toward Albany, New York, with an army of more than 9,000 Crown forces.

Within days of the first Battle of Saratoga, Burgoyne set his army to work on a series of field fortifications and waited for American Gen. Horatio Gates's next move. Finally, on October 7, 1777, Burgoyne launched a "reconnaissance-in-force" of over 1,700 soldiers against the left flank of the American fortifications. Advancing slightly less than a mile, they deployed in a line of battle across two fields and woods near the Barber Farm. American forces then attacked and drove the entire force back into the Balcarre's Redoubt on the right flank of Burgoyne's fortified lines. Despite having been relieved of command by Gates, Maj. Gen. Benedict Arnold rode on the field of battle. He encouraged and led advance after advance with bravery and tactical leadership.

After failing to breech the Balcarre's Redoubt, he galloped north to join American forces forming to assault the Breymann Redoubt and two fortified cabins in the gap between the redoubts. These undermanned fortified cabins were captured and thus uncovered the left of the Breymann Redoubt. As the bulk of Learned's Brigade and Morgan's Light Corps advanced against the front of the redoubt, Arnold stormed into the rear and left flank of it with part of Lt. Col. John Brooks's Massachusetts Continental Regiment and a collection of "15 or 20 rifleman." A Brunswick grenadier "platoon fired upon him" killing his horse and wounding him in the leg. As Brunswick colonel Heinrich Breymann fell, resistance collapsed. With the fall of the redoubt, almost all of Burgoyne's positions were exposed and became untenable. The Americans had won the second Battle of Saratoga and, by October 17, 1777, had forced Burgoyne's army to surrender.

PRIVATE COLLECTION

MASSACHUSETTS STATE ARCHIVES, PHOTO BY DON TROIANI

Brunswick Grenadier's Cap

In commemoration of the crushing defeat of the German and Loyalist forces at Bennington in August 1777, the American commander, John Stark, presented several battlefield trophies to the states of New Hampshire and Massachusetts, where they have been held since. Among the items preserved by the Commonwealth of Massachusetts is this splendid grenadier's cap of the Brunswick Regiment von Specht, bearing a stamped-brass front plate emblazoned with the coat of arms of the principality. The coarse, red woolen body originally was decorated with three brass flaming grenades around the band, all now missing, as is the yarn tassel or "pom-pom" once at the top.

TROIANI COLLECTION

Brunswick Cartridge Box Badge

Found in an orchard on the Bullard farm in the 1920s, this heavy cast-brass badge was from a Brunswick soldier's cartridge box. The farm had served as General Rediesel's headquarters during the battles near Saratoga. It bears the cipher of Carl I, Duke of Brunswick, and is thus far one of only two known Brunswick pouch badges to have survived as relics from the campaign.

Brunswick Grenadier Cartridge Pouch

Another Bennington memento is this cartridge pouch of a Brunswick grenadier, bearing a large oval plate with Brunswick horse and ducal cipher of Carl I, although only one of the four original brass grenade ornaments still remains. Battalion company pouches were similar, but trimmed with only the oval center plate.

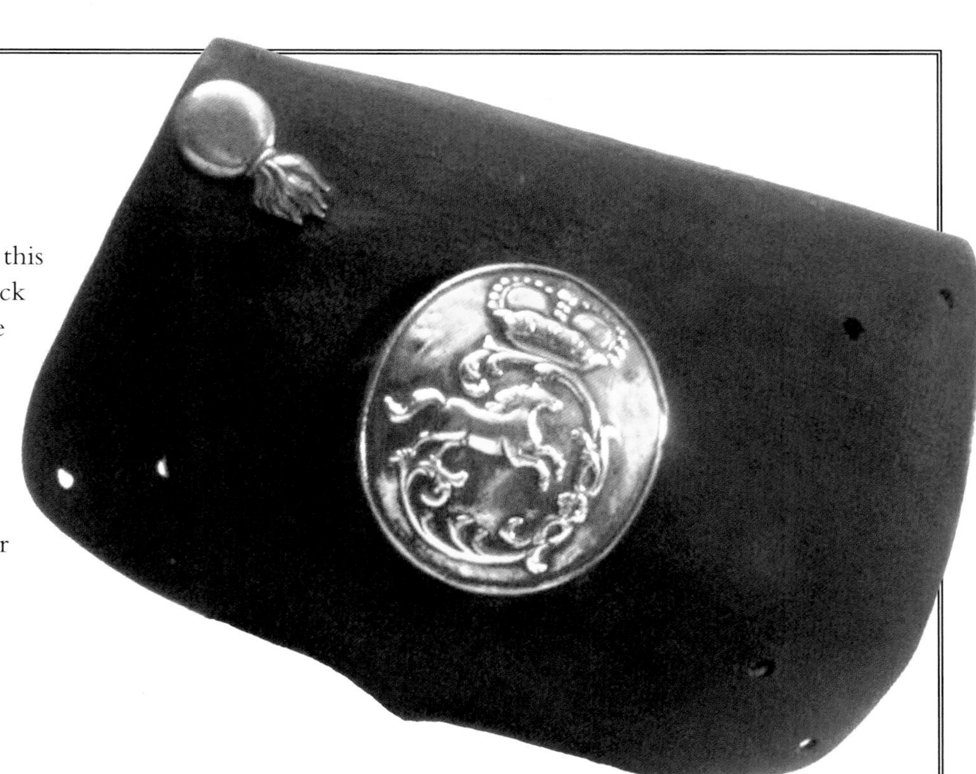

PHOTOGRAPH COURTESY OF THE NEW HAMPSHIRE HISTORICAL SOCIETY

Brunswick Grenadier Drum

An equally impressive Stark trophy of Bennington is this drum, captured from one of the grenadier companies present at the battle. It has a brass shell and wooden rims painted in a dark blue (or black) and red pattern. The shell bears the leaping or running horse and cipher of Duke Carl I, and the drum is complete with its buff leather sling, trimmed with a black and white "livery" lace of worsted and fastened to the drum with brass "clamshell" hooks.

MASSACHUSETTS STATE ARCHIVES, PHOTO BY DON TROIANI

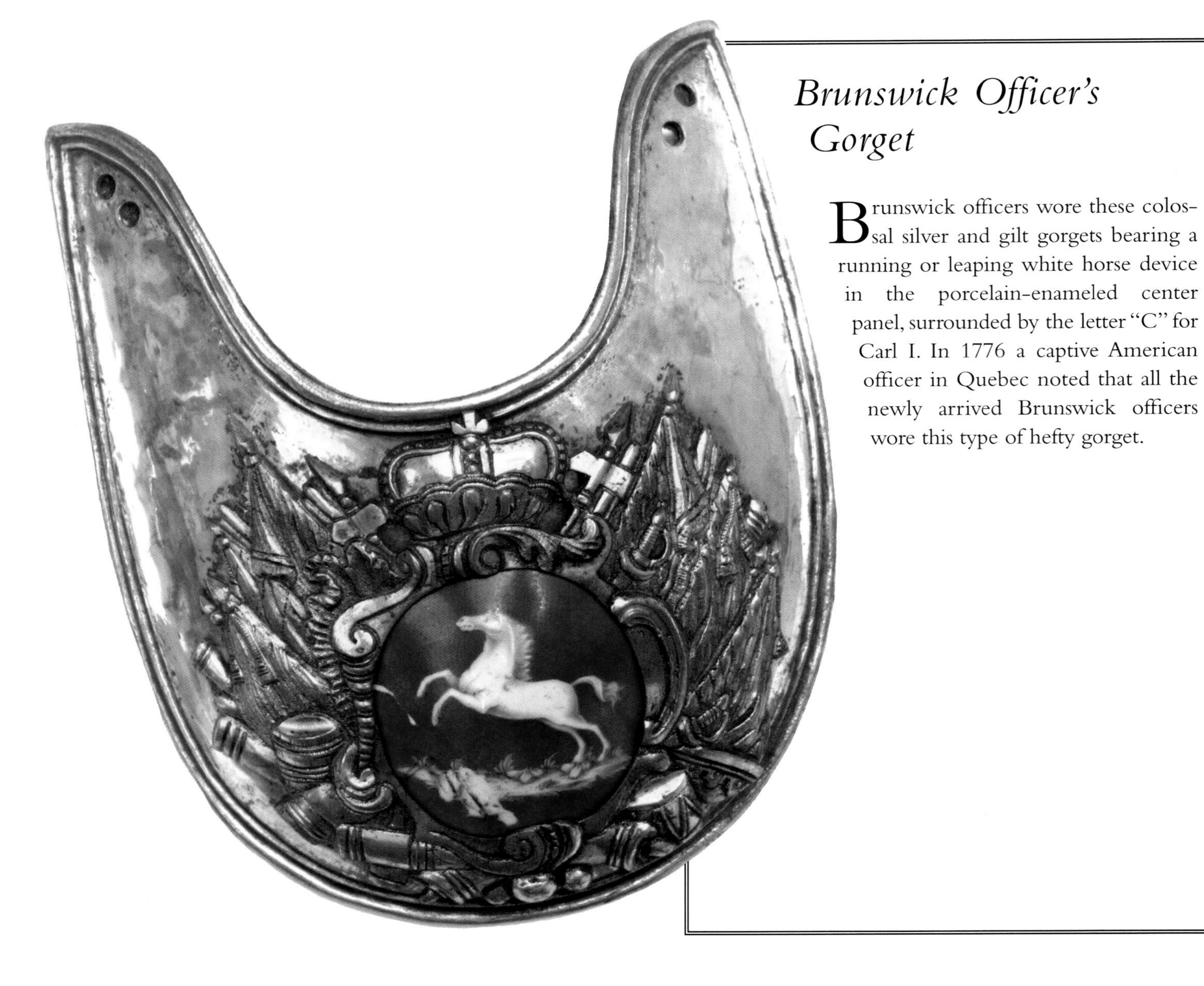

Brunswick Officer's Gorget

Brunswick officers wore these colossal silver and gilt gorgets bearing a running or leaping white horse device in the porcelain-enameled center panel, surrounded by the letter "C" for Carl I. In 1776 a captive American officer in Quebec noted that all the newly arrived Brunswick officers wore this type of hefty gorget.

TROIANI COLLECTION

Waldeck Waistbelt Plate

The Prince of Waldeck, Fredrich Karl August, "rented" one of his regiments of infantry (the 3rd) to the British for service in North America. This fine example of a Waldeck waistbelt plate was recovered in New York City during the 1920s, while several more were found on sites occupied by the regiment or its Spanish captors, during or following the siege of Pensacola in 1781.

COLLECTION OF THE NEW-YORK HISTORICAL SOCIETY (INV. 5631.18.)

WEST POINT MUSEUM, PHOTOGRAPH BY DON TROJANI

Ansbach-Bayreuth Color

This embroidered flag of silk was captured from one of the two Ansbach-Bayreuth regiments that surrendered at Yorktown in 1781. It bears the letters "SETCA" in an intertwined cipher, which is believed to be the motto *"Sinceriter ["Sincere"?] et Constanter"* and the initials of the principality's ruler, Christian Friedrich Karl Alexander. The "M.Z.B." below are the initials for *"Markgraf zu Brandenburg."* The 1st (or Ansbach) and 2nd (or Bayreuth) Regiments were described as "exceedingly fine troops" when brought into British pay in 1777. They fought during the siege of Rhode Island during 1778 and in the Virginia campaign of 1781. Four of the ten nearly identical company colors taken from these regiments still survive.

Hessian Cartridge Box Badges

Large brass cartridge box badges of the Hessian Regiments Erbprinz (left) and von Bose (formerly Regiment von Trumbach) that were discovered during 1930s excavations of redoubts at Yorktown, Virginia.

COLLECTION OF YORKTOWN NATIONAL HISTORICAL PARK

Hessian Bullet Mold

This Hessian iron single-cavity bullet mold was one of several excavated in the Inwood Hill campsite areas of upper Manhattan Island in the 1920s.

TROIANI COLLECTION

Brunswick Polearms

Both commissioned and non-commissioned officers in the Brunswick corps carried polearms during the 1777 Saratoga campaign—the partizan (left) by the latter and the spontoon (right) by the former.

TROIANI COLLECTION

The Patriots and Their Allies

BUNKER HILL

"The danger we were in made us think . . . that we were brought there to be all slain . . . for about 5 in the morning, we not having more than half our fort done, they began to fire." Thus wrote Pvt. Peter Brown to his mother the week following the momentous June 17, 1775. The night's work had produced a respectable redoubt and connecting breastworks. Intermittently, while the morning's work continued, British warships blasted the Charlestown Peninsula; although generally falling short of the fortifications, the gunnery set the old town ablaze. Half a mile across the bay, thousands of Boston residents watching from rooftops marveled at the destruction. By 1 P.M., they had also witnessed forty barges deliver about 2,200 British troops to that smoky shore.

In the scene shown here, about an hour later, the redoubt's garrison had withstood two massed frontal assaults, inflicting enormous casualties. Each time, His Majesty's regulars performed with remarkable fortitude, overcoming through sheer will the burdens of sixty pounds of gear per man. And each time, the New Englanders reserved their fire almost to the literal point of Col. William Prescott's "whites of their eyes" admonition. Now, though, piling knapsacks at the base of the hill and affixing bayonets, the redcoats were preparing to drive forward in irresistible, savage rage. For not a few of the now greatly outnumbered Yankees atop the hill, the cartridge just loaded was their final round.

In news that would reverberate throughout the empire for years to come, the cost of this terrible day in British military annals would be 268 killed and 828 wounded, a stunning 50 percent.

RICHARD ULBRICH COLLECTION

A Committee of Safety Pistol

Although somewhat ungainly, this pistol made by Nathan Bailey of New London, Connecticut, is one of the few surviving pistols made under contract by a Committee of Safety. It bears the "SC" mark of the state of Connecticut in the stock and Bailey's name on the face and interior of the lock plate. Bailey was listed as an armorer to the state and was repairing public arms in 1775.

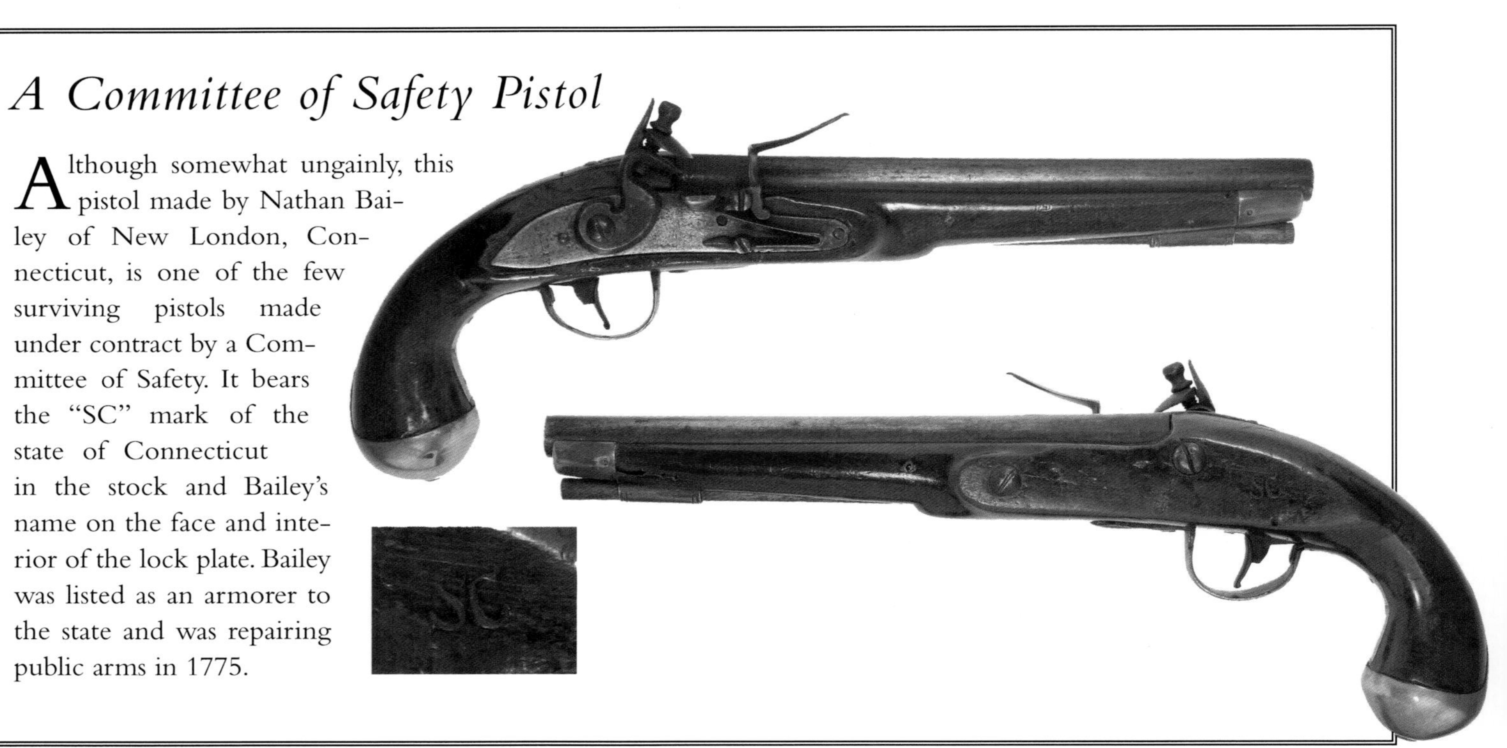

RICHARD ULBRICH COLLECTION

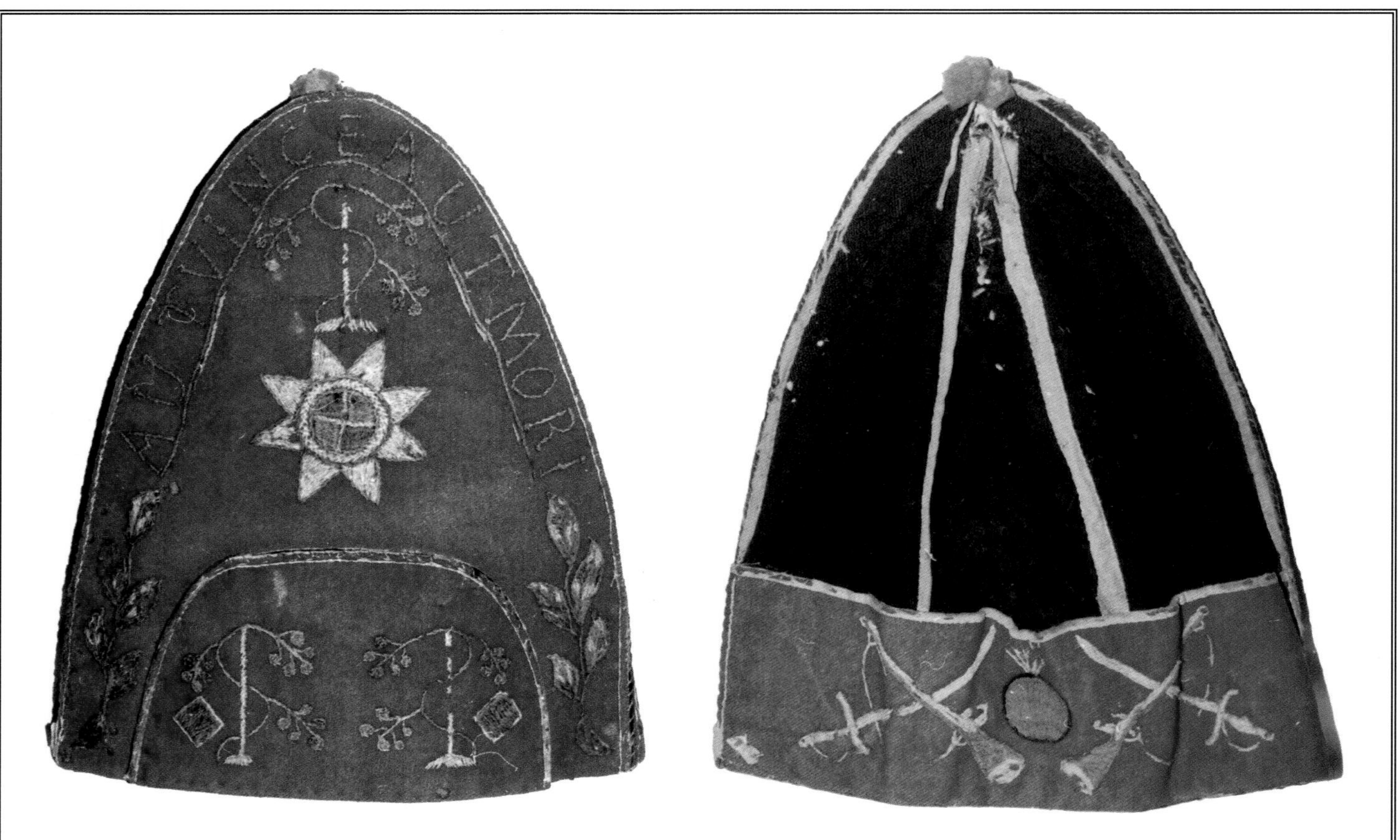

An American Grenadier's Cap

This cloth grenadier's miter cap, bearing the embroidered arms of the state of Connecticut, is believed to have been worn by the Governor's Foot Guard in New Haven just before the war. It copies its form from those worn by British grenadiers prior to the change in headgear prescribed by the Warrant of 1768.

NEW-YORK HISTORICAL SOCIETY, PHOTOGRAPH BY DON TROIANI

THE MINUTE MAN

Whether among those bold few aligned on the Lexington Common or those barring passage of the Concord Bridge, or those who stunned an empire by the fearsome toll their musketry exacted at Bunker Hill, he is resolute determination personified. His suit of matching broadcloth frock coat and breeches might suggest that he is, by education and profession, a gentleman, but its colonially favored modest brown and simplicity of cut and finish would have been apropos for virtually any social strata beyond a day laborer. Forestalling austerity, his waistcoat and stockings convincingly attest to the vibrant and diverse hues apt to be encountered in city or village. With obviously greater emphasis on practicality than fashion, his broad-brimmed fur felt hat is laced only at rear, and he carries only his powder horn and shot bag, normally used for hunting.

Whether as result of his own provincial military service fifteen or so years previously, or through secondary acquisition, his Model 1728/41 French infantry musket is typical of one among many varieties within the broad and diverse array of arms which America's defenders would employ during the first years of the Revolution.

RICHARD ULBRICH COLLECTION

A Carved Powder Horn

A soldier's powder horn owned by Ruben Hoar, inscribed "Made at Fort Miller, September 19 AD 1758," which was carved for him by his brother Leonard. He served with forty-eight men from Brimfield, Massachusetts, in a company of foot under the command of Daniel Burt as part of a regiment raised by the province. During the period from March 13 to November 20, 1758, Ruben Hoar marched in response to the alarm of April 19, 1775, to Cambridge, very possibly carrying this same powder horn. Later in the Revolution, he was first lieutenant. in Capt. Joshua Shaw's 15th Company of the 1st Hampshire County Regiment of Militia. This "Ft. Miller" horn is one of three recorded to have been carved by Leonard Hoar, an obviously skilled artisan.

COL. J. CRAIG NANNOS COLLECTION

Wooden Keg

This small wooden keg or "rundlet," dated 1772, was typical of the type a militiaman might have used to carry water or even rum.

WILLIAM H. GUTHMAN COLLECTION, PHOTOGRAPH BY DON TROIANI

A Pipe Tomahawk

A remarkable pipe tomahawk with the inscription "to your arms soldier and fight" engraved on the face of the blade. Popular among troops on the frontier, deadly in battle, and handy for a smoke, this higher quality specimen may have belonged to an officer.

WILLIAM H. GUTHMAN COLLECTION, PHOTOGRAPH BY DON TROIANI

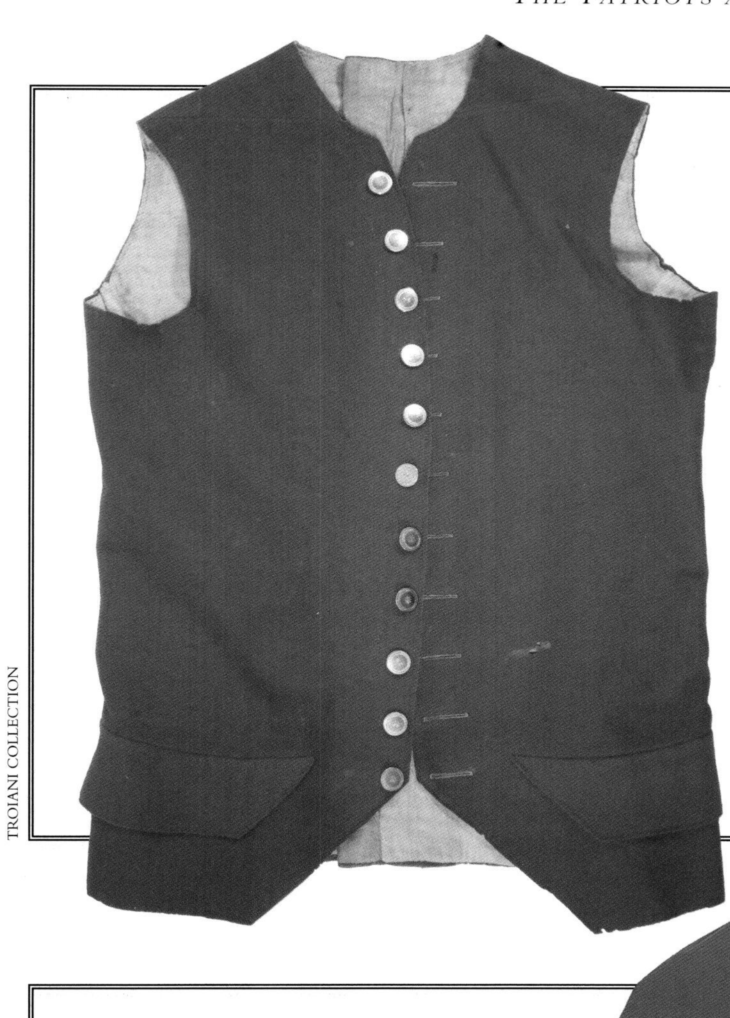

TROIANI COLLECTION

A Young Militiaman's Waistcoat

This plain scarlet woolen waistcoat with decorated Tombac buttons belonged to Simon Parker (born 1759) of Chelmsford, Massachusetts. Although legally underage for enrollment in the militia, he still may well have fought on April 19, 1775. A Simon Parker is recorded as serving along the Hudson in the 7th Middlesex County Regiment later in the war.

Cadet Coat

On April 22, 1772, the Independent Company of Cadets of Massachusetts Bay Colony adopted a scarlet-faced white coat—changing to buff facings the following year—with plain silver-plated metal repousse button with wooden backs. This coat in remarkable condition from the small, short-lived unit has survived with the loss of only a few of its original buttons.

FORT TICONDEROGA

CONTINENTAL INDEPENDENT RIFLE COMPANIES, 1775

On June 14, 1775, the Continental Congress authorized the formation of ten companies of "expert riflemen" to serve as light infantry, each to consist of four commissioned officers, eight non-commissioned officers, a drummer or hornist, and sixty-eight privates. Pennsylvania's quota was six companies (later increased to eight and subsequently formed into Thompson's Rifle Battalion) while the additional four were to be raised in Maryland and Virginia, two per colony. These were the first troops raised specifically for service as Continental regulars and also the first from the Mid-Atlantic to join their embattled Yankee brethren of the Provisional New England Army then engaged in the siege of Boston; together, they would form the nucleus of the newly established Continental Army. Daniel Morgan was appointed captain of the rifle company raised in Frederick County, Virginia, while Hugh Stephenson commanded the company from Berkeley County. Both of the Maryland companies were raised in Frederick County, the first led by Capt. Michael Cresap and the second by Thomas Price.

All of the companies were clothed in the curious yet practical outer garment that had evolved among Appalachian frontiersmen since the French and Indian War—the hunting frock or shirt. Typically made of linen or tow cloth, it was short, loose, and slit open down the front breast, often furnished with an integral shoulder cape (or two) to better protect the wearer from the elements. Sometimes dyed in various colors, it was more often left in the "grey"—that is, natural or undyed, usually a brownish, yellowish, or off-white color, depending on the flax or hemp linen used. It was usually fringed at the edges. The volunteer riflemen were expected to be of "sufficient property to Clothe themselves completely, find their own arms and accoutrements, that is,

Officer's Commission

In 1775 John Hancock signed this partially printed commission of Capt. Thomas Price of Frederick, Maryland, giving him command of an independent rifle company in Continental service. After serving with his company at the siege of Boston, Price became major of Smallwood's Maryland Regiment and, later, colonel of the 2nd Maryland until his resignation in 1780.

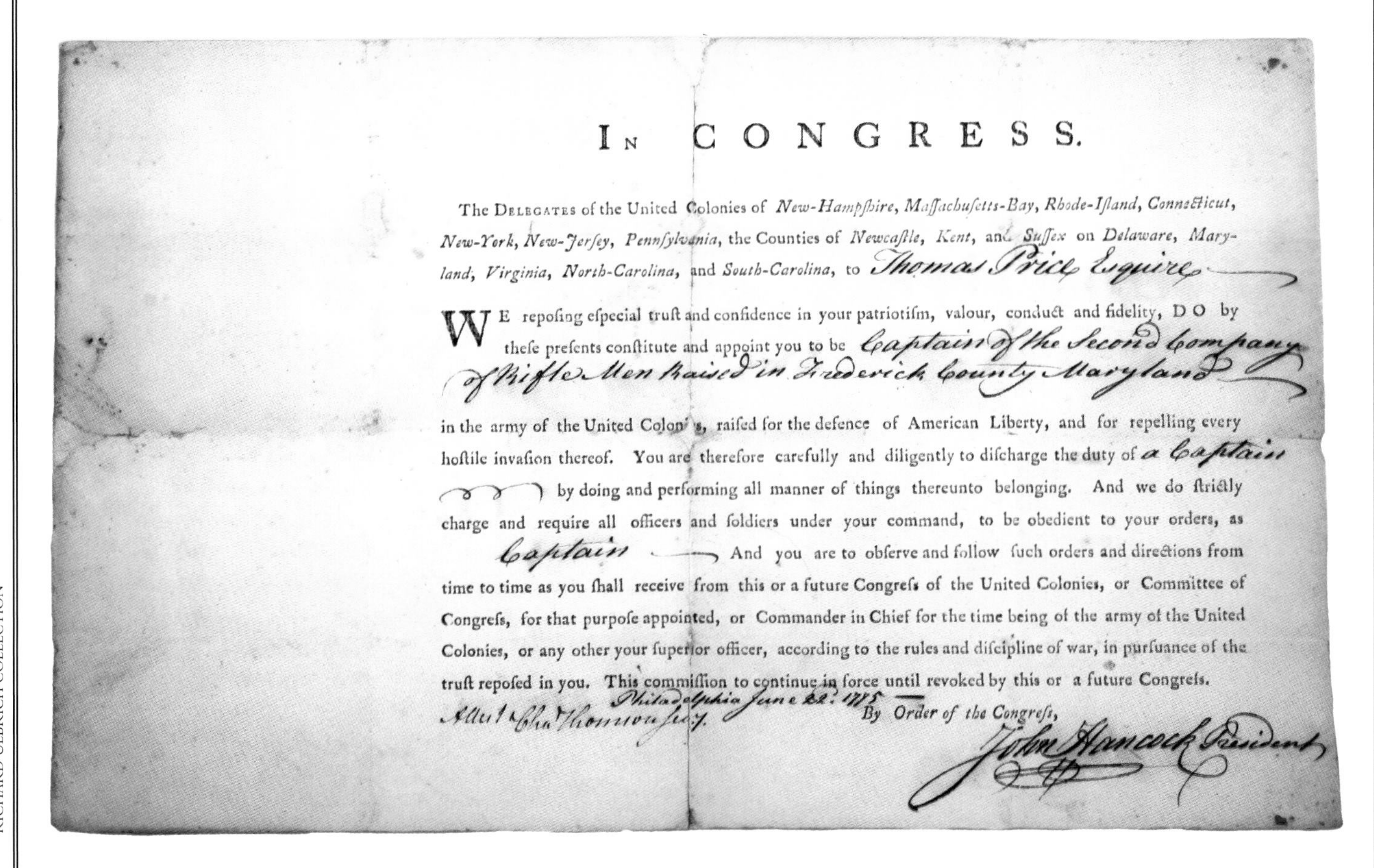

IN CONGRESS.

The DELEGATES of the United Colonies of *New-Hampſhire, Maſſachuſetts-Bay, Rhode-Iſland, Connecticut, New-York, New-Jerſey, Pennſylvania*, the Counties of *Newcaſtle, Kent*, and *Suſſex* on *Delaware, Maryland, Virginia, North-Carolina*, and *South-Carolina*, to Thomas Price Esquire

WE repoſing eſpecial truſt and confidence in your patriotiſm, valour, conduct and fidelity, DO by theſe preſents conſtitute and appoint you to be Captain of the Second Company of Rifle Men raised in Frederick County Maryland in the army of the United Colonies, raiſed for the defence of American Liberty, and for repelling every hoſtile invaſion thereof. You are therefore carefully and diligently to diſcharge the duty of a Captain by doing and performing all manner of things thereunto belonging. And we do ſtrictly charge and require all officers and ſoldiers under your command, to be obedient to your orders, as Captain And you are to obſerve and follow ſuch orders and directions from time to time as you ſhall receive from this or a future Congreſs of the United Colonies, or Committee of Congreſs, for that purpoſe appointed, or Commander in Chief for the time being of the army of the United Colonies, or any other your ſuperior officer, according to the rules and diſcipline of war, in purſuance of the truſt repoſed in you. This commiſſion to continue in force until revoked by this or a future Congreſs.

Philadelphia June 22. 1775

By Order of the Congreſs,

Attest Cha Thomson Secy.

John Hancock President

an approved Rifle, handsome shot pouch, and powder-horn, blanket and knapsack, with . . . a hunting shirt and pantaloons fringed on every edge and in various ways."

A Massachusetts veteran remembered the dress of Morgan's men as a "short frock made of pepper and salt colored cotton cloth like a common working frock . . . except that it was short and open before, to be tied with strings, pantaloons in the same fabric and color," while a Pennsylvania rifleman described his company's dress as a "deep ash colored hunting shirt, leggings and moccasins," further noting that it was "the silly fashion of the times for these riflemen to ape the manner of savages." Besides the sometime wearing of cloth or buckskin Indian leggings over their trousers or breeches, this meant the adoption of a breechclout of similar material to the leggings (often trimmed with colored tape bindings and beads, in the Indian manner) in lieu of such legwear, not to mention the occasional use of war paint.

While marching from Frederick, an eyewitness described "Cresap's formidable Company . . . painted like Indians," while thirty men of Stephenson's company purposely stopped before entering Lancaster, Pennsylvania, in order to apply paint, entering the town whooping like Indians. Their accurate fire inflicted such heavy casualties among British officers that the latter were permitted to remove the lace and other distinctions from their uniforms in order to reduce the likelihood of being singled out as targets.

Wooden Staved Canteen

This wooden staved canteen bears the inscribed name of Asaph Parmalee of Guilford, Connecticut, who served as a sergeant in Captain Dunning's Company of the 13th Connecticut Militia Regiment in 1776 and who likely saw service at the battles of Long Island and Kips Bay. The other side of this canteen bears the carved name of Asaph's nephew, James Parmalee, also of Guilford. James served with the 2nd Connecticut Regiment, Continental Line, from January 10, 1777, to January 10, 1780. In an 1818 pension, James remembered serving under Lafayette and observing the hanging of Major Andre.

FRANK KRAVIC AND PHILIP MEAD COLLECTION

An American Hunting Knife

An American hunting or utility knife which was recovered during construction excavations in central Philadelphia. It features a curved iron blade with a simple stag handle and a leather sheath worked with pricked decorative motifs and the inscription "ano 1759." This is typical of the type of the everyday tool rifleman and frontiersmen carried and may well be the earliest known American-made knife.

TROIANI COLLECTION

1ST CONTINENTAL RIFLE REGIMENT, SUMMER–WINTER 1776

U.S.ARMY HISTORICAL FOUNDATION

Upon assuming command of the 1st Continental Regiment, Lt. Col. Edward Hand took great pains to properly equip his riflemen and instill a sense of esprit de corps. New uniforms were ordered from Pennsylvania, in addition to a fine silk standard or color for the senior regiment of the army. The latter was described by Hand on

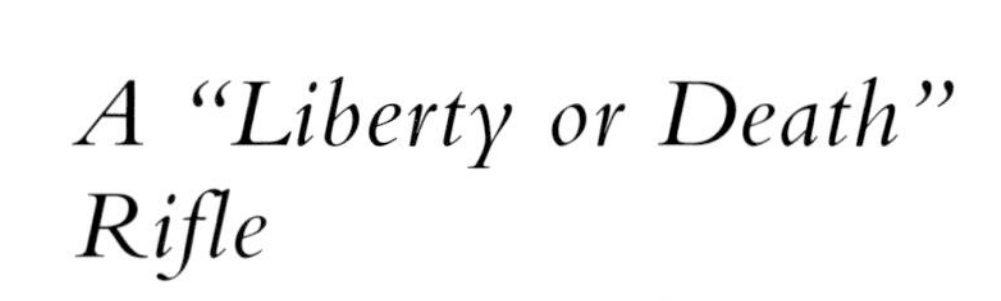

RICHARD ULBRICH COLLECTION

A "Liberty or Death" Rifle

The motto "Liberty or Death" boldly engraved on the patchbox of this graceful rifle was hardly an idle boast. With Pennsylvania rifles such as this, practiced frontier marksmen heralded death at a distance for many of the king's soldiers. Probably made in Bucks County or the Lehigh Valley, it has a military-style lock and has been modified to take a bayonet. A major flaw with most such rifles was the lack of a bayonet, which placed the users at a serious disadvantage against bayonet-armed troops in close-quarter fighting. The American riflemen suffered seriously at the Battle of Long Island, being unable to defend themselves when over run by fast moving regular troops.

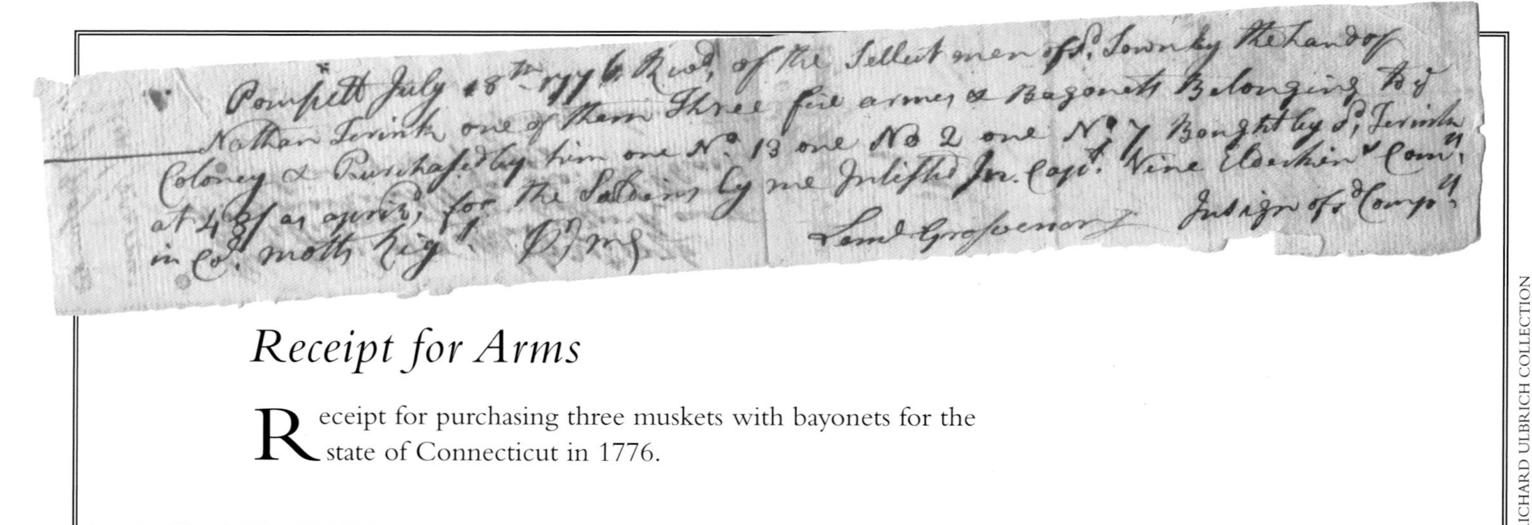

Pomfrett July 18th 1776 Recd of the Sellect men of sd Town by the hand of Nathan Smith one of them Three fire armes & Bagonets Belonging to ye Colony & Purchased by him one No 13 one No 2 one No 7 Bought by sd Smith at 4£ a peice for the Soldiers by me

RICHARD ULBRICH COLLECTION

Receipt for Arms

Receipt for purchasing three muskets with bayonets for the state of Connecticut in 1776.

March 8, 1776, as "a deep green ground, the device a tiger partly enclosed by toils, attempting the pass, defended by a hunter armed with a spear . . . on a crimson field the motto Domari nolo." Made in Philadelphia from Hand's description, the standard was forwarded to the rifle regiment, arriving in time to be carried during the fall 1776 campaign; this stalwart veteran of Revolutionary service has survived until the present, carefully handed down by descendants of Thomas Robinson (the regiment's third commander), until donated by them to the Pennsylvania Historical and Museum Commission.

The regimental uniforms were to match the colors of the standard: short green coats with scarlet or red facings, with buckskin breeches. However, most of the woolen uniforms sent for the enlisted men were in store at Fort Lee and captured when that post fell on November 20, 1776. Thus, most of the men continued to wear their traditional riflemen's dress of linen for the remainder of the fall and winter, while many officers, who had privately purchased their own uniforms, such as this ensign carrying the standard, were better clothed for cold weather. This rifle undress or campaign uniform was a short, fringed, green-dyed hunting frock and matching trousers, worn with narrow-brimmed "round" hats trimmed with white binding and plumes—typically bucktails or feathers, often to suit the whim of its wearer.

GRENADIER, 26TH CONTINENTAL INFANTRY, 1776

Elite grenadier companies dressed in tall, pointed caps is not normally the image that comes to mind when one thinks of the Continental Army, but a number of regiments did indeed have troops dressed in this manner. One of the earliest documented examples is that of Capt. Thomas Mighill's company of Col. Laomi Baldwin's 26th Continental, a regiment raised for one year's service in early 1776 which distinguished itself in the rear-guard action at Throg's Neck later that fall. The regiment was clothed in brown coats with buff facings which, according to one Hessian eyewitness, appear to have been cut with "collars and facings made in the English fashion." Waistcoats and breeches were probably of white cloth, based on Colonel Baldwin's inventory. During May 1776, Mighill purchased and issued both pewter and brass buttons for his men, including "plain" ones and others with "a rim on the edges," so the coats do not all appear to be uniform in that regard.

This grenadier's miter cap is based on a surviving example, now in the Smithsonian collections, which has a stiffened front plate of brick-red cloth, with buff "turn-up" and brown cloth "bag," a front embroidered with the regimental number and flaming grenade, as well as a "*GW*" cipher. The cipher was in honor of the Continental Army commander in chief, and the regiment was sometimes called the George Washington Regiment. Mighill also exchanged his company's old arms in July, drawing from the Continental Store some of "Manlys Guns" in their stead. These were Short Land Pattern muskets and bayonets taken from cargo of the British ordnance store ship *Nancy*, captured in November 1775 by the armed schooner *Lee*, Capt. John Manley commanding. Also issued with the muskets were Ordnance-issue "belly" boxes, belts, and frogs, part of the "stand of arms" of 2,000 pieces captured aboard the *Nancy*.

BRUCE HERMAN COLLECTION

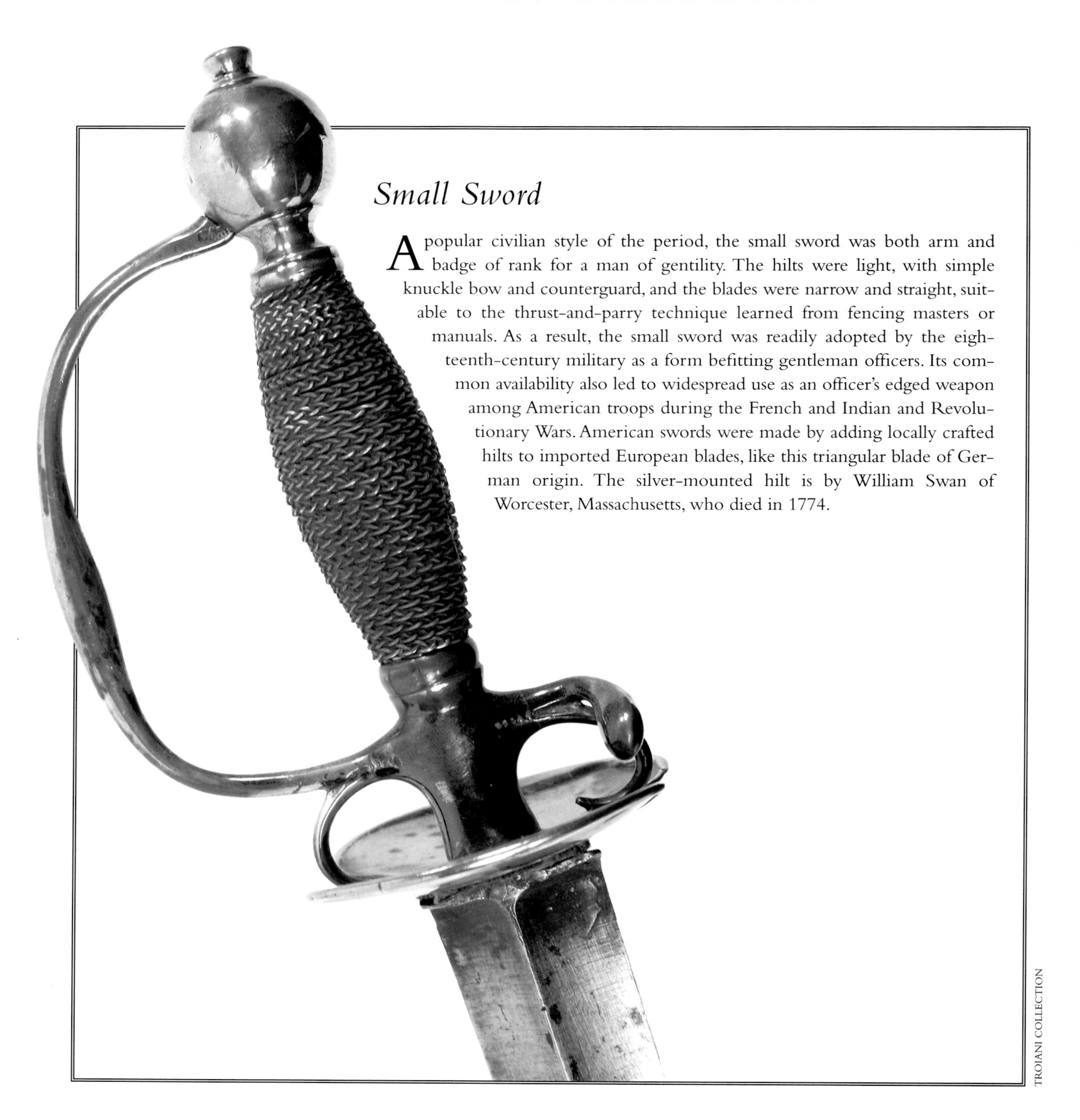

Small Sword

A popular civilian style of the period, the small sword was both arm and badge of rank for a man of gentility. The hilts were light, with simple knuckle bow and counterguard, and the blades were narrow and straight, suitable to the thrust-and-parry technique learned from fencing masters or manuals. As a result, the small sword was readily adopted by the eighteenth-century military as a form befitting gentleman officers. Its common availability also led to widespread use as an officer's edged weapon among American troops during the French and Indian and Revolutionary Wars. American swords were made by adding locally crafted hilts to imported European blades, like this triangular blade of German origin. The silver-mounted hilt is by William Swan of Worcester, Massachusetts, who died in 1774.

TROIANI COLLECTION

PRIVATE, 3RD NEW JERSEY REGIMENT OF 1776

Blue—a color long associated with the Whig or opposition party to the Tory government in England—was a logical color for the patriot forces being raised in America, and soon wartime demands exceeded available supplies. As a result, many regiments received coats of less popular colors, such as green, gray, and "drab"—an aptly named dye of brownish cast, ranging in shade from light to dark. After the 3rd New Jersey Regiment was established on January 10, 1776, a uniform consisting of coats and belted waistcoats of light drab (almost a tan shade) and buckskin breeches was procured. The short coats had narrow lapels, cape, and pointed cuffs of dark blue, with "slashed sleeves," that buttoned on the underseam. Coat and waistcoat buttons were pewter, cast with "New Jersey" in raised script letters, and the men's cocked hats were neatly bound with white tape. Accoutrements made by New Jersey saddlers were furnished with buff leather crossbelts of the new fashion, and muskets were drawn from colony stores, supplemented by market purchases. This soldier, shown here advancing while loading, carries a "NEW JERSEY"–marked, Wilson-contract musket of the type purchased by the colony during and following the French and Indian War.

RICHARD ULBRICH COLLECTION

Liberty Cartridge Box

The rectangular impressed panel on the face of this cartridge box was, in all probability, done with the same metal plate used to emboss patriotic leather wallets of the period. With its decorative leaf and vine motif, the raised word "Liberty" makes a courageous statement for all to see.

PRIVATE COLLECTION

A Mortar Shell

American thirteen-inch iron mortar shell with raised lip and lifting handles (one is missing), excavated near Fort Ticonderoga-Mount Independence. Large mortars using shells such as this were primarily for siege operations and large fortifications.

TROIANI COLLECTION

An Infernal Engine

Among the most primitive weapons and the earliest form of "land mine" almost unchanged from ancient times is this iron caltrop. Designed to puncture a foot or hoof, they could be spread about in front of earthworks, in river fords, or at any place where enemy troops might attempt to pass. The British were recorded as using them at Boston in 1775.

WILLIAM H. GUTHMAN COLLECTION, PHOTOGRAPH BY DON TROIANI

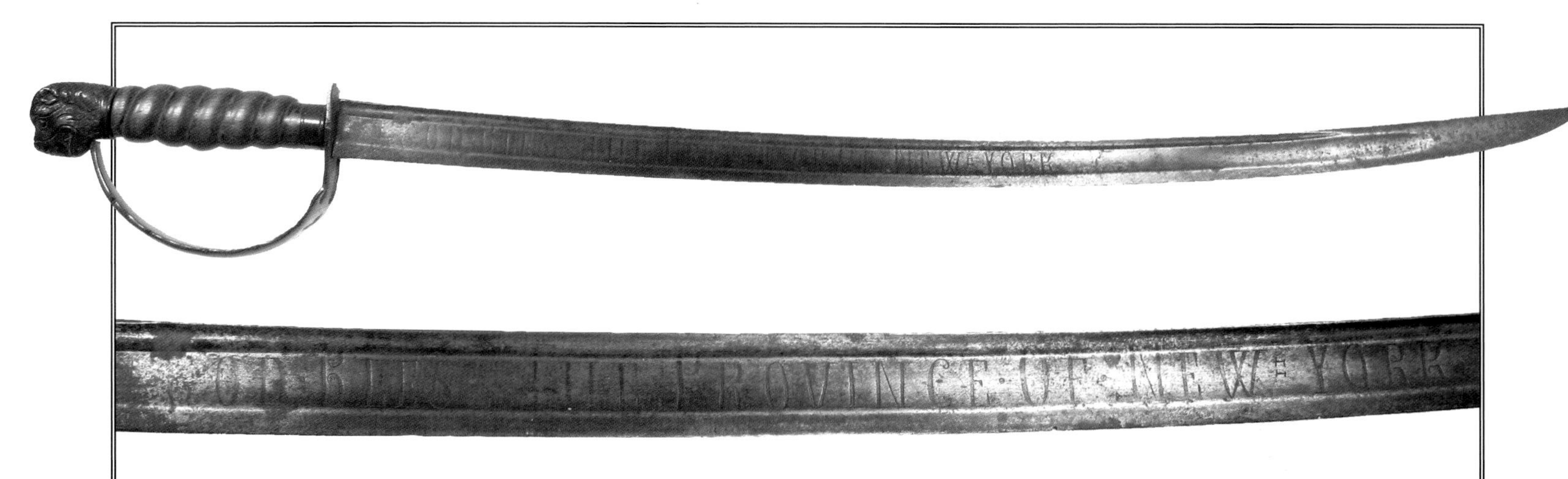

TROIANI COLLECTION

An American Officer's Hanger

An American officer's hanger with a brass guard and lion's head pommel featuring bulbous turned wooden grips. The blade displays in large letters "God Bless the Province of New York." Similarly inscribed swords featuring Massachusetts Bay and New Jersey are also known, and it has been theorized that these blades may have been imported into the colonies as early as the 1750s. This specimen was found in the Mohawk Valley of New York State.

BOB MCDONALD COLLECTION

Pewter Button

Pewter New Jersey soldier's button with the name of the state fully spelled out in script. These have been recovered from a site occupied by New Jersey troops in the 1776–77 period.

Despite its rather dull-colored uniform, the 3rd New Jersey was said "to be the completest and best Regiment" when formally mustered into Continental service at New York City on May 1, 1776. The eight-company regiment sailed up the Hudson as part of Gen. John Sullivan's brigade, intending to join the Northern Army in Canada. However, the 3rd was instead detached and marched to the Mohawk Valley to intimidate Loyalists from attempting to organize any armed resistance and to maintain, at the least, the neutrality of the Oneida Iroquois. A substantial portion of the regiment was stationed at Fort Stanwix, where it played a major role in the rebuilding of the crumbling fortification. In October the 3rd New Jersey was ordered to Fort Ticonderoga, where it remained in garrison until the end of February 1777, before marching homeward to Morristown, New Jersey, where its men were discharged on March 20, 1777.

PRIVATE, 3RD NEW YORK REGIMENT, 1777

MICHAEL FLANAGAN COLLECTION

In January 1777, Col. Peter Gansevoort of the 3rd New York wrote the governor of New York that "troops not paid and half naked can be but little expected from" and requested new uniforms for his regiment. The Continental storekeeper at Albany was able to issue a limited supply of short drab coats to alleviate the immediate needs of the regiment's worst-clothed men, but it would not be until spring and early summer that the regiment took to the field in their new regimental coats of blue with red facings and white linings. Further, many of the men were rearmed with new French Model 1766 muskets, in addition to drawing new cartridge boxes and bayonet belts. Thus equipped, the men of the 3rd New York would gallantly and successfully defend Fort Stanwix during late summer 1777 when besieged by an invading British force.

A Wrought Iron Grill

An unusually complete example of a soldier's wrought iron grill for broiling meat recovered during archeology work at Fort Stanwix. Items like this could have been crafted by one of the fort's blacksmiths or perhaps brought in from elsewhere.

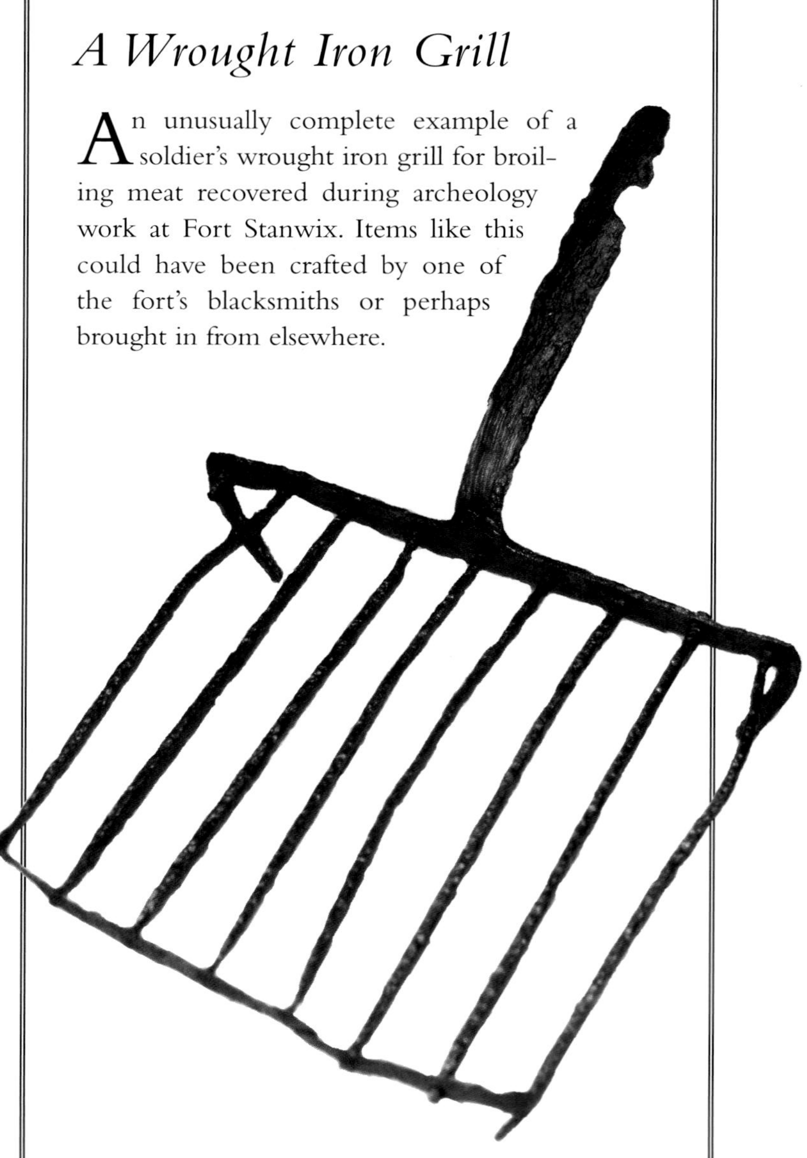

NATIONAL PARK SERVICE, PHOTOGRAPH BY DON TROIANI

TROIANI COLLECTION

A French Model 1728/1741 Musket

Essentially an improved version of the model 1717, the first standardized French pattern, this model 1728 musket was first updated in 1741, when iron ramrods replaced the earlier wooden ones. It had a 44-inch barrel of .69 caliber, firing a ball of slightly smaller diameter than that fired by its .75-caliber British counterpart. Further changes, principally in the configuration of the barrel bands, were incorporated in a new model, the 1746 musket, which probably also saw limited usage here during the French and Indian War. Well made and reliable, many of these muskets found their way into British and American hands and were later used during the Revolutionary War, not only by patriot forces, but also by some Loyalist troops.

TROIANI COLLECTION

A Serviceable Musket

A crudely fashioned American Committee of Safety musket made by Jesse Curtis of Waterbury, Connecticut, which conforms to the specifications laid out by the state in 1776. It has a forty-four-inch barrel and an imported Dutch lock (as provided to the gun makers by the state) marked "I. Curtis." Also, as required, the letters "SC" (State of Connecticut) are stamped on the top of the barrel. Curtis had two known contracts for a total of thirty-two muskets in 1778 and 1779, although he may well have made more. Very few signed Committee of Safety muskets survive today.

GENERAL GEORGE WASHINGTON, 1776

RICHARD ULBRICH COLLECTION

In 1774, "a Number of Gentlemen & Freeholders" in Fairfax County, Virginia, formed themselves into the "Fairfax Independant Company of Voluntiers" and elected Col. George Washington, who was then in Philadelphia as one of the Virginia delegates to the First Continental Congress, as their commanding field officer. The dress specified that the new patriotic corps was to be "a regular Uniform of Blue, turn'd up with Buff; with plain yellow metal Buttons, Buff Waist Coat & Breeches, & white Stockings." The adoption of blue and buff was not by mere accident or whim, as they were "*the antient Whig Colours* of England"—the Whigs being the opposition party to the Tory government then in power and with whom the colonists felt politically aligned. Washington's step-grandson and adopted son, George Washington Parke Custis, later claimed that Washington selected the uniform, and it is very likely that he had more than a little influence in this decision since the Virginians had conferred with him about such military matters prior to his departure in August.

Back home at Mount Vernon in November, Washington had "1 Suite Regimentals" made for himself, which then served as the pattern for the entire company. This uniform would accompany Washington on his return to Philadelphia to attend the Second Continental Congress. Worn by him to the May–June 1775 sessions, it served to remind his fellow-delegates that the tall, impressive-looking Virginian was not only a veteran soldier, but was willing to fight and possibly sacrifice his life in upholding their rights and liberties as free-born British subjects. Though we will never be sure of

Designed to Mutilate

These four .69-caliber musket balls with iron nails pounded through them were excavated years ago near Fort Ticonderoga. Projectiles such as these were contrived to cause as much damage to flesh as possible. Officially condemned in correspondence by both sides, it appears not to have been a frequent practice since such specimens are almost never recovered from wartime campsites.

TROIANI COLLECTION

An Officer's "Takedown" Fusil

American officer's fusil carried by Lt. Abraham Rose of the 1st Regiment of Minute Men of Suffolk County, Long Island, New York, in 1776. This gun is unique in that it is signed by two different makers: "Perkin" on the lock and "W. Allen fecit" on the barrel. Both were gunsmiths in New York City before and during the Revolutionary period. A superior quality officer's weapon, it is designed with a two-piece stock and easily removable barrel, allowing speedy disassembly for traveling purposes. This arm was found during the disposal of the Rose family homestead in Bridgehampton, Long Island, New York.

TROIANI COLLECTION

An Identified Cartridge Box

During the Revolutionary War and later, Americans frequently referred to all cartridge containers worn by soldiers as "boxes," as differentiated from the British system, which distinguished the more substantial shoulder "pouches" from the belly-mounted "boxes" discussed earlier.

This cartridge box was carried by a Connecticut militiaman during the 1776 New York Campaign, and the front of its wooden block bears the following inscription: "Benjamin Fogg is my Name and with my hand I wrote the same Bought at portland [Connecticut] price one dollar." It still contains two original paper-wrapped musket cartridges in the nineteen-hole block, which is enclosed within the early bag-style pouch of black leather. The shoulder sling is of linen upholstery webbing, with the ends inserted and sewn into place at the back seam of the pouch flap. This form of pouch was also commonly issued to Connecticut Continental troops, although by 1779 it had fallen out of favor in preference for improved models and was already being referred to as being of the "old construction."

TROIANI COLLECTION

the extent such martial attire played in convincing his peers that he was the most likely candidate for the challenging task at hand, Congress enthusiastically appointed Washington general and commander in chief of the Continental forces being raised for, or already engaged in, the siege of British-held Boston.

Arriving at Cambridge on July 4, 1775, to take command of the "troops of the UNITED PROVINCES of North America," Washington found a collection of New England farmers, tradesmen, sailors, and the like—largely dressed as they had come from the plow, shop, or masthead. Washington was shocked by the lack of discipline and proper sanitation, as well as the ragged and non-uniform clothing. In contrast, Washington cut a very martial figure among his men, as noted by Surgeon James Thacher, who described him as "truly noble and majestic; being tall and well proportioned" and wearing "a blue coat with buff-colored facings, a rich epaulette on each shoulder, buff under dress, and an elegant small sword; a black cockade in his hat." Finding that the generals and their staffs were not receiving the military recognition and courtesies of their rank, Washington issued a general order on July 10 to prescribe devices to distinguish the rank and status of officers; for the commander in chief,

Belt Axe

Typical of small-size belt axes excavated on campsites, the head of this specimen is stamped "US" on one side and "CC" on the other.

COL. J. CRAIG NANNOS COLLECTION

Musket Flints

French-style, amber-colored musket flints excavated from American campsites in the Hudson Highlands. The upper specimens are partly sheathed with flattened lead to prevent slippage while in the jaws of the musket hammer.

TROIANI COLLECTION

Wrapped Cartridges

Two American paper-wrapped cartridges of typical types. Occasionally, newspaper was used as a wrap, which, if bearing a date, allows placing the exact manufacture of the cartridge itself.

TROIANI COLLECTION

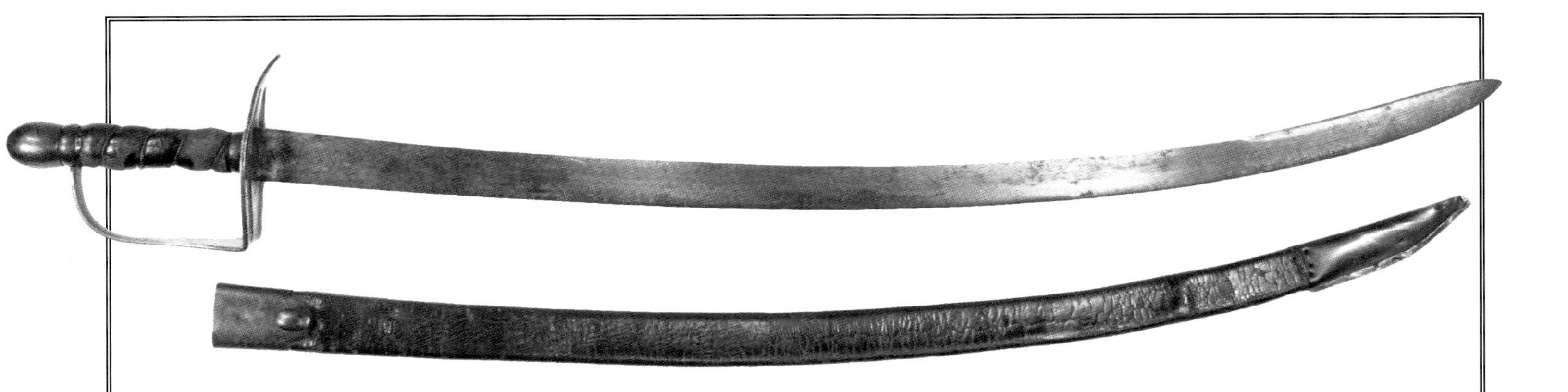

A Partisan Leader's Potter Saber

Dragoon saber with iron-mounted scabbard made by James Potter of New York City during the Revolution. Potter's well-known, robust sabers were issued to Loyalist cavalry and were also heavily used by the patriot light horse in large numbers. This example was owned by mounted partisan leader Richard Mead (1758–1826) of Greenwich, Connecticut, and was passed down through his family with an accompanying note from his granddaughter. Mead and his small band defended the local area from Tory Cowboys and Refugees, who terrorized Westchester County and the Connecticut coastline. Local tradition holds that he and his band lived outdoors all year round in order that the Loyalists could not locate him. In 1780 he was captured and spent six weeks in the infamous Sugar House prison until exchanged. Quite likely, this saber was taken by Mead from a Loyalist horseman at some point during the war. His granddaughter is buried adjacent to him in the Second Congregational Church Cemetery in Greenwich, Connecticut.

TROIANI COLLECTION

Buckshot and Ball

American buckshot and .69-caliber ball excavated from a campsite of late 1778 and found together where a cartridge was dropped. Favored by the Americans in particular, "buck and ball" was an effective load, particularly at close range.

TROIANI COLLECTION

Buckshot Mold

A large brass gang mold for casting several sizes of buckshot with the maker's name, "N Dominy," and the date, 1779, engraved into the side.

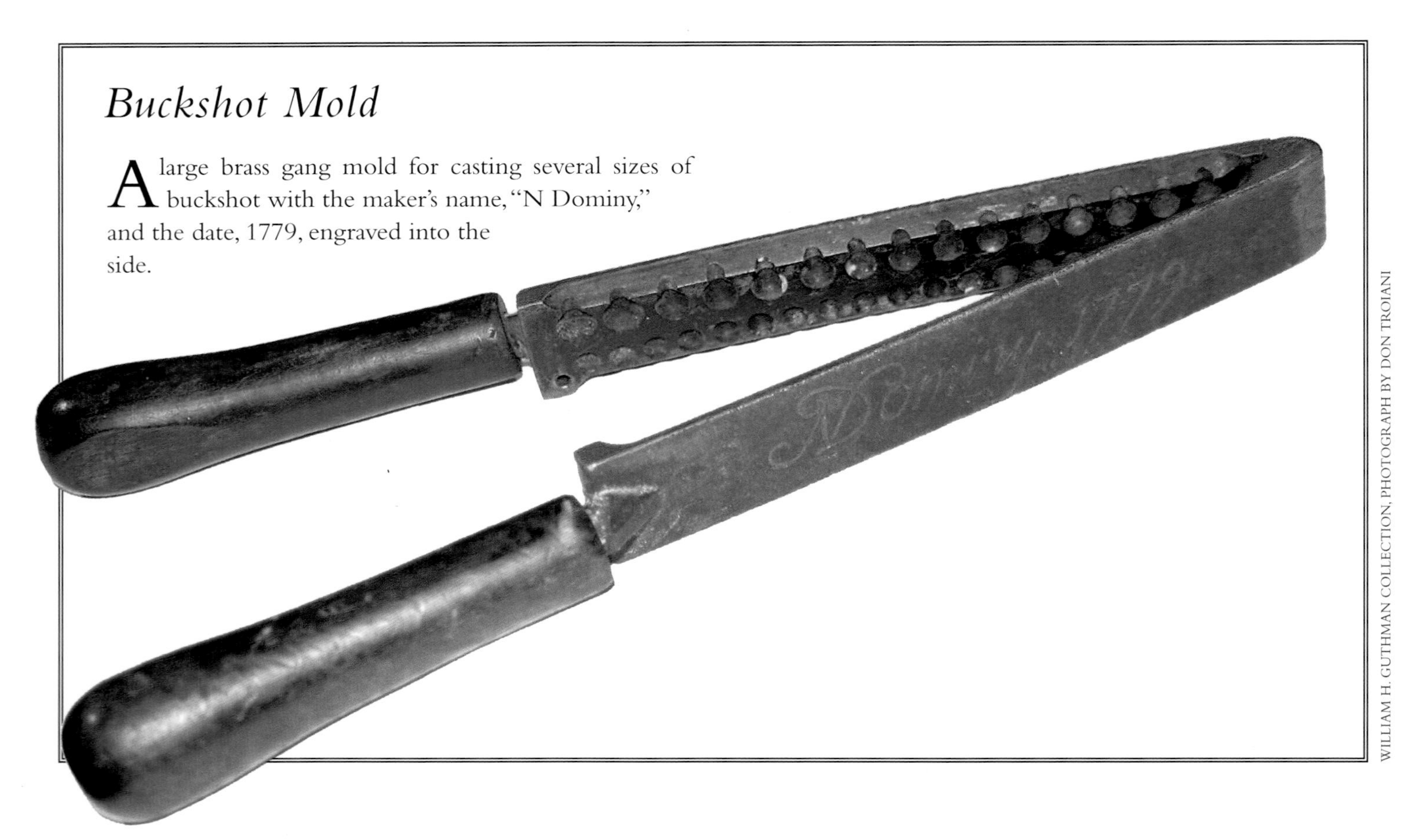

WILLIAM H. GUTHMAN COLLECTION, PHOTOGRAPH BY DON TROIANI

this was to be "a light blue Ribband, wore across his breast, between his Coat and Waistcoat."

Washington is shown as he would have appeared during the Battle of White Plains during the New York campaign of 1776 (and subsequently in the retreat across New Jersey and the victories at Trenton and Princeton). Washington's deep blue "regimental" coat is faced and lined with buff and trimmed with plain, flat, gilt buttons. The three buttons on each sleeve are set "long" with "dragoon" cuffs—period terms denoting the placement of buttons up rather than around the cuff and the use of indented cuffs and worked buttonholes of herringbone form. Each shoulder bears an epaulette made of gold lace finished in a "rose knot" trimmed with fine gold-bullion fringe. A silver-hilted smallsword is suspended at Washington's left hip, the so-called "State" sword still preserved at Mount Vernon, known to have been worn by him during at least the first two years of the war. His buff waistcoat is edged with foliate embroidery, and his breeches are of buckskin leather. Considered the "horseman of his age," Washington preferred the saddle to

"Liberty, This is Fair" Pouch

One of the finest examples of an American cartridge box of the Revolutionary War, this extraordinary example has a large embossed figure of a grenadier or light infantryman with his musket at rest, who is flanked on either side by hand-painted bell tents. The legend dauntlessly proclaims, "Liberty, This is Fair." Most likely embossed with a metal or wooden plate, logic would dictate a number of pouches like this were so ornamented, but this example appears to be the only survivor. The shoulder strap is of black leather.

FORT TICONDEROGA

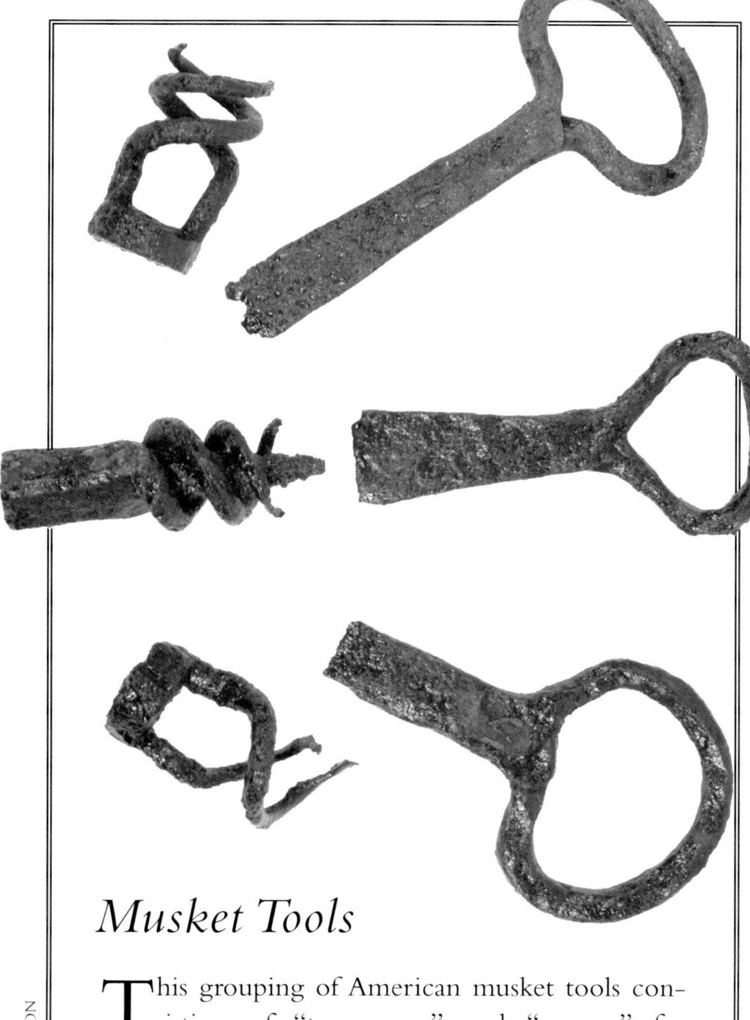

Musket Tools

This grouping of American musket tools consisting of "turnscrews" and "worms" for extracting lead balls was excavated near the Camden, South Carolina, battlefield.

TROIANI COLLECTION

any chair and wore out numerous pairs of buckskin riding breeches—normally durable, long-lasting garments. Disregarding current fashion extremes, he preferred his breeches "roomy in the seat and not so tight in the thigh," noting that snug ones can only "with difficulty . . . be drawn on, to which I have an utter aversion."

Behind him are a mix of militia and short-term "regulars" that made up his force during that hard-fought action, most wearing civilian clothing and a few the short, "bounty" coats furnished by the colony of Massachusetts in 1775 as an incentive to military service. They are armed with a mix of long arms—civilian fowlers and military muskets of British manufacture or Committee of Safety copies, not to mention a few captured "French relics" from prior colonial service. While many of the colonies strove to furnish proper uniforms for their regiments, Congress had failed to issue a regulation that governed the dress of its general officers, much less the entire Continental Army. However, Washington's aides-de-camp seemed to have quickly adopted his uniform, as did many of the general officers. Soon blue and buff became the widely used, but as yet still unofficial, dress of the army's general staff. As seen here, one of Washington's aides-de-camp (who held commissions as lieutenant colonels) wears such a uniform and the green ribbon sash of his position, as well as the pink cockade denoting a field-grade officer. Little did Washington realize, when he first donned blue and buff, that such would continue in his wardrobe for the remainder of his life. Nor did he dream that it would come to symbolize not only his own service and sacrifices as a citizen-soldier, but those of his Revolutionary compatriots, to future generations of Americans.

Saddle Holsters

Leather saddle holsters with blue cloth covered flaps used by Col. Heman Swift of the 7th (and later the 2nd) Connecticut Regiments of the Continental Line. Swift's Regiment fought at the Battle of Germantown and wintered at Valley Forge.

TROIANI COLLECTION

Marquis de Lafayette's Sash

This crimson sash of sprangwork was, by tradition, used by the Marquis de Lafayette to bind his leg wound at the Battle of Brandywine. Col. Heman Swift, who was standing nearby, placed his own sash around the general's waist. Before Lafayette returned to France, he presented the colonel with this sash and a pair of epaulettes. Besides being draped across the shoulder as a badge of rank, a sprangwork sash could stretch amply to form a sling or impromptu stretcher when not wrapped around its owner's waist.

FRAUNCES TAVERN ® MUSEUM, SONS OF THE REVOLUTION IN THE STATE OF NEW YORK, PHOTOGRAPH BY DON TROIANI

"Wilson" Military Fusil, 1750–60

Fusils, or "fuzees," were essentially lightweight versions of the smoothbore muskets typically carried by officers. Military-type fusils generally had the same furniture as their heavier counterparts but were scaled down in size. Barrels were lighter and smaller, both in caliber (usually .65 to .68) and length (36 to 42 inches). Marked "WILSON" on the lock plate, this 42-inch-barreled fusil was made by the firm of Richard Wilson and closely resembles the Long Land Pattern musket that inspired it.

This weapon's furniture and workmanship are much simpler than that usually found on an officer's privately purchased fusil, suggesting a similar contract procurement or common issue. Commercially produced military arms were purchased by British colonial governments in North America, including New Jersey, Virginia, Massachusetts, South Carolina, and New York City, during the French and Indian War period. A small number of Wilson muskets marked "NEW JERSEY" or "CITY OF NEW YORK" still survive.

TROIANI COLLECTION

"Rose Knot" Epaulettes

These silver "rose knot" epaulettes, a form popular with British officers, are believed to have been worn by Anthony Wayne during his 1776–77 colonelcy of the 4th Pennsylvania Battalion. Showing no sign of having ever been backed with a ground of cloth, they were apparently sewn flat to the coat shoulders.

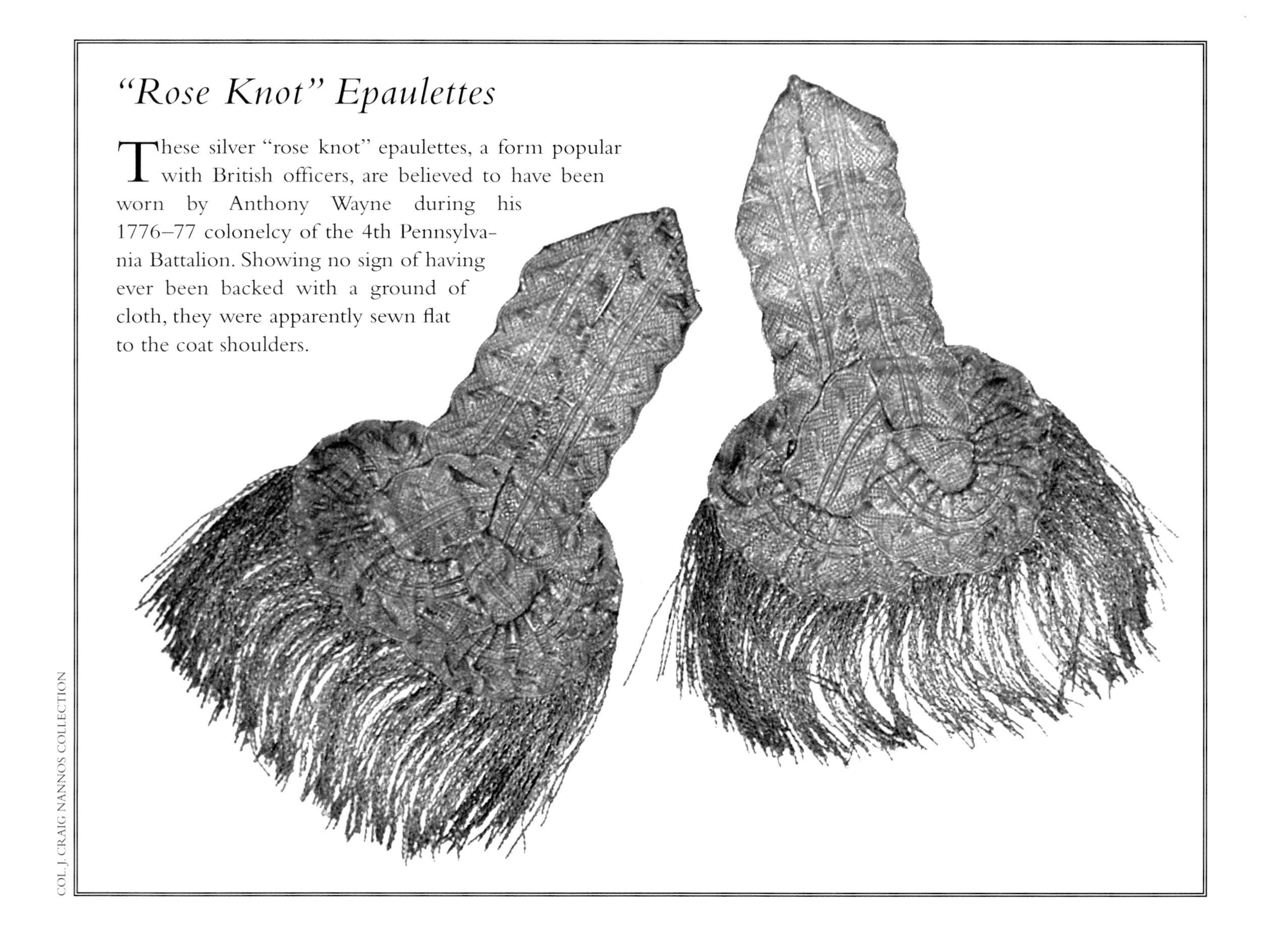

COL. J. CRAIG NANNOS COLLECTION

American Wooden Canteen, 1776

This unpainted canteen is of a form known to collectors as a "cheesebox" canteen, because of its resemblance to a wooden cheesebox. Typically made of white cedar, it was formed by wrapping a one-piece wooden band around two circular wooden faces and pegging or nailing the band into place.

Carved into one face of this canteen is the following inscription: "JOSEPH AMES x THE 10 x Day 1776 AD." One "J. Ames" served in the 2nd Continental Artillery Regiment, raised principally in New York, and "Pitckills" refers to the town of Peekskill, New York, a major Continental Army supply center on the Hudson River.

TROIANI COLLECTION

Linen Knapsack

This linen knapsack was carried during the war by Benjamin Warner (1757–1846), who first enlisted in Wooster's Connecticut Regiment on May 8, 1775, then served in the siege of Quebec, returning eastward in 1776 in time to participate in the battle for Long Island. He completed his wartime service in Crane's 3rd Continental Artillery Regiment and was discharged in 1779. Warner later settled in Ticonderoga, New York, after the war. The knapsack is now missing its straps but still retains traces of the Spanish brown paint that once coated its flap.

FORT TICONDEROGA

Wooden Canteen

This wooden canteen of stave, or "keg," construction is a fine specimen of a form well documented as Continental Army issue. This example has "U. STATES" deeply branded into one of its faces, one of several canteens of this pattern bearing such markings. The initials "JG" or "IG" also stamped in the wood may be the maker's mark.

AMERICAN REVOLUTION CENTER, PHOTOGRAPH BY A PRIVATE COLLECTOR

FIRST TROOP OF THE PHILADELPHIA CITY CAVALRY

Silk Standard, Light-Horse of the City of Philadelphia

The Light-Horse of the City of Philadelphia was composed of twenty-eight young men from the Philadelphia upper classes who completely armed and outfitted themselves as a volunteer troop of horse in 1774. Attached to the Philadelphia Associators, they escorted Washington on various occasions and served with great merit at the Battle of Princeton and in other actions. Their richly embroidered, yellow silk standard was presented in 1775 and remains in excellent condition to this day. The canton of the flag was originally a British union but was over-painted with the thirteen stripes of the United Colonies (later States) during the war.

"Cheese Box" Canteen

Sgt. Tobias Oakman of Captain Turner's Company, Colonel Brooks' Massachusetts Regiment of Guards, carved his name and dates of service into this simple wooden "cheese box" canteen. He was stationed at Cambridge, 1777–78.

BOB MCDONALD COLLECTION

THE COMMANDER IN CHIEF'S LIFE GUARD, 1777

PRIVATE COLLECTION

The Life Guard originated in March 1776 as a company-sized unit responsible for safeguarding Gen. George Washington and his military family, as well as the headquarters papers, baggage, and camp equipage. They provided the guard mounts, set up and broke down Washington's tents, and performed the myriad duties associated with headquarters interior police and administration. They were dissolved in February 1777, but reestablished on May 1, 1777, to consist of one captain, one lieutenant, four corporals, one drummer, and forty-seven privates. All of the men were required to be between five feet, nine inches and five feet, ten inches in height and "American born." Of the original cadre, most were drawn from the Virginia Line, although the unit was commanded by Capt. Caleb Gibbs, a Massachusetts Yankee. This elite corps was later expanded to 150 picked men from all the State Lines serving with the main army and served in every campaign with Washington until disbanded in 1783.

Captured Equipment

A patriot soldier ingeniously converted this captured British bayonet and waist belt frog into a shoulder belt arrangement by stitching webbing straps to the top. Captured British equipment of all types was a precious resource, and it was put to good use.

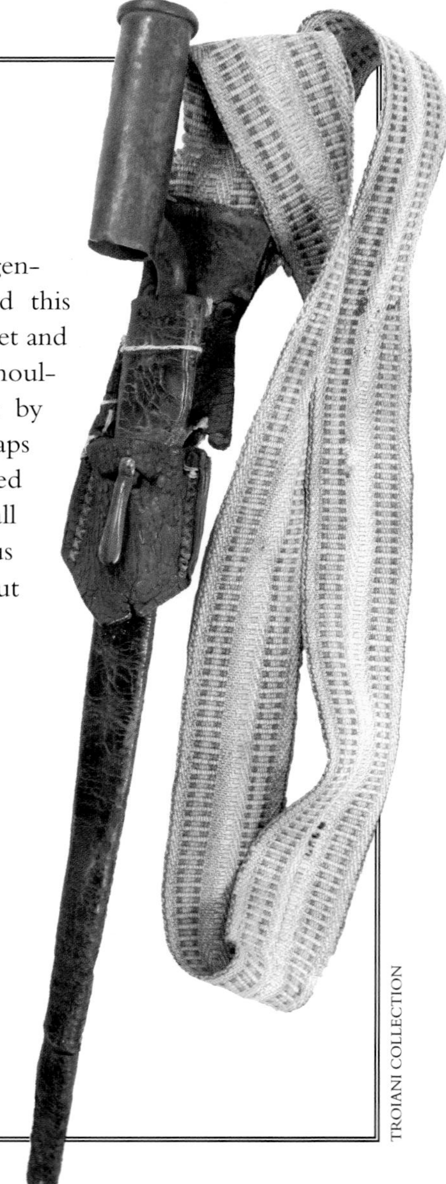
TROIANI COLLECTION

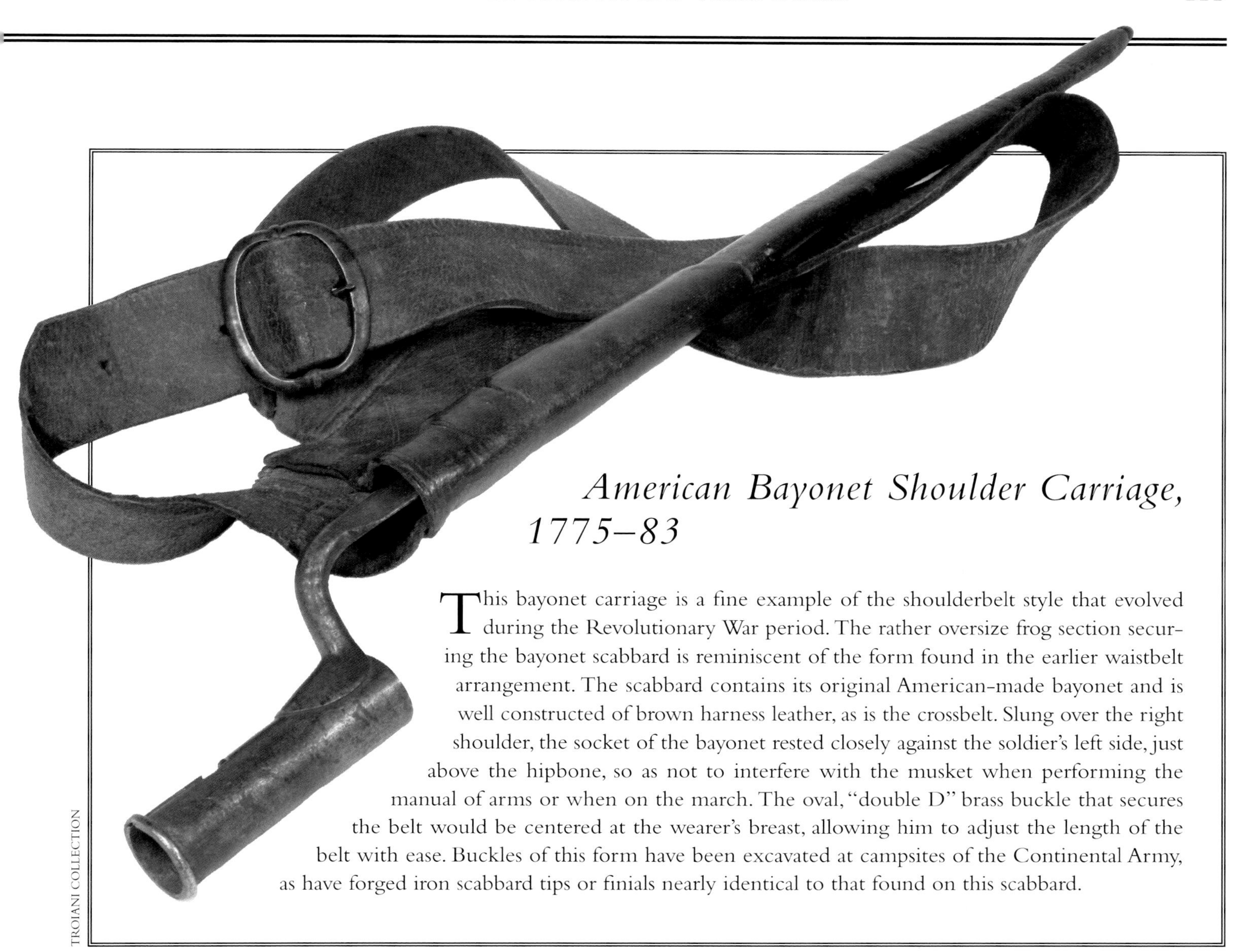

American Bayonet Shoulder Carriage, 1775–83

This bayonet carriage is a fine example of the shoulderbelt style that evolved during the Revolutionary War period. The rather oversize frog section securing the bayonet scabbard is reminiscent of the form found in the earlier waistbelt arrangement. The scabbard contains its original American-made bayonet and is well constructed of brown harness leather, as is the crossbelt. Slung over the right shoulder, the socket of the bayonet rested closely against the soldier's left side, just above the hipbone, so as not to interfere with the musket when performing the manual of arms or when on the march. The oval, "double D" brass buckle that secures the belt would be centered at the wearer's breast, allowing him to adjust the length of the belt with ease. Buckles of this form have been excavated at campsites of the Continental Army, as have forged iron scabbard tips or finials nearly identical to that found on this scabbard.

TROIANI COLLECTION

A Signed Bayonet

An American-made bayonet found during construction work in Philadelphia, still in remarkable condition considering its long burial. It is marked "US" and "Thos. Wylie" (Thomas Wylie), who was a known contractor for bayonets in 1776 New Jersey and Carlisle, Pennsylvania. There is no record of him after 1780.

COL. J. CRAIG NANNOS COLLECTION

Continental Army Buttons

From left to right, top row: 1) Officer's button of the 8th Massachusetts Regiment, 1781–83. Made of silver-plated copper over a wooden backing, these very elegant buttons bear the number of the regiment over a skull-and-crossbones motif. 2) Pewter button of the Georgia Battalion raised in January of 1783. 3) Pewter specimen of the 10th Regiment, Massachusetts Grand Army of 1775, found near Lake Champlain. 4) The "USA" pattern button. Adopted in early 1777, this button was widely used in all theaters of the war by many Continental units. 5) Pewter USA North Carolina button. 6) Button of the 3rd South Carolina Regiment. 7) 1st Pennsylvania Battalion of 1776. The center of this button bears the raised device "1 B.P" surrounded by the words "Continental Army." 8) Officer's button of the Continental Artillery, imported from France about 1780–81. 9) Bronze officer's button of the Delaware Regiment found near Camden, South Carolina.

TROIANI COLLECTION

When discussing clothing for his new Life Guard in April 1777, Washington requested that "if blue and buff can be had, I should prefer that uniform, as it is the one I wear myself." However, the Clothier General was unable to locate enough cloth of that popular color for even the facings of this small unit and reluctantly informed the commander in chief the following month that he was obliged to use yellow cloth "which although tis a little to strong colourd, does pretty well," but promised to do better for them in future clothing issues. Washington left the style of hat to the Guard's commander, who selected round hats which were then trimmed with bearskin crests. Arms and accoutrements were the best that could be procured and, at least with the former, appear to have been captured British Land Pattern muskets.

Button Mold

Excavated near the Fishkill, New York, barracks site, this die was for embossing officers' buttons for one of the New York regiments. Strangely, examples made from this mold have yet to be unearthed.

WILLIAM H. GUTHMAN COLLECTION, PHOTOGRAPH BY DON TROIANI

NEW HAMPSHIRE HISTORICAL SOCIETY

New Hampshire Flags

The 2nd New Hampshire Regiment lost these two colors to the 9th Regiment of Foot near Fort Anne or possibly at Hubbardton, Vermont, in July 1777. They were transported to England by Lt. Col. John Hill and remained there until 1912 when they were purchased from his descendants and returned to New Hampshire. The blue flag bears a painted device and the motto, "The Glory Not the Prey," and the buff (perhaps originally light yellow) flag has a circle of interlocking chain links bearing the names of the thirteen colonies and the motto, "We Are One." The cantons are the British-style union made up from strips of silk and paint.

Painted Wooden Drum

Magnificent painted wooden drum with the arms of the state of Connecticut and military trophies. In 1781 Connecticut drums were required to be painted with the arms of the state and number of the regiment. This may well be one of those drums.

CONNECTICUT MUSEUM OF HISTORY, PHOTOGRAPH BY DON TROIANI

CORPORAL, BREST DIVISION OF FRENCH MARINES, 1778

PRIVATE COLLECTION

The *Corps Royal d'Infanterie de la Marine* was formed in 1774 by a reorganization of the infantry elements from the previous *Corps Royal de la Marine*. A division of Marines was stationed at each of the three major French naval bases (Brest, Toulon, and Rochefort), from which detachments were drawn for sea service. The *Ordonnance* of December 26, 1774, established the new dress of the marine infantry, which was to consist of a coat, waistcoat, and breeches of royal blue cloth, with red facings, blue linings, and brass buttons bearing an anchor device. A British Marine officer left this detailed description of French Marines from this division serving aboard the frigate *Licorne* after her capture at sea in 1778:

> *They are all stout Men and of a good size. . . . Uniform, Blue faced with Red, red lining, Yellow Buttons with an Anchor on them, Blue Vest and Breeches, with [yellow] laced Hats, and each man has a foraging Cap, to do Common duties in, made of blue Cloth. The Serjeants have two rows of Worsted lace on their cuff and the Cape. The Corporals one row on the Cuff only. The private Men no lace on any part. The Cuff of their coat about the size of ours.*

French Musket Hammer

This hammer from an imported French Model 1774 musket complete with huge lead sheathed amber gunflint still in position, was unearthed from a late-war American campsite in the Hudson Highlands. Notice how the flint is flush against the left edge of the hammer yet still protrudes on the right. As the flint edge wore down, the user could easily reposition the unused edge portion by continuously sliding it to the left.

CHARLES SALERNO COLLECTION

Cartridge Box

Militia private Jotham Wade used this bag-style cartridge box during three months of service at Claverack, New York, with Col. John Jacobs' Massachusetts Regiment in late 1780. Containing a wooden block with nineteen holes, it features a decorated flap bearing his initials and is suspended by a narrow, whitened buff leather shoulder strap closed with a pewter buckle.

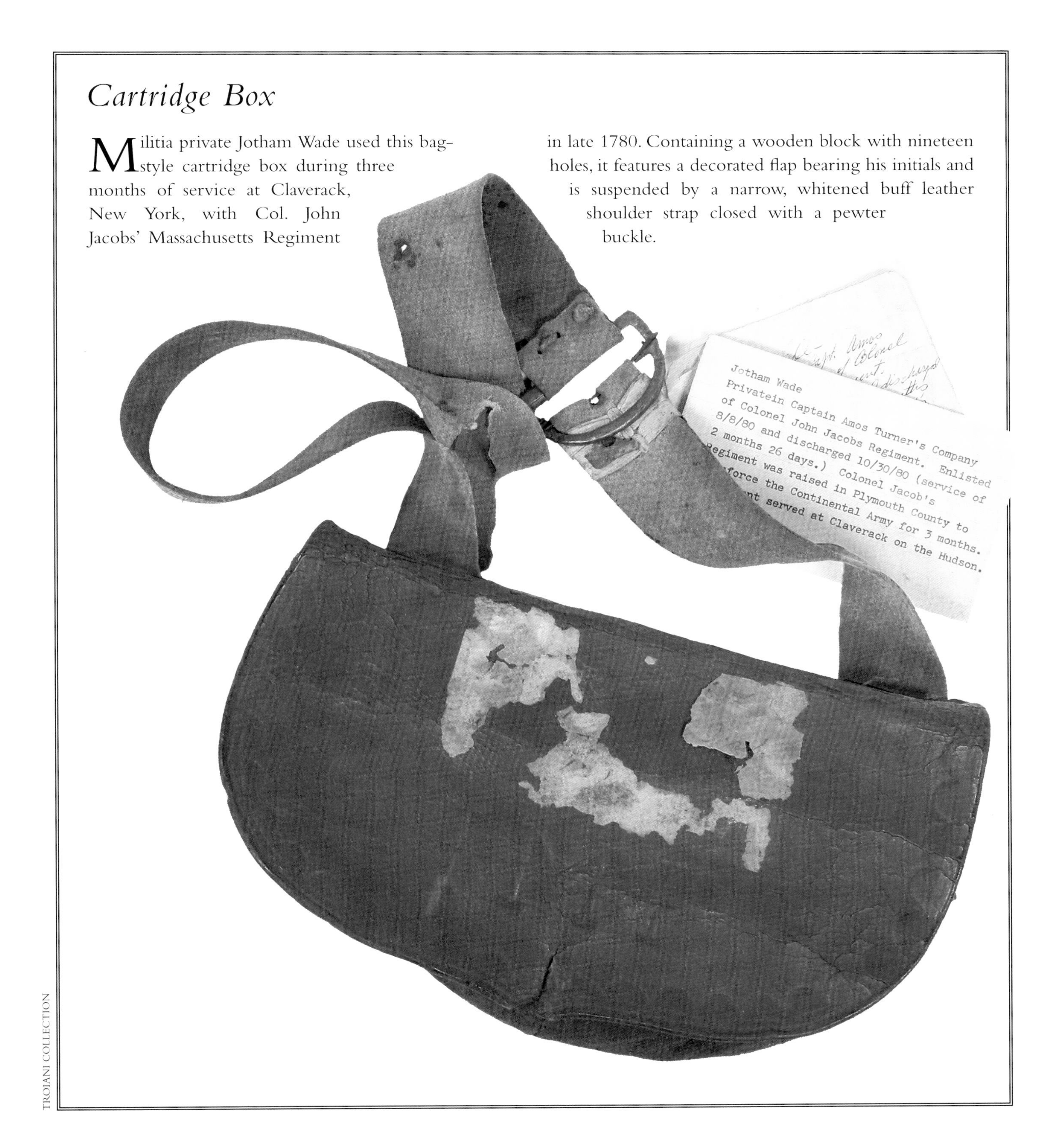

TROIANI COLLECTION

These were apparently uniforms originally provided for the pre-1774 Marine regiments, altered to conform to the new 1774 regulations using available stocks of cloth and trimmings. As uniform coats were issued only once each three years, it is very likely that the Marines of the Brest Division aboard the *Licorne* were still wearing "suitable" coats first received in 1775, made by utilizing the red serge still on hand for linings, instead of the prescribed blue that was not yet procured.

This fusilier corporal of Marine infantry wears a chevron on his left sleeve denoting eight years of honorable service, in addition to his cuff-mounted rank insignia. He carries the standard 1767 *briquet* issued to noncommissioned officers in the fusilier companies of Marines (grenadiers and bombardiers carried their own unique variants of these swords), in addition to his Model 1766 Marine musket and bayonet. Dressed for guard mount, he wears breeches and high gaiters (white in summer, black in winter), rather than the trousers normally worn in daily fatigue duties.

Sailor's Hat

Construction work in lower Manhattan resulted in excavations that revealed the original Revolutionary War waterfront of New York. Numerous artifacts were found perfectly preserved in the wet mud, including this knitted "Dutch" sailor's hat. Made of brown woolen yarn, it still retains traces of a tarred or other waterproofing substance.

ROBERT NITTOLO COLLECTION

French Model 1763/1776 Pistol, Second Manufacture, 1770–79

The most common pistol imported to the United States during the war seems to have been the second production of the French model 1763/1776. This production incorporated the modifications of 1769, which included a shorter barrel and simpler furniture. More than 23,000 pairs were fabricated between 1773 and 1779, the year production ceased. All French pistols made during the *ancien regime* had brass mountings; those with iron fittings are from the later French Revolutionary period, iron being a cheaper, stopgap substitute.

Thousands of these brass-banded 1763/1776 pistols were purchased by Continental and state agents in France for use as both cavalry arms and naval boarding weapons. Horse pistols were always in short supply among the Continental light dragoons; a trooper was lucky if he had a pistol of any pattern in good, firing order, and the receipt of a fine weapon like the model 1763/1776 must have been a very welcome addition to his armament. These pistols were fabricated at St. Etienne, Maubeuge, and Charleville.

TROIANI COLLECTION

French Model 1766 Marine Musket

Both the infantry and bombardier companies of the French Marines were issued the same musket pattern during the Revolutionary War. Until they were replaced (starting in mid-1778) with muskets of the improved 1777 Marine pattern, these sea soldiers carried ones modeled on the French Army's *Fusil d'Infanterie Modele 1766.* Both the 1766 and 1777 Marine muskets differed from their well-known army counterparts in one major respect: the "mountings" were of brass rather than iron—much more practical for weapons constantly subjected to wet and salt. As the Model 1777 Marine musket became available, the 1766 Model was largely disposed of by gift and sale to France's new American allies and was subsequently issued to the Continental Marines and Navy. Only a handful of the Model 1766 Marine muskets survive today, all of which are found in the United States. Two of them bear "U.S." surcharges.

Although the majority of the Ministry of Marines' firearms were produced exclusively by the Tulle Manufactory throughout the first half of the eighteenth century, in 1761 the other royal manufactories were permitted to manufacture Marine arms. This superb example of a Model 1766 Marine fusil was fabricated at the Royal Manufactory of St. Etienne. The barrel, as well as every brass mount, bears an inspection mark of this arsenal. Although extremely well-made, the rather slight mountings and delicate stock of this light musket would seemingly be inappropriate for the robust nature of service afloat, which is probably why the Brest Division of French Marines' muskets were described in 1774 as being in disrepair after only a year's use and which likely accounts for their rarity today.

JAMES L. KOCHAN COLLECTION

French Model 1777 Pistol

The French Model 1777 pistol was a simple and innovative departure from previous models and made in both cavalry and naval versions. It was so successful that after the war it became the model for the first United States martial pistol, produced by North and Cheney of Berlin, Connecticut, under a 1799 contract with the federal government.

TROIANI COLLECTION

CAPTAIN, CONTINENTAL NAVY, 1776–83

BENNINGHOFF COLLECTION

This captain wears the uniform first prescribed for officers of his rank by the Marine Committee of the Continental Congress on September 5, 1776: a coat of "blue cloth with red lapels, slash cuff, stand-up collar, flat yellow buttons, blue britches, red waistcoat with narrow [gold] lace." This remained the official uniform throughout the war (despite an attempt by Capt. John Paul Jones and other senior naval officer to have the facings changed to white with gold-laced buttonholes in 1777—disapproved, but apparently worn, by Jones and some of his officers for at least a short period) and can be seen in portraits of navy officers that survive from the period. Further details, such as the use of red linings and gilt anchor buttons, are also corroborated by such artwork and a list of uniform articles to be purchased in France. Many examples of the French-made uniform buttons survive, including ones from the uniform of Jones.

Rigging Cutters

Cast-iron bar shot, expanding bar shot, and chain shot were primarily used to cut down a ship's rigging and were fearsome cannon projectiles indeed. There were a myriad of forms and sizes of these cannon projectiles in use during the muzzle-loading artillery era.

TOP: TROIANI COLLECTION; MIDDLE: WEST POINT MUSEUM; BOTTOM: RICHARD ULBRICH COLLECTION

PRIVATE, 4TH NEW YORK REGIMENT, 1778–79

WILLIAM RODEN COLLECTION

The 4th New York Regiment was authorized in November 1776 and organized during the early part of 1777. Commanded by Col. Henry Beekman Livingston until his resignation on January 13, 1779, the regiment continued in service until its disbandment with the reduction of the New York Line in January 1781. Assigned to the Northern Department and attached to the New Hampshire Brigade in August 1777, it fought bravely and well during the battles at Freeman's Farm. Reassigned with the brigade to the Main Army in October, it again proved its mettle during the Battle of Monmouth—the last pitched battle in which the regiment would fight.

On September 3, 1778, army clothiers in Boston complained to the Board of War that Maj. Gen. John Sullivan had requested them to provide the 4th New York with "400 suits of white regimentals turned up and lined with scarlet" and a corresponding number of "caps with black hair," plus brass knee and shoe buckles, black worsted knee garters, white stockings, and black or scarlet stocks with clasps (a unique and generous uniform allotment that they considered exceptional to normal Continental Army supply procedures). Livingston and his officers had already provided themselves with such distinctive uniforms, however, and political pressure was brought to bear on the regiment's behalf.

By late 1778 the 4th New York appears to have received white uniforms with red or scarlet facings, trimmed with brass buttons. Leather caps were unavailable, but caps were made from felt hats and trimmed with hair crests per Livingston's specifications. Overalls were issued in lieu of buckskin breeches and knee garters, and it seems more likely that black, rather than scarlet or red, leather neckstocks were received, black-dyed leather being commonly used for both that item and accoutrement belts. The entire 4th New York drew newly imported French model 1766 muskets in June 1777, part of a shipment earmarked for the New Hampshire regiments.

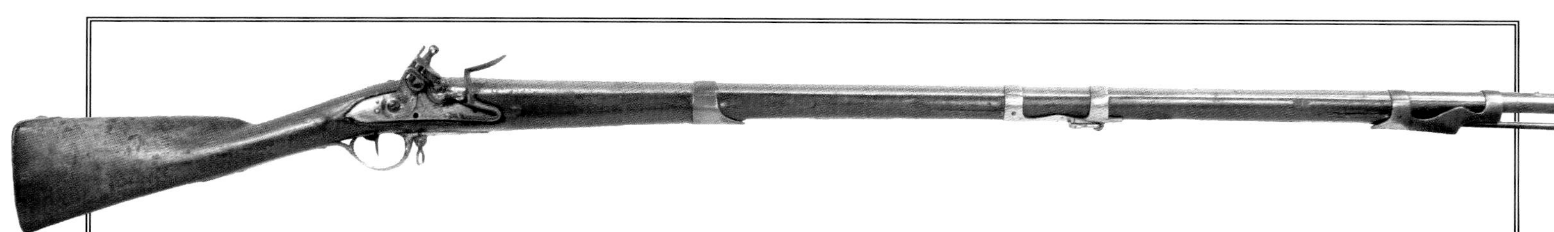

TROIANI COLLECTION

French Model 1770 Dragoon Musket

With the exception of distinctive barrel bands and brass mountings—notably the upper and lower barrel bands, trigger guard, and side plate—the model 1770 dragoon musket has a similar overall configuration to the French infantry muskets of 1770 to 1774. Only about 5,000 were produced between 1772 and 1778 before it was superseded by the model 1777 dragoon musket. Originally intended for the French dragoons, who functioned as a cross between mounted infantry and light horse, surplus model 1770 dragoon muskets were also used by American troops, the center band of at least one specimen being found on an American artillery campsite. At the surrender of Charleston in 1780, the British noted "French cavalry fusils" among the captured arms.

Continental Property

This American-made cartridge box of the "new construction" bears the large brand "U.States" on the interior face of its body. It is fitted with an iron swivel closure, and its black leather shoulder strap is painted white, in imitation of whitened buff leather.

TROIANI COLLECTION

THE 4TH CONTINENTAL LIGHT DRAGOONS, 1779–81

U.S. CAVALRY MUSEUM, FORT RILEY, KANSAS

Stephen Moylan, a former Philadelphia merchant, was named colonel-commandant of the 4th Regiment of Continental Light Dragoons on January 5, 1777, four days after the corps was authorized by the Congress. Raising and equipping a regiment of horse was no small feat, and Moylan put his not-inconsiderable talents, connections, and experience (he had previously served as an aide-de-camp to Gen. George Washington and as Quartermaster General of the Continental Army) to work in achieving just that. Moylan's efforts paid off, and by early summer, three well-equipped troops of the 4th had already joined Washington's main army at Bound Brook, New Jersey, serving with merit during the Philadelphia campaign of 1777, the Battle of Monmouth, and the subsequent campaigns of Washington's main army during 1779–80. As with most of the Continental light dragoons during 1777–80, the 4th was principally deployed in small detachments, primarily performing reconnaissance duties and skirmishing, but also serving as military escorts, couriers, and foragers.

Moylan's dragoons were originally clothed in the captured red coats of the British 8th and 21st Regiments of Foot in 1777. These were exchanged in the winter of 1778–79 for new "regimentals" consisting of short green coats with red facings (colors reversed for trumpeters), red woolen waistcoats, leather breeches for mounted duty, and, apparently, green woolen overalls for dismounted and stable duty during winter. Surmounting this dress were leather helmets with bearskin crests, trimmed around their crowns with bands of "livery lace"; as a further distinction, those of the trumpeters also had a brass "4 LD" device mounted to the "shields" or upright fronts of their caps, and trumpeters were provided with turbans of scarlet durant (a glazed wool). Also provided were horseman's cloaks of green, with red "capes" (collars), to be worn in cold or inclement weather and otherwise carried rolled behind the saddle. While most of the troopers were well-armed with sabers and pistols, carbines were always in short supply and, after 1780, were no longer issued to Continental light dragoons. Both the officers and

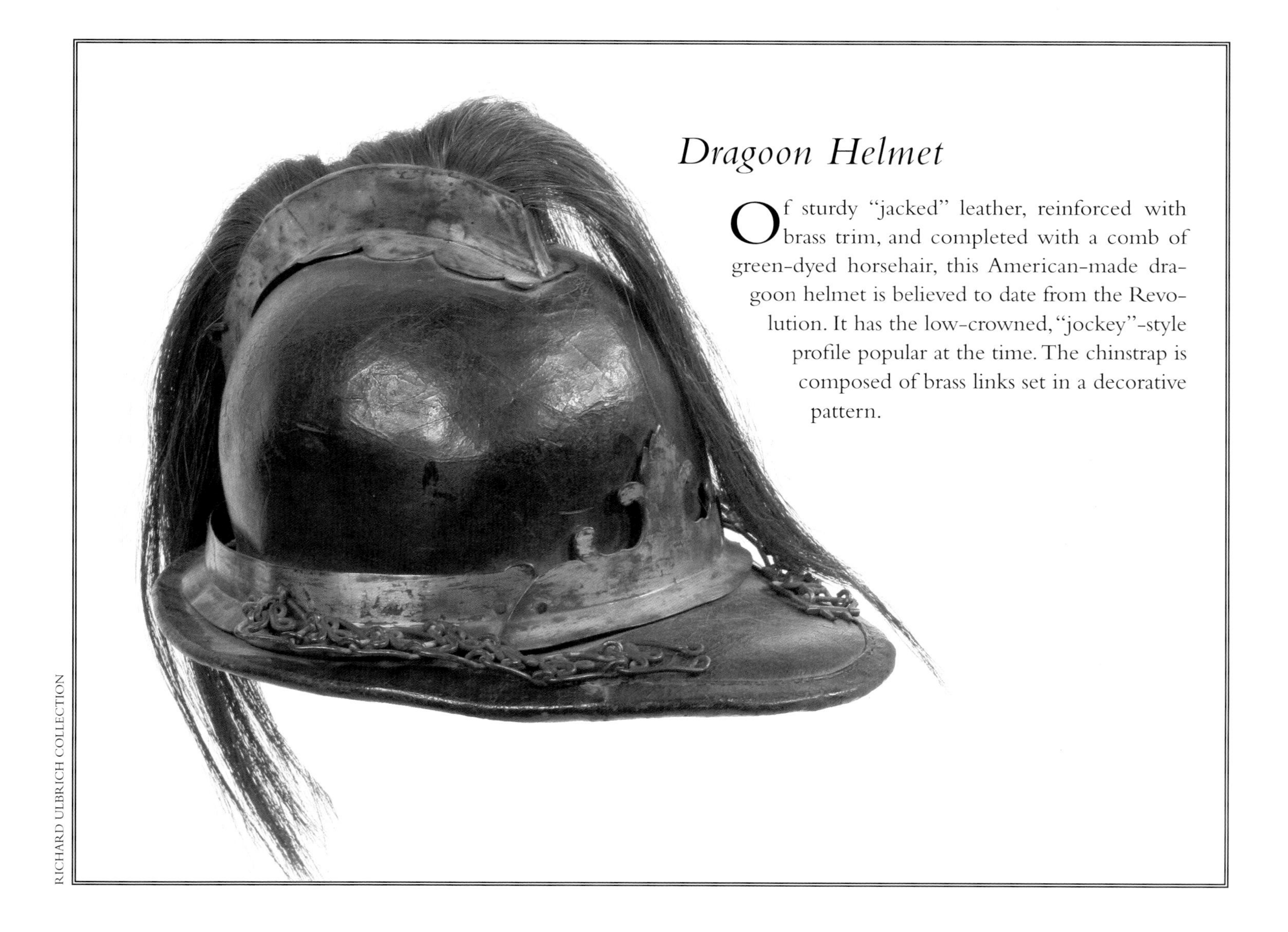

Dragoon Helmet

Of sturdy "jacked" leather, reinforced with brass trim, and completed with a comb of green-dyed horsehair, this American-made dragoon helmet is believed to date from the Revolution. It has the low-crowned, "jockey"-style profile popular at the time. The chinstrap is composed of brass links set in a decorative pattern.

RICHARD ULBRICH COLLECTION

Regimental and Troop Standards, 2nd Continental Light Dragoons

This splendid red and white striped silk regimental standard of the 2nd Continental Light Dragoons was captured during the skirmish at Poundridge, New York, on July 2, 1779. Surprised by a numerically superior raiding party, Col. Elisha Sheldon and his dragoons were forced to abandon the color, along with most of the regimental baggage, in a house around which they were encamped. Lt. Col. Banastre Tarleton, who commanded the British raiding force, later sent it to England as a trophy or souvenir.

PHOTOGRAPH COURTESY OF SOTHEBY'S

MUSEUM OF CONNECTICUT HISTORY, PHOTOGRAPH BY DON TROIANI

Blue silk troop standard of the 2nd Regiment of Continental Light Dragoons, 1777–84. Several other troop flags of various colors exist for this regiment. The design of a winged sphere with rays and lightning bolts surmounting a ribband with the Latin inscription *"Pata Concita Fulmnt Nati"* is painted in the center of the field.

enlisted men had swordbelts made of webbing or whitened leather; officers' saddles were furnished with saddle cloths, while the men's had sheepskin housings—like their uniforms, probably in imitation of those used by French dragoons. As the war progressed and the resources of Congress and the states diminished, keeping the regiment up-to-strength in men, horses, and equipment (especially the latter two) proved increasingly difficult. Writing to Washington on November 5, 1779, Moylan reported that he had finally obtained a new supply of "coats and waistcoats for the 4th. Regiment," but still needed leather breeches, shirts, stockings and boots before it could "be enabled to Keep the field"; four months later, the unit was still reported "non effective for want of" such necessary articles. Although sporadic influxes of equipment, arms, clothing, and horses provided some relief, the 4th was never able to field more than fifty or sixty well-equipped mounted troopers at any time during 1779–81.

WEST POINT MUSEUM, PHOTOGRAPH BY DON TROIANI

Tin Cartridge Canister

Tin cartridge canister with hinged lid and loops to be hung from a shoulder sling. Nearly identical versions of this type of ammunition holder were in use by both the American and British forces during the war.

ERIK GOLDSTEIN COLLECTION

Colonial Currency

A New Jersey "script" or paper note of 1776 for the value of three pounds.

SERGEANT, 2ND CONTINENTAL LIGHT DRAGOONS

PRIVATE COLLECTION

One of the first troops of the 2nd Continental Light Dragoons to be raised and mounted was that of Capt. Thomas Young Seymour. The troop was sent north to reinforce Gen. Horatio Gates in time to participate in the Saratoga campaign, serving as couriers and attached to Gates's headquarters. One eyewitness noted that they wore "blue coats with white facings with bearskin [covered] caps and long white hair streaming in the wind." However, in 1778 brass helmets were sent to the regiment from France and artist John Trumbull chose to portray Seymour wearing that headgear—although with the same regimentals as above—in both his postwar portrait and his painting of the surrender at Saratoga. On July 2, 1779, Banastre Tarleton and 360 Loyalist and British troops surprised the 2nd Continental Light Dragoons and American militia at Poundridge, New York, and pushed back the patriots, resulting in the loss of its colors and regimental baggage, including most of its uniforms and helmets. The following year, the regiment received a new uniform of green faced with white but returned to the original blue and white uniform by 1781. The cut of this sergeant's short-skirted "coatee" is based on contemporary artwork that depict this regiment (including a sketch of a brass-helmeted dragoon "doodled" on a return for forage drawn from Elisha Williams, deputy commissary general of Connecticut). He wears one of the imported French dragoon helmets, trimmed with a pale blue turban, and is armed with one of the captured Brunswick dragoon swords that were issued to the 2nd in 1778.

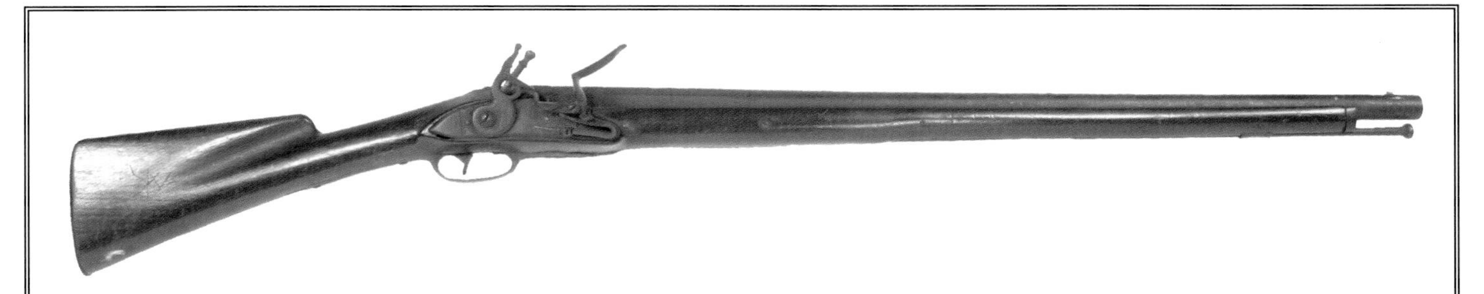

TROIANI COLLECTION

American Cavalry Carbine, 1776–83

Perhaps a unique survivor of the Revolutionary War, this light horse or cavalry carbine was cheaply "cobbled" together from various musket parts and resembles no other known example. The lock plate is marked "J. VALET" over "A. LIEGE," and the 28 ½-inch barrel has "ROUGET FOUBIER" marked on it, as well as a "US" surcharge. Liege, now in eastern Belgium, was the center of arms production in what was then the Austrian Netherlands in the eighteenth century. Though the carbine may have been assembled in the Netherlands, it could possibly have been created by an American gunsmith working from imported parts. Great numbers of lock plates and other parts were shipped from the Netherlands and France during the Revolutionary War. This carbine has a sling bar on the reverse side opposite the lock plate, which was used to clip the weapon to the leather shoulder sling of a cavalryman.

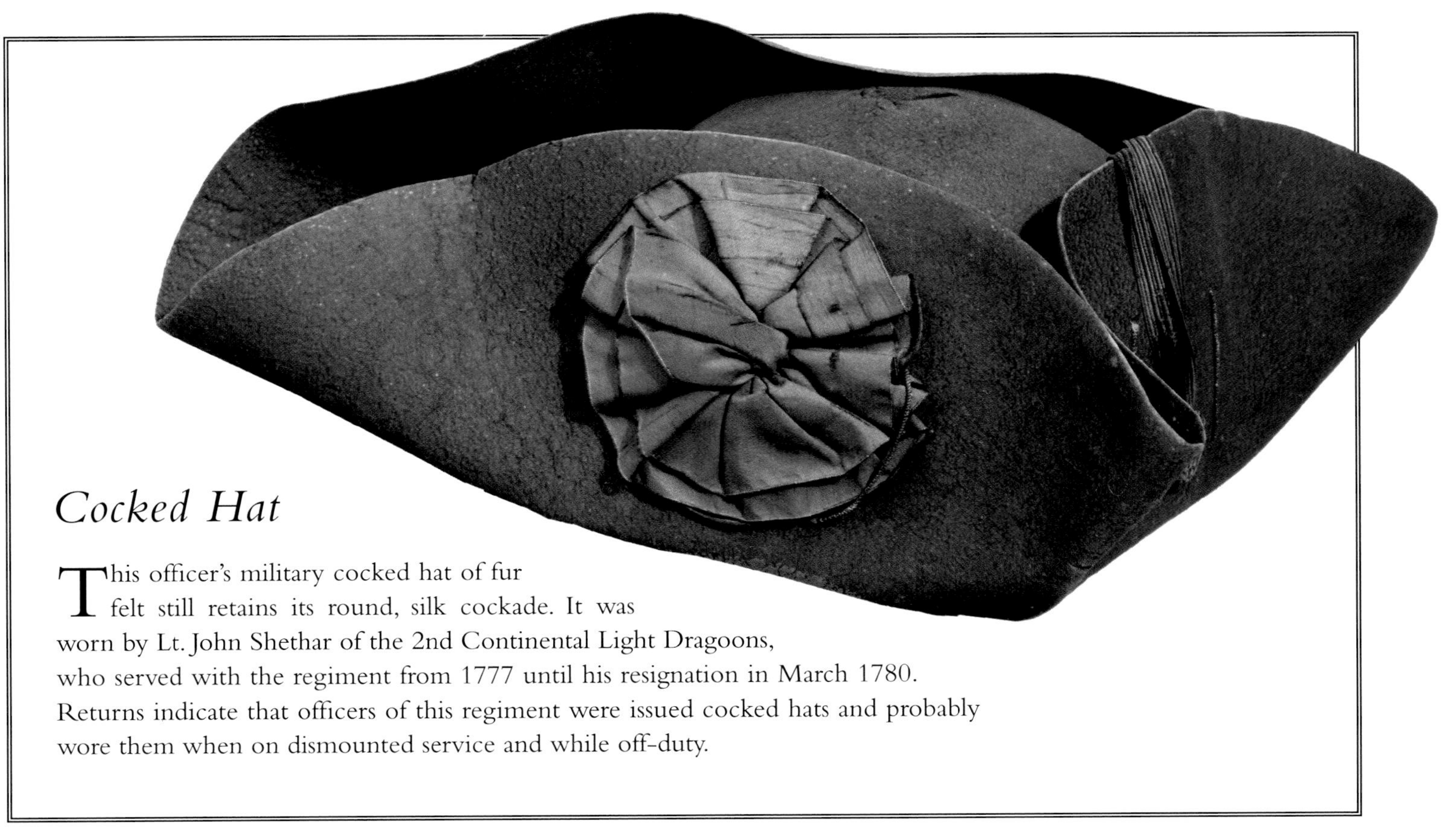

COLLECTION OF THE NEW-YORK HISTORICAL SOCIETY (1927.104.)

Cocked Hat

This officer's military cocked hat of fur felt still retains its round, silk cockade. It was worn by Lt. John Shethar of the 2nd Continental Light Dragoons, who served with the regiment from 1777 until his resignation in March 1780. Returns indicate that officers of this regiment were issued cocked hats and probably wore them when on dismounted service and while off-duty.

A "BLACK IRISHMAN" OF THE 2ND PENNSYLVANIA REGIMENT, WINTER 1778–79

COL. J. CRAIG NANNOS COLLECTION

The 2nd Pennsylvania Regiment was constituted in 1777 by the merger of the 2nd Pennsylvania Battalion of 1776 with the 13th Pennsylvania Regiment, and command of the regiment was given to Col. Walter Stewart. As part of Brig. Gen. Anthony Wayne's 1st Brigade of the Pennsylvania Division, the 2nd suffered through the winter at Valley Forge and stood up to the British grenadiers in the hard-fought Battle of Monmouth on June 28, 1778. Late that year, the 2nd, along with the rest of the Pennsylvania Division, took up winter quarters near Middlebrook, New Jersey, constructing log hut cantonments along the rocky hillsides during the short, cold days of December. While the troops felled trees and cleared the land at their encampment area in the tattered remnants of last year's clothing, the long-promised new uniforms were finally delivered.

The Pennsylvanians drew royal blue coats with red facings, along with white woolen waistcoats and breeches and gray yarn stockings. These ready-made uniforms were drawn from a stock of more than 30,000 suits received from France earlier that year. They had been procured by the American commissioners in Paris, Silas Deane and Benjamin Franklin, who contracted for uniforms equal in quality of materials and workmanship to those made for the Royal Army of France. Although cut in the three standard sizes used for French uniforms, the clothing was made to specifications and patterns developed by the commissioners.

American Horsemen's Sabers, 1775–83

Although the national origin and form of such edged weapons varied greatly among the patriot mounted troops, the preferred style was clearly that favored by British light dragoon regiments. From left to right:

An incredibly massive iron-hilted saber with slotted guard originally discovered in a barn in Rhode Island decades ago. With a proportionately long and imposing curved blade, it dwarfs even the largest sabers of the period.

An elegant brass-mounted saber with tall oval pommel and turned cherry grips. This sword utilizes a blade by the famed James Potter of New York City but was presumably hilted by another maker, as several other examples of this hilt with other types of blades are extant.

This simple iron hilted pattern, marked with an "H" stamped in the guard, is believed to have been made by James Hunter at Rappahanock Forge in Virginia, who had several sword contracts during the war.

According to family tradition, Capt. Samuel Mills of the 2nd Continental Light Dragoons carried this rudimentary saber during the war; its bone grip and circular iron pommel make it a rather singular variant.

TROIANI COLLECTION

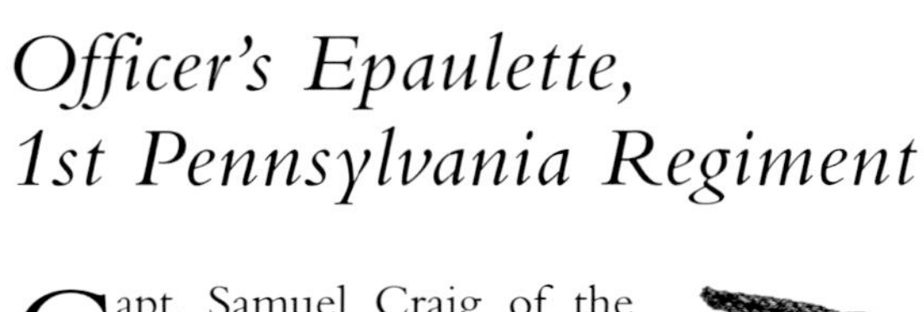

Officer's Epaulette, 1st Pennsylvania Regiment

Capt. Samuel Craig of the 1st Pennsylvania Regiment wore this British-style epaulette sometime between 1775 and his retirement from the service in 1781. It is backed with scarlet wool, the facing color of the regiment. Craig was wounded during the British surprise attack on Anthony Wayne's camp at Paoli, Pennsylvania, on September 19, 1777.

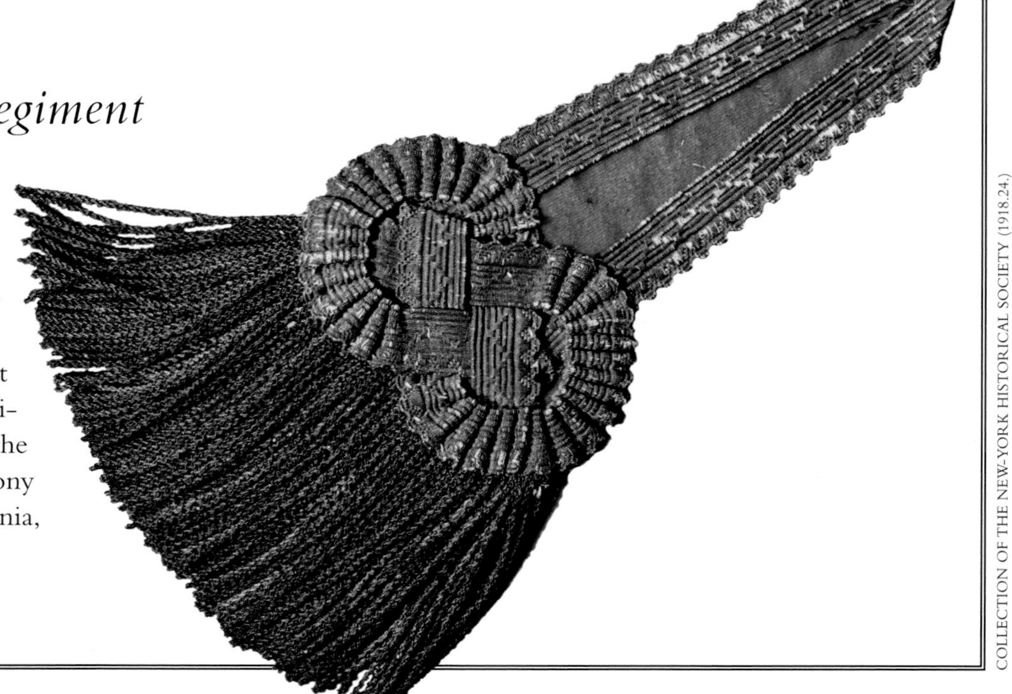

COLLECTION OF THE NEW-YORK HISTORICAL SOCIETY (1918.24)

Officer's Epaulette, 4th Pennsylvania Regiment

Made of silver bullion, this officer's epaulette was worn by Capt. Henry Bicker, Jr., and afterward was passed down through his descendants. Bicker was commissioned as ensign in the 3rd Pennsylvania Battalion and taken prisoner at the fall of Fort Washington. He was later exchanged in 1778 and rejoined his old regiment, which had been subsequently reorganized and numbered as the 4th Pennsylvania Regiment, serving until the close of the war.

TROIANI COLLECTION

Rather than copying the French military fashion of half lapels, the coats were made with full lapels capable of fully covering the torso when buttoned over—a critical feature given the cold American winters. Cuffs were slashed in the French manner, buttoning at the underseam of the sleeve. The bodies of the coats were lined with twilled, white serge and finished with plain-faced, pewter buttons.

New hats had not been included in the shipment, and the Pennsylvanians' old hats were in terrible condition and of varied styles. This led Wayne to order that all hats "which do not Admit of been Cockd" in the proper military fashion be converted into caps by cutting off all "but About half An Inch" of the brim around the crown and leaving one side of the brim intact. The remaining flap was to be cocked up, and the cap was "bound Round with White Tape Linnen," achieving at least some degree of uniformity in the headgear of his command. That the 2nd Pennsylvania wore such caps with their French-made uniforms is confirmed by a "wanted" ad for one of its privates, one Andrew McCarty, who stole a horse while on furlough in February 1779. He was described as being "about five feet seven or eight inches high, black hair, pitted with the small pox; had on a blue regimental coat lined with white, a ruffle shirt, red flannel leggings, and a sort of cap dressed up with fur." The Irishman is armed with a captured Hessian musket and bayonet, and his accoutrements include a cartridge box "of the new Construction," one of thousands first issued to the Pennsylvania and Maryland Division at Middlebrook that winter.

PRIVATE, CAPTAIN GEORGE LEWIS'S TROOP, 3RD REGIMENT OF CONTINENTAL LIGHT DRAGOONS, 1777–78

NATIONAL PARK SERVICE

Although he received authorization to raise the 3rd Regiment of Light Dragoons on January 9, 1777, newly-promoted Col. George Baylor had proceeded with only limited success by spring of that year. Recruits and horses were relatively easy to obtain in his native state of Virginia and nearby Maryland, but horse equipage, weapons, and clothing were scarce commodities as stocks in Virginia were virtually depleted when equipping the 1st Continental Light Dragoons in 1776–77. That spring, only George Lewis's troop was fully supplied and able to join the Main Army. General Washington ordered Baylor to send up detachments from the regiment as soon as they could be mounted—with or without arms and uniforms—so great was the need for cavalry. Lewis, a relation of Washington's, was attached with his troop

Matched Set of Accoutrements

A complete matched set of accoutrements was discovered in the attic of an eighteenth-century New England home. The pouch-style box with large flap and British fusil bayonet are suspended from heavy natural-colored, wide-woven shoulder straps.

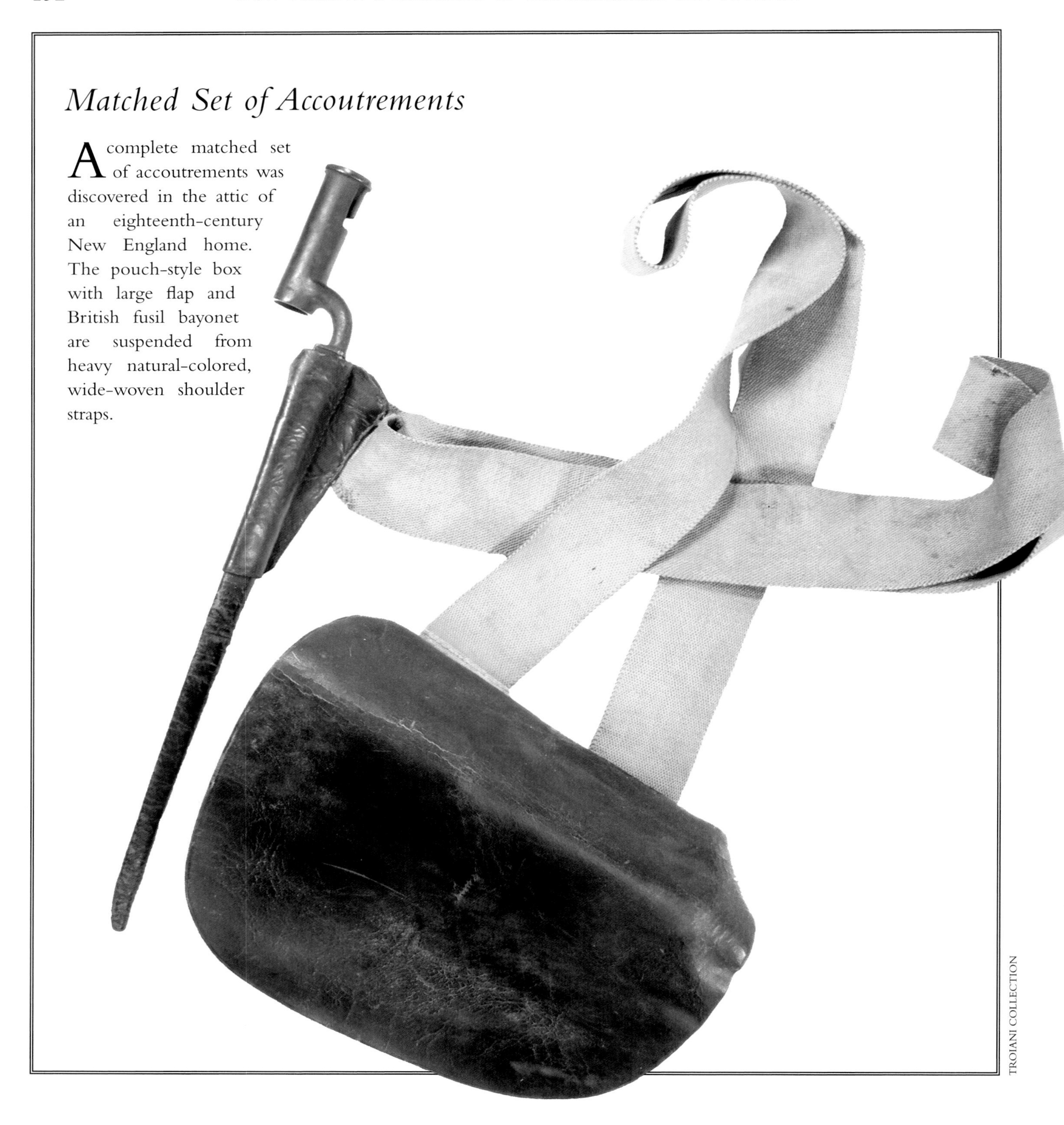

TROIANI COLLECTION

to Washington's headquarters guard, the men serving primarily as couriers and escorts. Soon Lewis's troop became referred to as "Washington's Bodyguard" or the "Lady Washington Horse." This troop continued on headquarters duty until late 1778, when it rejoined the regiment.

Baylor and 104 men from his regiment were surprised in their billets near Tappan, New York, by British light troops under Maj. Gen. Charles "No Flint" Grey on September 19. Fewer than half escaped death or capture, and of the latter—Baylor included—most had been repeatedly bayoneted. The regiment was re-raised from its survivors and new recruits but never reached full strength. A squadron of horse under Lt. Col. William Washington, consisting of men from this regiment and the 1st Light Dragoons, served during the southern campaign of 1780–81 with great merit, notably at the battles of Cowpens, Guilford Courthouse, and Eutaw Springs.

Committee of Safety Bayonet

This petite American copy of a British bayonet bears the markings "SC" and "No 1" on the blade, indicating it was accepted by the State of Connecticut.

TROIANI COLLECTION

Cartridge Pouch

An American cartridge pouch of the bag body style with the front flap boldly inscribed "Independence 1778" with a decorative row of stars. It was alleged to have been used by a militiaman from Rhode Island.

WILLIAM H. GUTHMAN COLLECTION, PHOTOGRAPH BY DON TROIANI

The 3rd wore a distinctive uniform of white coats with blue facings for most of the regiment's existence. During 1777–78, it was cut in the French dragoon fashion, featuring interrupted half lapels, slashed cuffs, and small collars of light or medium blue cloth. Pewter buttons of the regiment, bearing the letters "LD" in an intertwined script cipher, have been excavated at the site of Baylor's Massacre. Sergeants' coats had shoulder straps edged with silver lace, and officers' uniforms were similar, but made of finer materials and furnished with silver epaulettes on the right shoulder. A helmet cap worn by a member of Lewis's troops during 1777–78 still survives and is made of jacked leather with a white horsehair crest and bears "several rows of small chains" around the crown, as prescribed for such caps. Black feathers were provided to trim the caps of the officers in Lewis's troops during 1778.

This reconstruction shows a private of Lewis's troop during its headquarters service. Under his coat he wears a white, belted waistcoat, and his leg wear consists of buckskin breeches and boots. He is fully armed with saber, holstered pistols, and carbine. Accoutrement straps are of black leather, including the "belt for the carbine with a running swivel," by which that arm is suspended, and its nose secured a carbine "boot" strapped to the saddle. Few if any of the other troops in the 3rd were better armed and equipped; carbines were scarce from the start and after 1779 were no longer carried by the regiment.

MOLLY PITCHER

On June 28, 1778, the Battle of Monmouth began with a morning attack launched by the advanced elements of George Washington's army against Sir Henry Clinton's rear guard. Poorly coordinated and executed, the attack turned into a withdrawal before many troops were even engaged, their officers astounded when ordered to retire. After the increased professionalism and esprit gained from the Valley Forge training efforts, the sight of some of his best troops in inexplicable retreat shocked and infuriated their commander in chief when he arrived on the battlefield. Determined to force a stand until reinforcements could be brought up, Washington deployed the retreating troops and rode to their front to take "observation of the advancing enemy," according to Pvt. Joseph Plumb Martin, who noted that he "remained there some time upon his old English charger, while the shot from the British artillery were rending up the earth all around him."

With the temperature nearing 100 degrees, the overwhelming humidity and glaring sandy fields became unendurable. In more than a few units of both armies, the heat killed more men than did enemy fire. After Washington brought forward a large body of Continentals to anchor an extended main line in the rear of the hedgerow, 500 "picked men," including Private Martin, were skillfully moved undetected to the left flank. The 42nd Royal Highland Regiment, the renowned Black Watch, was attempting to use a nearby orchard as cover from which to launch a turning movement around the American left. Immediately upon discovery of this threat, several field pieces were rapidly moved to support the arriving "picked" New England infantrymen. It was as this

PRIVATE COLLECTION

Powder Horn

This priming horn is similar to those used by the British, with a threaded wooden knob set into the wooden plug by which the container could be easily refilled with gunpowder. It bears a "U. States" surcharge on its side, indicating Continental Army ownership.

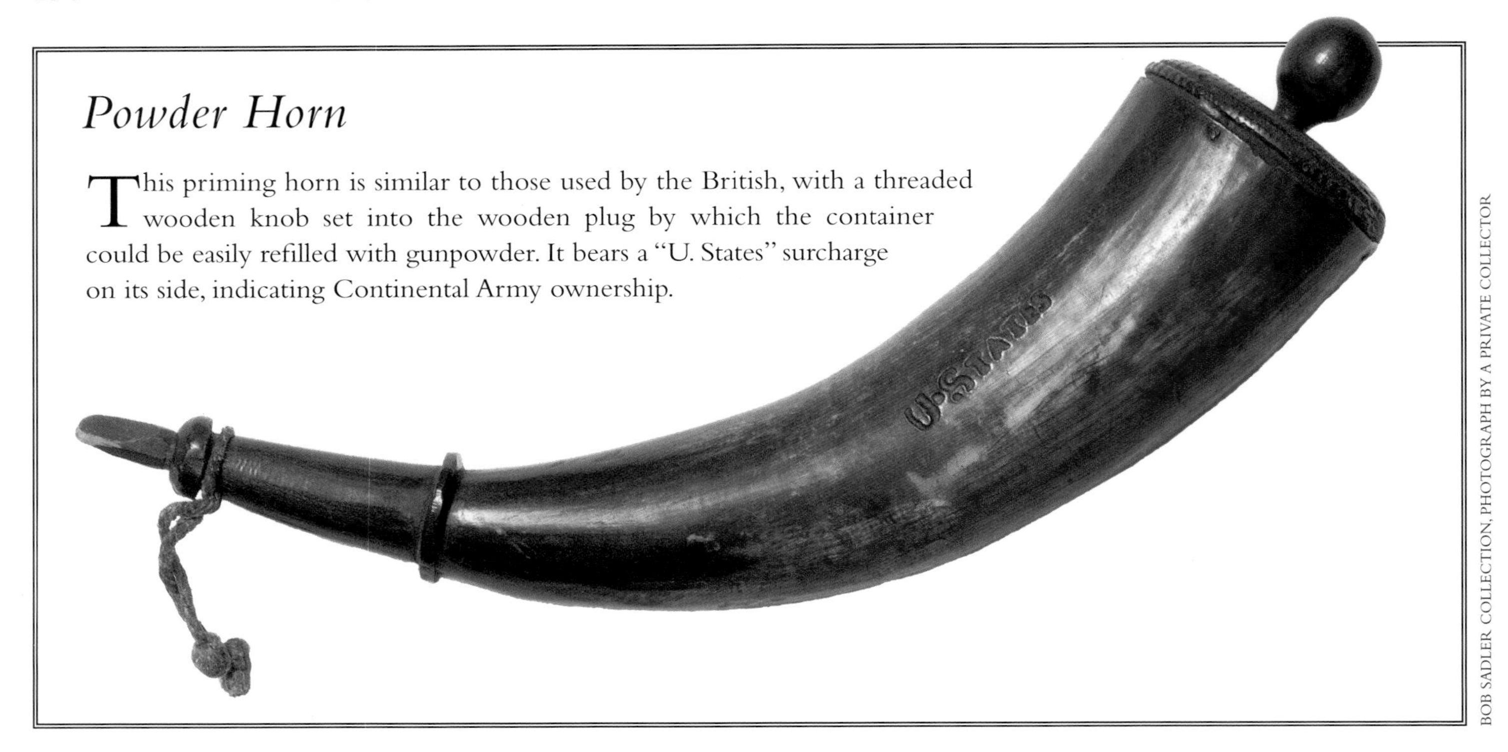

BOB SADLER COLLECTION, PHOTOGRAPH BY A PRIVATE COLLECTOR

Tomahawk

Fine example of a typical soldier's tomahawk with combination blade and hammerpoll. The "US" surcharge indicates this was property of the Continental Army.

RICHARD ULBRICH COLLECTION

critical response team opened a heavy and well-coordinated fire on the Highlanders that Martin saw

> *A woman whose husband belonged to the artillery and who was attached to a piece in the engagement, attended with her husband at the piece the whole time. While in the act of reaching a cartridge and having one of her feet as far before the other as she could step, a cannon shot from the enemy passed directly between her legs without doing any more damage than carrying away all the lower part of her petticoat. Looking at it with apparent unconcern, she observed that it was lucky it did not pass a little higher, for in that case it might have carried away something else, and continued with her work.*

The wife of William Hays of Proctor's Artillery Regiment, Mary was in her mid-twenties, common in appearance, but compact and strong. There was probably little to distinguish her from the many hundreds of other women attached to the army—that is, except exchanging the role of water bearer (a role performed by many "camp followers" of the army during combat) for that of combatant. Thus, Mary Ludwig Hays became "Molly Pitcher." Following William's discharge from service, the pair settled in Carlisle, Pennsylvania, where their only child, a son, was born about 1783. Widowed about five years thereafter, she remarried, becoming Mary Hays McCauley. In 1822, Pennsylvania's governor signed a legislative act awarding "Molly McColly" a quite generous lifetime pension, she being one of only three women granted pensions for services performed during the Revolution. When she died at age seventy-nine in 1832, Carlisle's militia turned out to march in her funeral procession.

Imported "Virginia" Grenadier and Artillery Swords, 1778–83

In late spring 1778, Jacques LeMaire returned to his native France after a year in Virginia, newly commissioned as a captain in the Virginia State forces and carrying with him letters of introduction signed by Gov. Patrick Henry. LeMaire also brought with him lists of much-needed ordnance and war materiel for Virginia's Continental and state regular forces, as well as the militia, in whose capacity he was to act as military agent. LeMaire was from a prominent French family, and Henry recognized that his political and social connections would open doors more readily than the more formal diplomatic channels then being pursued by William Lee, the state agent already in France. Lee was the younger brother of Arthur Lee, one of the three commissioners to Europe appointed by the Continental Congress to secure treaties of alliance and acquire military goods on behalf of the United States.

William Lee had departed Paris for Vienna in search of ordnance when LeMaire arrived, and Arthur Lee instructed the young Frenchman to travel to Strasbourg "to engage the sabres, etc. for the light horse." By June 1778 he was already in negotiation with the sword and tool manufacturers for edged weapons, shovels, axes, and other military tools. Forwarding William Lee quotations for such materials, Lee wrote back on June 27, advising him that "time will not allow for our waiting till the Sabres are made" and that "we must find them ready made to be transported immediately." Before Lee's letter reached LeMaire, "he had made contract on the 4th [of July] . . . at a higher price than the manufacturer's first price." These swords were custom-manufactured for Virginia at Klingenthal, located southwest of Strasbourg in France's Alsace region, where the French government had established its sword manufacturing center in the early eighteenth century.

Two of the three pattern swords were intended for Virginia foot troops and had brass hilts that conformed closely to the French model 1767 hanger or briquet. The hilts were two-piece castings, consisting of a ribbed grip with large capstan-pommel and a stirrup-shaped guard. The first pattern had "Grenadeer of Virginia" inscribed below a panoply of arms on its blade just above the hilt, with "Victory or Death" similarly marked on the reverse. The second type of sword had "Artillery of Virginia" marked on it, with flat, slightly curved blades—$26\frac{1}{2}$ inches long for the former and $23\frac{3}{4}$ inches for the latter. The artillery hanger's blade was slightly wider, while the grenadier saber had a rather unique, wider upper blade section with false edge, running approximately eight inches to the tip. A third pattern sword for dragoons was also manufactured, with different form hilt and straight blade.

The estimated 1,500–2,000 swords were completed in early 1779 and eventually shipped to Virginia, arriving in August. Initially stored at Cumberland Court House, they were dispersed by direct issue to regular and militia troops, as well as shipment to other military depots. During April 1781, Gov. Thomas Jefferson ordered that militia cavalry troops be formed to augment the limited existing horse, and "grenadier swords" were authorized for issue in lieu of cavalry sabers, ensuring "that the want of that Article need not keep them from the field." State regular corps, including Dabney's Legion and Clark's Illinois Regiment, were also furnished with grenadier sabers and artillery hangers, which were variously referred to as "sergeants swords" and "cutlasses." Postwar issue of the weapons continued from Point of Fork Arsenal during the 1790s until its closure, when the remaining 900 swords were shipped to Richmond. During the first decade of the nineteenth century, many of the grenadier sabers were cleaned, refurbished, and engraved with Virginia militia regimental markings at the Virginia Manufactory of Arms before issue to militia artillery companies.

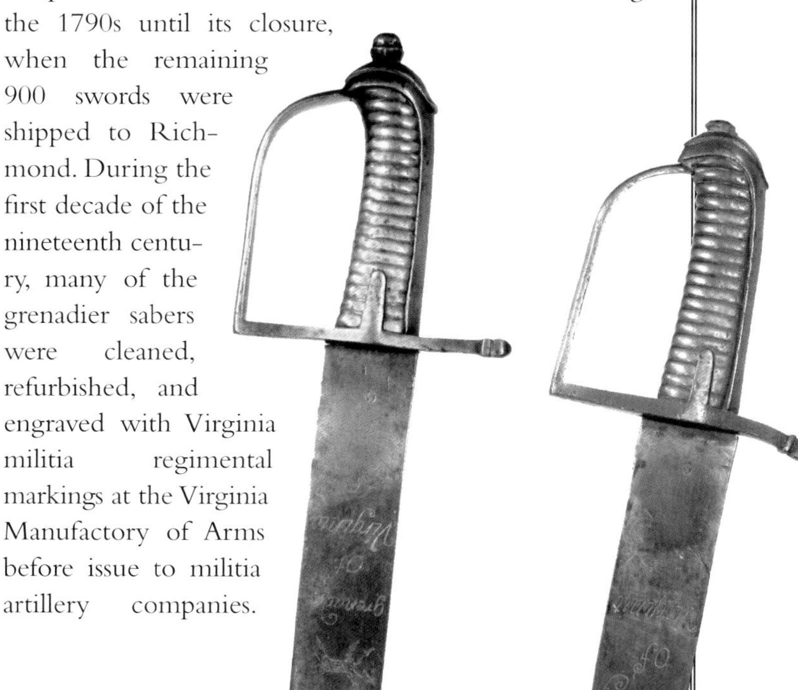

TROIANI COLLECTION

SERGEANT, CLARK'S ILLINOIS REGIMENT, 1782

PRIVATE COLLECTION

In anticipation of George Rogers Clark's intended expedition against the Ohio Indians in 1782, the state of Virginia sent what supplies it could spare that would prove useful on such a frontier campaign, including two bronze 3-pounder "grasshopper" guns and approximately 150 ready-made uniforms for the use of his Illinois Regiment of Virginia state regulars. These uniforms were French-made and may have originally been intended for Continental regiments of some southern state, as they appear to conform to the Congressional specifications of 1779: royal blue coats with blue facings and "USA" buttons and lined with white serge. Also purchased were white woolen waistcoats (similarly trimmed), and linen overalls, as well as hats. The uniforms were purchased by Virginia's agent for use by her state forces and, in addition to the Illinois Regiment, were used to clothe Dabney's Virginia State Legion. Shipped from Richmond in April, they arrived at Fort Nelson (present-day Louisville, Kentucky) that summer and were issued to the men during August. This sergeant is armed with a Spanish Model 1752 musket and bayonet, as well as a cartridge box bearing the cipher of King Charles III, all procured from the governor of Louisiana in 1780. Befitting his rank, he also carries one of the French-made "Grenadiers of Virginia" sabers.

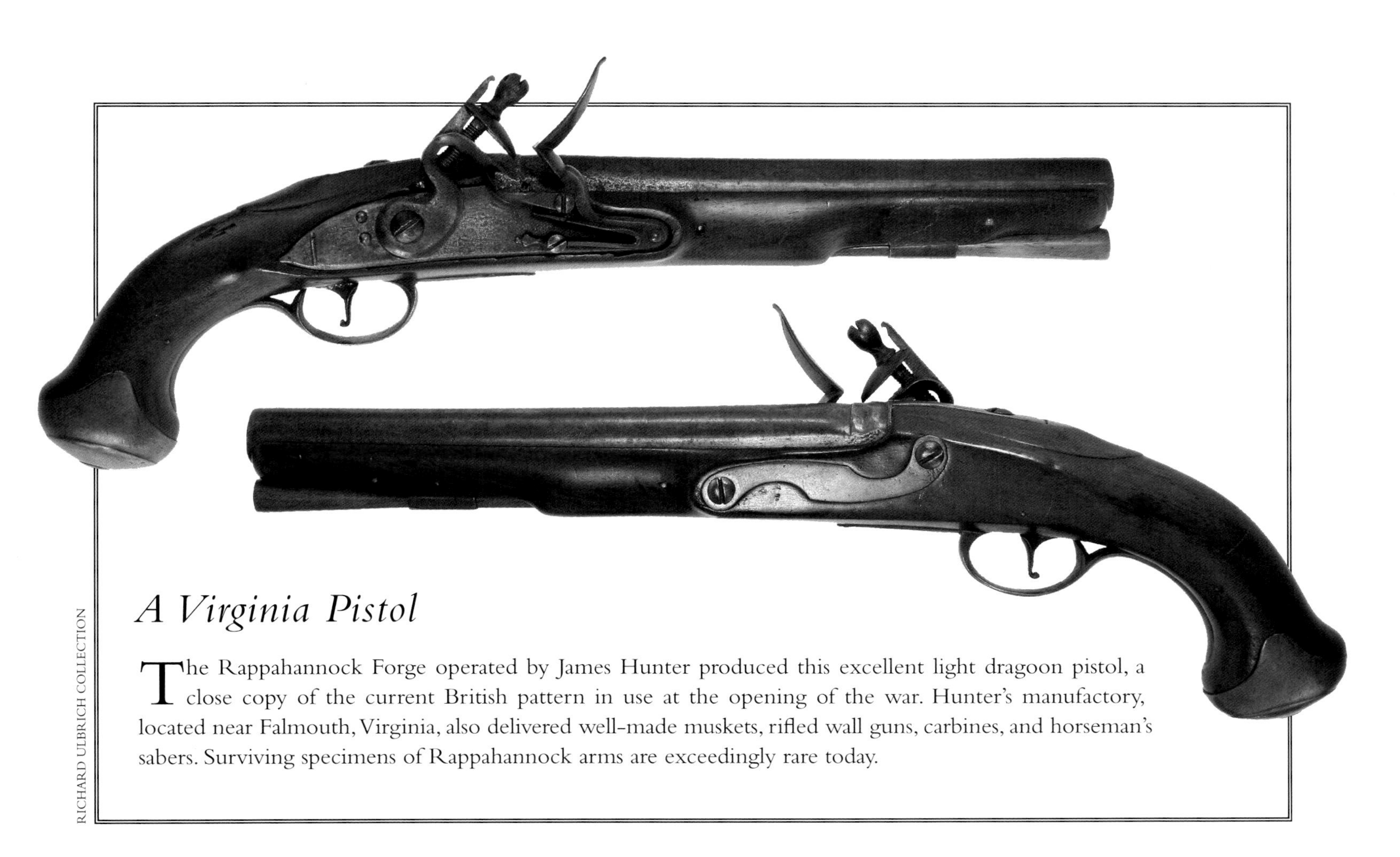

RICHARD ULBRICH COLLECTION

A Virginia Pistol

The Rappahannock Forge operated by James Hunter produced this excellent light dragoon pistol, a close copy of the current British pattern in use at the opening of the war. Hunter's manufactory, located near Falmouth, Virginia, also delivered well-made muskets, rifled wall guns, carbines, and horseman's sabers. Surviving specimens of Rappahannock arms are exceedingly rare today.

Trench Spear Head

The head of this "trench spear" is one of several excavated on a circa 1778–83 fortification site in the Hudson Highlands. Note the flat leaf blade and long reinforcing side straps. Valuable for their long reach, they were generally used to defend fortifications against attackers scaling the walls. Trench spears were used with deadly effect by the defenders of Fort Griswold at New London, Connecticut, in 1781.

TROIANI COLLECTION

THE CONTINENTAL ARMY RIFLE CORPS, 1778–1779

PRIVATE COLLECTION

In May 1777 Gen. George Washington created a "corps of rifle troops" under Col. Daniel Morgan, consisting of expert marksmen drawn principally from the Pennsylvania, Virginia, and Maryland Lines. The rifle corps was not intended as a permanent body, but was instead to serve as a temporary detachment of picked men. At the conclusion of the summer 1778 campaign, the corps was partially disbanded and the remainder, approximately two companies strong, was sent under the command of Maj. Thomas Posey to reinforce the beleaguered settlements on the New York frontier against British-Indian incursions. In December Posey was recalled to the Main Army, and Maj. James Parr assumed command of the corps. Under Parr, the rifle corps would continue in frontier service on Sullivan's Expedition against the Iroquois, after which it was dissolved and the men returned to their parent units.

When the Continental Rifle Corps was formed, the men wore the same uniforms drawn earlier when serving with their parent regiments, supplemented by occasional issues of shoes, overalls or breeches, shirts, stockings, blankets, and the occasional hat, coat, or waistcoat. On November 7, 1778, eighty suits of French-made uniforms were drawn for the use of the rifle corps, consisting of brown coats with red facings and white linings, white small clothes, and grey woolen stockings. These were part of approximately 35,000 suits contracted for by the American commissioners and made up under contract by clothiers to the French army, although the cut of the coats was altered to accommodate American preferences. Instead of half lapels, lapels were to be made full length and "made to buttons over the Brest and Belly completely," while sleeves were "slashed"—that is, with a slit along the underseam of the sleeve and buttoned close by four small, pewter buttons.

While in garrison at Schoharie, Major Parr requisitioned 114 "light infantry" caps or hats, 114 hunting shirts, 228 pairs of linen overalls, 114 stocks and clasps, and 114 each of canteens, knapsacks, and haversacks for his corps on May 1, 1779. However, when inspected at Otsego Lake on July 6 (at the beginning of the Sullivan expedition), Parr's Rifles were still wearing the French-made uniforms, described as "Pretty Good, But Too Heavy In the Duty They Are Upon." It was noted that no hunting shirts were on hand and that the rifles and pouches were "Indifferent," while the horns were "Pretty Good." This rifleman represents the appearance of the corps between late fall 1778 and early summer 1779. No hats were provided with the French uniforms, and he wears a battered and rusty round hat from a previous issuance; a black silk kerchief serves in lieu of a neckstock; and his legs are protected by cloth "Indian leggings." His "necessaries" are rolled up in a blanket worn in a webbing tumpline across his breast. In addition to rifle and tomahawk (worn on a shoulder sling), he is armed with a folding spear of the form designed and issued to the corps in 1777 at Washington's behest in an attempt to remedy the deficiency in the American rifles, which had no means of mounting.

Cartridge Box

This "new constructed" cartridge box is an American adaptation of a British twenty-nine-hole cartridge "pouch." First issued during 1779, it was intended to replace the inferior forms carried by Continental troops earlier in the war that were incapable of shedding rain or carrying sufficient ammunition. This example retains its original whitened buff leather strap, and its flap is marked in white paint to a 2nd Company of a 6th Regiment. Being found in Connecticut, this box may well have been used by a soldier of Colonel Meigs' 6th Regiment of the Connecticut Line. When the 6th first received this pattern of box in 1780, its commander requested permission to affix the white belts of their earlier cartridge boxes to the new ones.

TROIANI COLLECTION

American Swordbelt, 1775–83

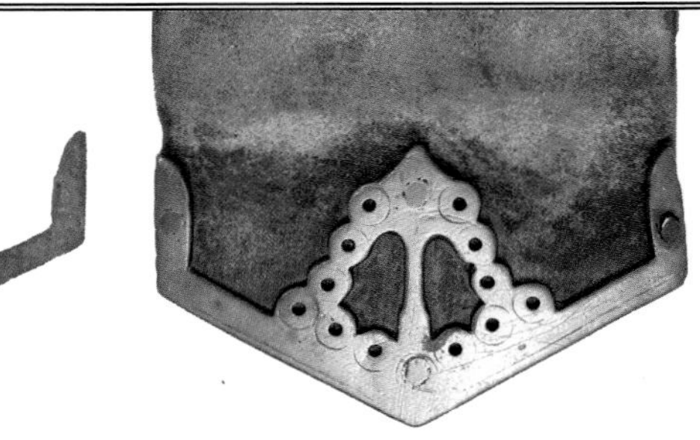

Rare indeed are eighteenth-century military swordbelts of American origin; scarcer still are artifacts of this nature with Revolutionary War provenance. This buff leather shoulderbelt was probably made prior to or during the war, and was apparently altered or modified in that conflict. The belt is $2^{3}/_{8}$ inches wide but has been tapered near the top to accommodate the brass ornament that was clearly added during the swordbelt's eighteenth-century refurbishment. Metallic ornamental tips of various patterns are frequently encountered in paintings of both Continental Army officers and cavalrymen.

This tip ornament is particularly interesting because an identical one has been excavated at a Continental Army cantonment site in the Hudson Valley. The excavated example, however, still retains its original brass clasps or tongues on the back, which were used to cling the device on to a leather belt. The brass tip of this particular swordbelt is attached by small iron pins driven through the face and peened over the buff belting on the reverse, a period repair to replace the fragile original attachments. Perhaps most exciting is the actual design of the ornament, the center of which forms a triangular shape made of an arrow supporting thirteen rings. It is derived from one of the most famous patriotic motifs of the Revolution—a circle of thirteen interlocking rings symbolizing the unification of the thirteen colonies.

TROIANI COLLECTION

A Work of Art in Silver

American silver-mounted horsemen's sabers of the Revolution are extremely rare. Most cavalry officers preferred a sturdier arm, with hand protection of iron or brass, rather than of soft silver. This lion-headed specimen with spiraled white ivory grips exhibits the finest workmanship and design. Originally found in Providence, Rhode Island, it bears a similarity to the work of New York silversmith William Gilbert (active 1767–1818). The imported Spanish blade has triple fullers and was a type in wide use throughout the colonies during much of the eighteenth century.

Swords with pommel caps of animal heads were highly popular, and although lions were the most favored, dogs and eagles were also in use. American-made swords of this era are often somewhat more rustic in design and craftsmanship than those of their British cousins. This magnificent lion's head, however, is certainly worthy of any good London maker.

TROIANI COLLECTION

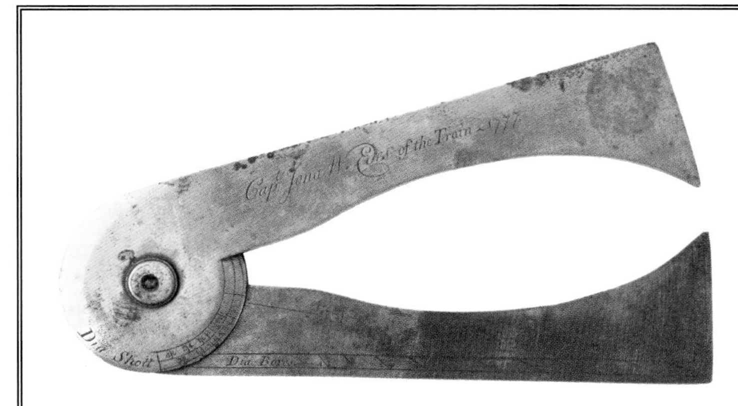

Gunner's Caliper

This brass gunner's caliper is engraved with the inscription of a Massachusetts officer, "Capt. Jona[than] W. Edes of the Train 1777." Calipers were used to calculate a cannonball's weight from its diameter and vice versa.

WILLIAM H. GUTHMAN COLLECTION, PHOTOGRAPH BY DON TROIANI

Shoe Buckles and Neck Stock Buckle

This sturdy set of brass shoe buckles and a neck stock buckle were excavated on a campsite of New England troops dating from 1780–82 in the Hudson Highlands. A number of identical specimens were recovered, including a few unfinished examples. Evidence from the site points to British beltplates captured at Yorktown being melted and recast into shoe buckles.

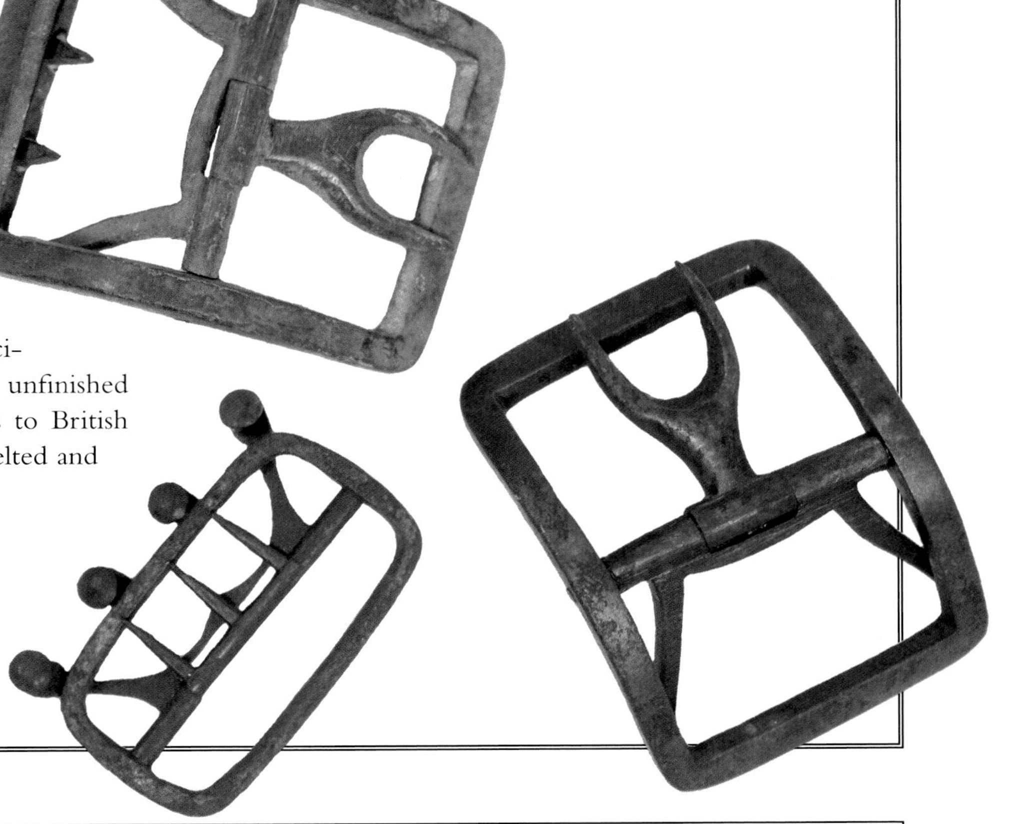

TROIANI COLLECTION

A French Bayonet

A French bayonet with "US" surcharge on the flat of the blade, which was bent to use as a brush or meat hook. This specimen was excavated on a 1780–1782 campsite in the Hudson Highlands.

TROIANI COLLECTION

LIEUTENANT JAMES GILES, 2ND REGIMENT OF CONTINENTAL ARTILLERY, FALL–WINTER 1780

PAUL SCHIERL COLLECTION

The 2nd Continental Artillery, also known as "Lamb's Artillery" after its commander, Col. John Lamb, was created on January 1, 1777. Raised primarily in New York but incorporating companies or men from Connecticut, Rhode Island, and New Hampshire, it served through the entire war. Like the three other Continental artillery regiments, it rarely served in its entirety; instead, companies or sections were often detached to serve with the various infantry brigades, manning the light battalion guns—usually 4- and 6-pounders—that accompanied such formations. Other companies of the regiment manned the artillery at fixed fortifications, such as the works at West Point and Constitution Island, as well as Fort Stanwix on the New York frontier. Most of the regiment marched to Virginia with the combined Continental and French armies in 1781, serving much of the heavy siege cannon in the American batteries.

From its formation until 1780, the regiment was clothed in the red-faced, black uniforms selected for the Continental Artillery by its commander, Brig. Gen. Henry Knox. However, the enlisted men of the 2nd Artillery received new coats of blue with scarlet facings in March 1780. Seven months later, Colonel Lamb prescribed the officers' new uniforms, which were to consist of deep blue coats faced with scarlet cuffs, lapels, and cape, all 2 1/2 inches wide. The cuffs were slit on the underside and closed with hooks and eyes. There were ten large, plain gilt buttons on each lapel with the "Button holes bound with Vellum—the Buttons on the Lappels, Cuffs & Pocket flaps to be Pair'd." A strap, or contra-epaulette, also bound with gold vellum lace, was placed on the shoulder opposite the fringed epaulette. Waistcoat and breeches were white, with small yellow buttons. The cocked hat was "Large with a Gold Button and loop, and Cock'd up with Gold Loopings."

Elisha Grose's Knapsack and Cartridge Box

The 3rd Continental Regiment of Artillery (sometimes called Crane's Massachusetts Artillery Regiment) was organized during spring 1777. It was known as a crack corps, and elements of the regiment fought in most of the major engagements from 1777 to 1780, including Brandywine, Germantown, Saratoga, Monmouth, the siege of Rhode Island, and the Battle of Springfield. Its ranks were composed largely of Massachusetts men, including veterans from Knox's Continental Artillery Regiment of 1776. One such veteran was Elisha Grose of Scituate, who joined the regiment in March 1777, having previously served in the siege of Boston and the Canada campaign of 1776. In March 1779 Corporal Grose was promoted to sergeant, serving with great merit until mustering out of service on January 6, 1783.

Returning to Scituate, Grose brought with him some of the articles he had carried through much of the war, including his knapsack, cartridge box, shoe buckles, and a 1780 furlough pass from the Continental cantonment at Morristown. Grose's knapsack is one of only two documented knapsacks that survive from the Revolutionary War. It is well-constructed in the fashion of British goatskin knapsacks, but it has a body made from the skin of an American black bear, while its straps are of buff leather. His cartridge box contains a wood block drilled to accomodate nineteen cartridges, seventeen of which still remain. It is a pattern that was in use by Massachusetts and other troops from the start of the war and is nearly identical to one recently recovered by archaeologists from the Valcour Bay wreck of one of Arnold's Lake Champlain flotilla of 1776. Together, Grose's relics of service compose a unique and rare assemblage of the accoutrements carried by the common soldier of the Continental Army.

JAMES L. KOCHAN COLLECTION

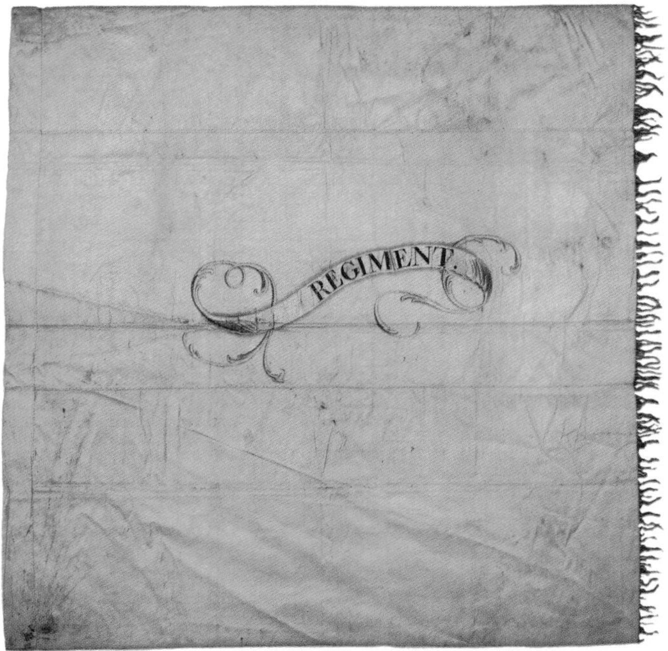

"The Waxhaws Colors"

This "stand" of three colors was posted at the center of the battle line formed by a 350-man detachment of the Virginia Continental Line when they made their stand against a pursuing Anglo-Loyalist force under Banastre Tarleton at the Waxhaws, South Carolina, on May 29, 1780. The American commander, Abraham Buford, made two strategic errors that proved their tragic undoing: first, he kept his field artillery on the march to prevent their capture, thereby allowing the British Legion and other light troops to form up just outside of musket range; secondly, he ordered his men to hold their fire until the attackers were fifty yards away, thereby allowing the massed cavalry charge to break through the thin line before being broken by opposing, concentrated fire. In the desperate action, numerous Virginians lost their lives under the sabers of the Tory light horse, including the standard bearers.

As trophies of war, the flags were sent home to England by a jubilant Tarleton and were carefully preserved by his descendants until the present day. The regimental "standard" is made of yellow silk, bearing a painted device of a beaver gnawing on a tree in its center, under which is a scroll bearing the motto *"Perservando"* (a patriotic motif also found on Continental currency). The canton is of blue silk, on which are painted thirteen silver stars—the "new constellation" first adopted in 1777. This is the seventh of thirteen regimental standards described in a Continental Army return of 1778, and of the three standards that still survive, this is the only one that contains nearly all of its design elements intact. It is also the only one still accompanied by its two "grand division" colors, in this case two slightly smaller colors of blue and yellow silk, respectively, on which are white scrolls bearing "Regiment" in black lettering. It had been intended that these division colors would have the number or name of the regiment painted on them once issued out, but since they were being carried by a battalion-sized detachment, hurriedly organized as a reinforcement to the Southern Army, the spaces for such remain blank.

PHOTOGRAPHS COURTESY OF SOTHEBY'S

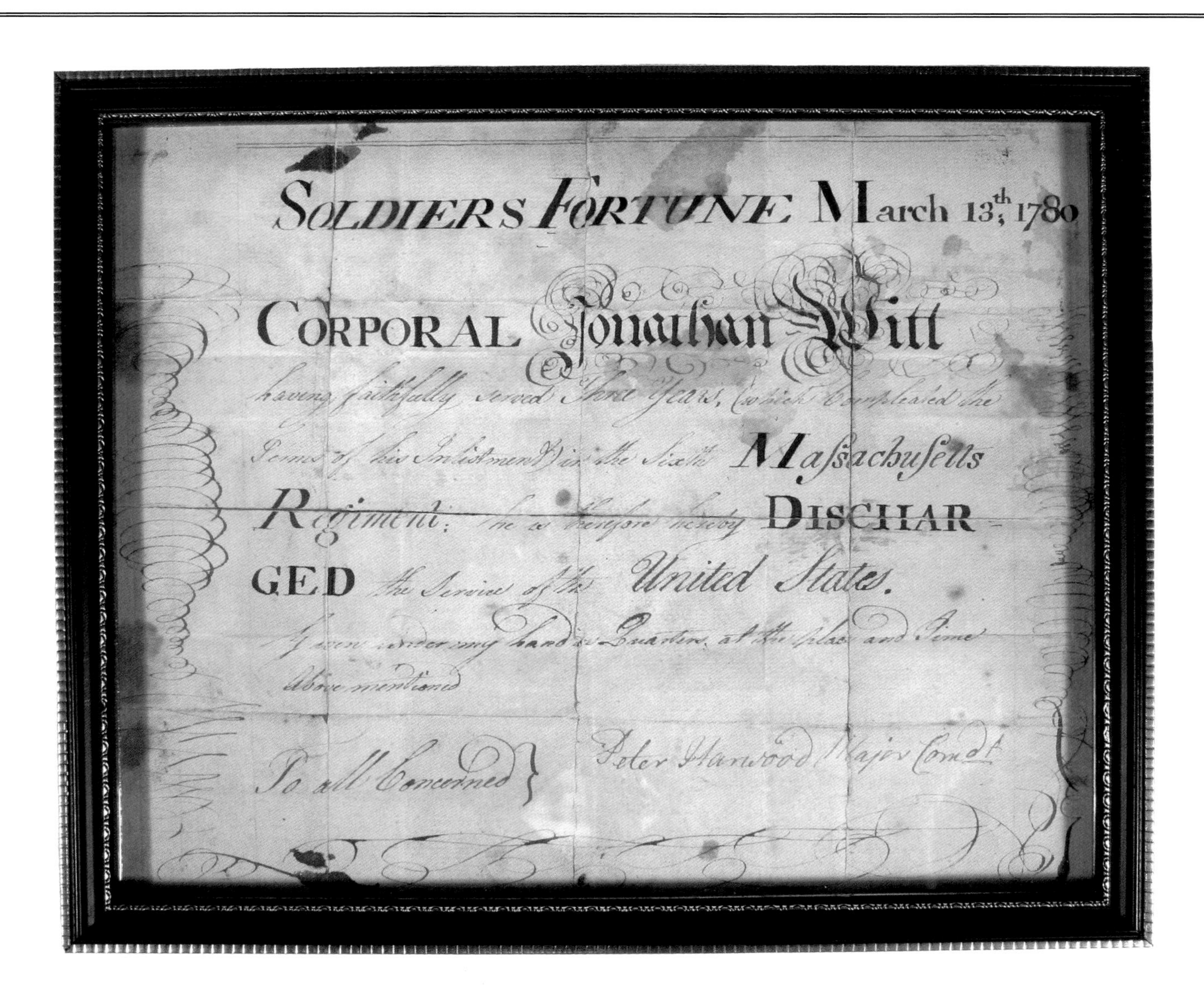
SOLDIERS FORTUNE March 13th 1780

CORPORAL Jonathan Witt

having faithfully served Three Years, (which Compleated the Terms of his Inlistment) in the Sixth Massachusetts Regiment; he is therefore hereby DISCHARGED the Service of the United States.

Given under my hand at Quarters, at the place and Time above mentioned

To all Concerned} Peter Harwood Major Comdt

WILLIAM H. GUTHMAN COLLECTION, PHOTOGRAPH BY DON TROIANI

Soldier's Discharge

After three years of faithful service, Cpl. Jonathan Swift of the 6th Massachusetts Regiment received this calligraphic discharge on March 13, 1780. The title, "Soldier's Fortune," refers to a winter Continental Army cantonment site on the east side of the Hudson River across from West Point.

During the late summer of 1780, Capt. George Flemming and his company of the 2nd were attached to the 2nd Brigade of the Light Infantry Division, commanded by the Marquis de Lafayette. In a September 23 letter to Colonel Lamb, Fleming wrote that the "Marquis has gave fresh instance of his munificence by presenting each Officer in his Division with a neat gold gilt small Sword" and "has got a French Merchant to supply us with superfine blue Cloth & Trimmings for a regimental Coat, Waistcoat & Breeches, for four Guineas each." Four days later, Lt. James Giles of Fleming's company signed for 1 1/2 yards of blue cloth, 1 3/8 yards of white cloth, and lining and trimmings for a uniform suit. This reconstruction of Giles is based on two postwar portraits, his clothing bill, and the uniform regulations of his regiment. His cocked hat sports the "black & red Feather" of the Light Infantry, also a gift of the marquis. His French Pattern 1767 smallsword is based on the original one presented to him by the marquis, which still survives.

THE BATTLE OF KING'S MOUNTAIN, OCTOBER 7, 1780

In September 1780, Lord Charles Cornwallis invaded North Carolina. While the British army advanced north toward Charlotte, Maj. Patrick Ferguson led a small, flanking force farther to the west. The backbone of Ferguson's command consisted of 100 of his American Volunteers, a detachment of "picked men" drawn from various Provincial "regular" regiments, still in the uniforms of their parent corps. However, he did his best to instill a sense of group cohesion by enforcing uniformity in the style of their cocked hats and hair. Ferguson also succeeded in procuring short, British military rifles for half of his "Rangers," the others being armed with muskets. He trained his men to fight in a loose, two-rank formation with the riflemen posted in the rear rank, protected by the bayonets of the musketeers in front, responding to his commands executed by sound of whistle or waving of the hat. The majority of Ferguson's command, however, consisted of nearly a thousand Loyalist militia from the Carolina backcountry. Ferguson had previously been appointed Inspector of Militia and had trained some of them to fight in the same manner as his American Volunteers. They were armed with a mix of their own guns, mostly long rifles or fowlers, along with captured French muskets. Needing a dependable cavalry force, Ferguson created a small cadre of "rifle dragoons" from the American Volunteers and issued naval cutlasses to them for fighting while on horseback.

Ferguson marched toward the North Carolina border and issued a warning that threatened "fire and sword" to those who resisted British rule. By late September more than 1,800 Patriot militia and "over mountain" men—mostly mounted riflemen—were on the march against him. Learning of this, Ferguson began a slow retreat but took post on the summit of King's Mountain on October 6, awaiting reinforcements and the return of a 200-man scout from his own command. It was a ridge that was nearly treeless at top but had rocky slopes wooded with old-growth hardwoods. That evening, the Patriots divided their force, sending a fast-moving column of some 900 of the "best horsemen" ahead to trap the Tories before it was too late. Riding all night through a heavy rain, they were reinforced by approximately 600 others prior to reaching their destination by midday. The riflemen began to encircle the perimeter of the mountain, and by three o'clock, most of them had reached their prearranged positions before an alarm was sounded. Overrunning the Loyalist outposts, "they were able to advance in three divisions . . . to the crest of the hill in perfect safety . . . and opened an irregular but destructive fire from behind trees and other cover." Ferguson countered this by having the American Volunteers push them back, with the "mountaineers flying whenever there was danger of being charged by the Bayonet, but returning again so soon as the . . . detachment faced about to repel another of their parties."

For nearly an hour, the battle raged in this seesaw fashion. Running out of ammunition, some of the Loyalist militia broke; others became confused and crowded the flanks of the regulars. Ferguson, realizing that the situation was desperate, called for another bayonet charge before their position was overrun. While the regulars formed, he led a handful of mounted men—two militia officers and the few "dragoons" of the Volunteers yet alive—down the hill, hoping to cut a swathe through the advancing riflemen. Although he was dressed in a hunting shirt, the Patriots had been told to be on the lookout for an officer wielding a sword in his left hand (his right incapacitated by an earlier war wound), and Ferguson fell with at least seven balls in his body. With his death, further Tory resistance crumbled, and this crushing defeat signaled the beginning of the end for British ascendancy in the Carolina backcountry.

Metal-Bound Wooden Canteen

A metal-bound wooden canteen with a dark blue-gray paint finish bearing an old nineteenth-century label "Canteen carried in-war 1776. Revolution by the Continental line of New Jersey." This is a typical style that remained fairly unchanged from the mid eighteenth century into the nineteenth. The various sets of initials carved in the sides may indicate this canteen had several different owners over time.

TROIANI COLLECTION

American-Made Officers' Swords

These three specimens, with completely American-made hilts and imported blades, are admirable examples of early American folk art. This type of sword is classified as a "cuttoe," which is a military version of the civilian hunting sword.

This silver-hilted example at the right was found in a home in the Connecticut River Valley and is capped with an unusually massive lion's head pommel and white, spiral-twist Mammoth ivory grips. It still retains the original silver-mounted leather scabbard.

The cuttoe in the center is of similar form but has a rudimentary brass animal head pommel, with features that are both leonine and canine. It has a white ivory grip that is carved with spiraling, tightly spaced, incised lines and has no ferrules. A large linked chain of twisted brass wire connects the mouth of the pommel to the pierced brass counterguard. The blade is single-edged and exhibits the remains of a French or Spanish inscription. Gen. Ethan Allen is known to have carried a similar weapon, still in existence today.

The example on the bottom is an imitation of many contemporary British swords, with a finely molded and chased silver lion's head pommel. The grip is a piece of arsenic-green stained ivory, a popular choice on sword hilts during this era. The blade is slightly curved, with a narrow fuller and a false edge on which is etched "Drawn to Defend Innocence 1775." New York City newspapers of the period advertise for sale silver-hilted swords with a variety of similar sentiments.

TROIANI COLLECTION

THE BATTLE OF COWPENS, JANUARY 17, 1781

It is Wednesday morning, January 17, 1781, at a place in northwestern South Carolina known to locals as "the Cowpens." Brig. Gen. Daniel Morgan has positioned his mixed command of troops wisely, taking full advantage of their abilities and weaponry, as well as the existing terrain. The first and second lines are composed of militia and volunteers from the Carolinas, Georgia, and Virginia. The riflemen in the front are to act as sharpshooters, skirmishing with the British from long distance. Morgan entreats the militia of the second line to fire two volleys into the British at close range, then retire to safety behind the third line. The third and final line of battle consists of the Corps of Light Infantry, "picked men" drawn from the remnants of the Maryland and Delaware Lines, augmented by one Virginia company and another small one from North Carolina. These 380 Continentals are under the command of Lt. Col. John Eager Howard of Maryland and are posted on the rising ground at the northern end of Cowpens. The regulars are masters of their trade, hardened from constant deprivation and severe hardships, and Morgan depends on them to deliver a victory or at least to prevent a complete rout.

From a distance, Howard's light infantry looks impressive, most dressed in the blue-faced red uniform prescribed in 1779 for Continentals of the Mid-Atlantic states. Although reclothed in October through the efforts of their state, the Maryland and Delaware regulars' new, short regimental coats already show wear from an active winter campaign. Seemingly forgotten by their state, the Virginia troops wear even more ragged uniforms of apparently ancient issue—supplemented with new clothing loaned from Maryland stores, principally overalls, shirts, and shoes. All of the mens' overalls are torn and stained from constant marching along muddy traces and through rain-choked streams, while shoes are in an even more miserable state. Hats, always in short supply, are mostly tattered remnants of the previous year's issue. The men's muskets are in good repair, however, and primarily of French make. Their bayonets are keen-bladed, and each man's cartridge box holds forty "buck and ball" cartridges—the standard combat load of the Continental Army.

As the dawn light begins to filter in from the east on this cold, crisp day, Lt. Col. Banastre Tarleton files his British and Loyalist troops across the southern terminus of the intended battleground. Although he cannot see Morgan's dispositions clearly, the open woods are ideal terrain for the swift form of warfare waged by his mixed force of horse and foot. "Bloody Ban" knows that Morgan's line of retreat to the north is cut off by the rain-swollen Broad River. Tarleton's right wing consists of four crack companies of light infantrymen while the infantry of his own British Legion compose the center and the proud 7th Regiment of Foot, known as the "Royal" or "British Fuzileers," takes up the left. Two 3-pounder cannon and their Royal Artillery crews move forward with the line, with one cannon placed between the two divisions of the 7th and the other in the interval between the fusiliers and the legion infantry. Each flank of the line is further covered by a troop of horse, ready to gallop in for the kill once the Americans are broken. The 1st Battalion, 71st Regiment (Frazier's Highlanders), is posted in reserve, along with Tarleton's remaining cavalry.

U.S. ARMY NATIONAL GUARD BUREAU

PRIVATE COLLECTION

Brigadier General Daniel Morgan, 1781

Of the 200 fusiliers, probably fewer than half had been with the regiment when it first came to North America in 1773. Although well-drilled under the watchful eyes of veteran commissioned and non-commissioned officers, they do not have the steadiness normally expected in such an "ancient" and famous regiment. Also left behind are the tall but impractical bearskin caps traditionally worn by fusiliers in the British Army, replaced with cocked hats bound and looped with white worsted tape. Officers and sergeants carry their traditional fusils as befitting a fusilier regiment, while the men carry Short Land muskets. Blue facings to the brick-red fusilier coats and royal livery lace festooning drummers' clothing still clearly identify the 7th Foot as one of the "king's own" regiments, and one cannot mistake the script "RF" motif on their accoutrement plates.

Tarleton opens the battle at sunrise "by the Discharge of two pieces of Cannon and three Huzzas" from his men. They march forward in the loose, open-file, two-rank formation that the British Army has employed to advantage for the past six years of the American rebellion, allowing the battle line to move forward quickly through the pine and oak trees with a minimum loss of order. The fusiliers soon begin suffering casualties, notably among their officers, whose scarlet and gold uniforms set them off as special targets for the riflemen of the American first line.

Some of the 7th, excited, confused, and enraged over their losses, open fire although no command has been given. The officers restore order, but Tarleton, impetuous and impatient for battle, moves the line forward before the 7th is completely reformed. Soon the sharpshooter fire withers away as the retreating militia dodge "from One tree to another" to escape the bayonets and fire of the British troops as they get within closing range. The second American line is now attacked, and more soldiers lie writhing in the grass after they receive its general discharge. The fusiliers now charge bayonets. Cheering madly as they advance, the British push the militia from the field. Only now do they clearly see the closely massed ranks of Howard's Continentals on the ground to their front. Tarleton orders a general halt and carefully redresses his battle line, which has become disordered by the charge. The fusiliers are on the left, facing the right center of the Continentals, with the Highlanders now drawn up into line of battle to the left of the 7th Foot.

As they prepare for a final thrust to break the right wing of the American third line, Tarleton orders the fifty dragoons posted on the British right flank to charge around the left flank, behind which the militia from the second line are reforming. The troopers are a detachment from the 17th Regiment of Light Dragoons.

Charging in compact formation around the American left flank, they are soon hacking away at the militia in the rear with their heavy sabers. Morgan and a few officers rally some of the sharpshooters, who reload and hit the dragoons with well-directed rifle fire, "emptying many a British saddle." Already disorganized by the success of their charge, the 17th are now charged in turn by Col. William Washington's 125 American cavalrymen who have been held in reserve. Supported by volunteer militia horse, the white-coated 3rd Light Dragoons and other veterans from the 1st Light Dragoons smash into the redcoats. Outnumbered nearly three to one,

PRIVATE COLLECTION

the redcoats "pretty much scattered" after "leaving in the course of ten minutes eighteen of their brave 17th dragoons dead on the spot." The success of Tarleton's strategy is now completely dependent on the British infantry.

The regulars advance briskly against Howard's Continentals. As the acrid, black powder smoke disperses in the wind, they see the Continentals in their front begin to withdraw by platoons. Cheering and huzzahing wildly, they charge bayonets and rush on, their loose order now deteriorating completely. Suddenly, the seeming Continental retreat is no more, and once again, a wall of blue and red—bristling with bayonets—confronts the British. First one platoon volley, then another, crashes into the confused redcoats. Under such a withering fire, few officers and noncoms are left standing to exert any control over the dazed redcoats. Howard, sensing his opportunity, orders his men to charge bayonets and counterattack. Panic is now at near-epidemic proportion among all the British and Loyalist infantry. Although small pockets of men still try to defend themselves or escape, most throw down their arms in desperation or club muskets to signify surrender to the Continentals, whose mad, scrambling charge has completely disordered their own ranks. Colonel Howard slashes down from his mount at a fusilier corporal who resolutely stands his ground in defense of the regimental colors. But the effort is futile, and both regimental and royal standards are seized as trophies of war. Next taken are the two cannon and final resistance melts among the British and Loyalist infantry—all witnessed by Morgan and his staff from their vantage point on the hill behind. The battle ends in a stunning American victory.

LEE'S PARTISAN LEGION, 1778–81

SCOTT FERRIS COLLECTION

In April 1778 Capt. Henry Lee was authorized to create an "independent corps" of two troops to be expanded from his original 5th Troop of the 1st Continental Light Dragoons. The following month an additional troop was added, with Lee in overall command with the rank of major. Lee, once described as having "sprung from the womb a soldier," had demonstrated his mastery of the *petit guerre* while on outpost duty near Philadelphia the previous winter, skirmishing with the enemy and forwarding vital intelligence, cattle, and other necessities to the army wintering at Valley Forge. The ambitious Virginian wasted no time in obtaining smart uniforms for his new command from his home state, which consisted of green-faced, buff coats and waistcoats trimmed with brass buttons, buckskin breeches, and leather jockey caps with bearskin crests. When his new mounted unit joined Washington's main army, they were described as "compleatly uniformed and extremely well mounted."

In June 1779 Capt. Allen McLane's light infantry company, officially part of Patton's Additional Regiment but long operating in an independent capacity similar to that of Lee's, was attached to Lee's "Partisan Corps." It was formally annexed as its 4th Troop on July 13, 1779. McLane's original command was augmented with the dismounted dragoons from the other troops, and this overstrength "light infantry" command soon became known as the "Partisan Rangers." It was McLane who had performed the reconnaissance that enabled the capture of Stony Point by "Mad Anthony" Wayne that month and, in August, the taking of Paulus Hook by Lee. McLane and his Rangers also distinguished themselves in the assault. McLane's men were poorly outfitted when they first joined Lee's corps, but in September 1779 they procured "Uniform light linnen Jackets dyed a Purple & all there Ovrehalls the same." Completing this rather whimsical costume were leather caps with green turbans, surmounted by a bearskin "roach" or crest—the same as worn by Lee's mounted dragoons. During July and August 1779, ninety-six muskets (apparently British Short Lands), along with cartridge boxes, bayonets, and black crossbelts, were drawn by McLane for his men.

On February 14, 1780, Lee's command was designated the "Partisan Legion" and reorganized to consist of three mounted and three dismounted troops. For much of that year, they received little in the way of new clothing issues and apparently continued wearing their old buff and green uniforms. While attached to the Marquis de Lafayette's Corps of Light Infantry in late summer and fall, each Legion officer and enlisted man was presented with the distinctive red and black plume of that corps—personal gifts from the gallant French nobleman. Lee was said to be "horse-proud," and his unit was perhaps the best mounted command on either side during the war. Each troop was distinguished and known by the color of its horses: for example, the Sorrel Troop and the Gray Troop. This well-armed dragoon holds a Rappahannock Forge pistol—a Virginia copy of the British light dragoon model—while a carbine and a captured "Potter" saber are slung from his black crossbelts.

The command eventually marched southward following their official transfer to the Southern Department on October 31, 1780. Described as now being virtually "bare of clothing", the entire legion received "short green coats, with other distinctions exactly resembling some of the enemy's light corps" just prior to their departure. An eyewitness described the uniforms as "jackets," and as Lee's Legion was

Cartridge Box Plate, Foix Regiment, French Army, Savannah, Georgia, 1779

The Foix Regiment of French line infantry, part of which had been sent to the West Indies in 1776, was one of the units that participated in the unsuccessful attempt, by French admiral d'Estaing, to capture Savannah in the fall of 1779.

From 1776 to 1779, the uniform of the Foix Regiment, a unit raised in 1684, was white with green cuffs and lapels, yellow collar, and brass buttons. It also would have been worn later, however, especially by the detachment in America, as the French Army reclothed only a third of the men in each regiment every year. The oval brass cartridge box plate model illustrated was introduced by the royal regulation of April 25, 1767. The royal regulation of May 31, 1776, specifically abolished the use of badges on cartridge box flaps, but as with many other items in what proved to be one of the most unpopular regulations in the history of the French Army, unit commanders simply went on using the badges until new equipment, which now came without badges, was issued.

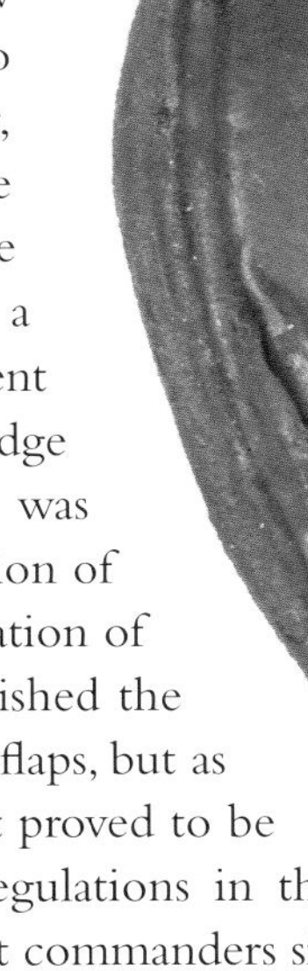

TROIANI COLLECTION

WILLIAM RODEN COLLECTION

frequently mistaken for the Queen's Rangers and the British Legion, the new uniforms must have been green stable or "round" jackets similar in form to those worn by the Loyalist light corps. "Light-Horse Harry" Lee and his men wore this practical uniform while performing many notable exploits during the numerous engagements of the 1781 campaign, including the taking of Forts Motte and Granby, the Battle of Guilford Courthouse, Orangeburgh, and the Siege of '96. This dragoon officer of the famous command is shown in such attire, privately purchased but closely matching that issued to his men, although of finer quality and tailoring. Gilt buttons and a gold bullion epaulette, a gift of the Marquis de Lafayette, proclaim his status as an officer, as do his well-fitted "jockey" boots.

PRIVATE COLLECTION

FUSILIER PRIVATE, SAINTONGE REGIMENT OF INFANTRY, 1780–82

PRIVATE COLLECTION

The Saintonge Regiment composed part of the French expeditionary force dispatched to North America under command of the Comte de Rochambeau in 1780, arriving in Rhode Island that July. As with most French infantry regiments at this time, it was organized in two battalions. Each consisted of four "fusilier" or battalion companies and one elite flank company; a grenadier company was attached to the first battalion and one of "chasseurs" (light infantry) to the second. Since the close of the Seven Years' War, the French army had undergone massive reforms in organization, tactical doctrine, and equipment—all of which went toward rendering it an extremely formidable force—and their new American allies were more than impressed upon viewing the drill, arms, and uniforms of Rochambeau's men. Elements of the Saintonge Regiment took part in various small actions around New York, including the July 12, 1781, raid on the Loyalist post at Lloyds Neck. However, it was during the siege of Yorktown that their military prowess was most clearly demonstrated, in both the conduct and operations of siege warfare, from construction of batteries and parallels to the assault of fortified positions.

New uniform regulations were put into effect for the French Army in 1779 by which the cut and even the facing colors of most regiments were changed. The body color of the coat for the Saintonge (as well as all line infantry regiments) remained the traditional white of France, but its facings were changed. Gone, at least on paper, were the sky blue collar and "*aurore*" (yellowish-

Pattern 1767 French Grenadier's Saber

This Pattern 1767 French grenadier's saber was the type carried by such elite troops when they served in America during the 1779–82 campaigns. It bears the cipher of Louis XIV engraved on its blade, in addition to a flaming grenade device and the "Grenadier" appellation.

TROIANI COLLECTION

orange) cuffs and lapels of the 1776 pattern, replaced instead by green cuffs and white facings edged with green, trimmed with brass buttons bearing "85" on their faces. However, a French soldier received a new uniform coat only once each three years, with approximately one third of a regiment receiving the new issue each year. Thus, at Yorktown, more than 200 men in the Saintonge were described as still wearing their pre-1779 coats. This Saintonge fusilier is distinguished by his green-edged shoulderstraps, as well as the bayonet frog attached to his cartridge box belt. The elite grenadier and chasseur companies instead wore red and green epaulettes, respectively, and carried short sabers in a crossbelt arrangement, in addition to the Model 1777 musket and bayonet. His cocked hat bears the white and black "Alliance" cockade, emblematic of the 1778 treaty of cooperation between the French and American nations.

French Brass Button

Brass soldier's button of the 79th Dillon Regiment, which was composed of Irishmen in French service. In 1779 they were renumbered as the 90th Regiment, but buttons with both numerical designations have been found at American sites.

MILITARY AND HISTORICAL IMAGE BANK

COMPANY OFFICER, CONTINENTAL LINE INFANTRY REGIMENT, MID-ATLANTIC STATES, 1780–83

NATIONAL PARK SERVICE

On October 2, 1779, the Continental Congress established blue as the ground for all Continental Army uniforms. White facings were prescribed for regiments from New England states, buff for those of New Jersey and New York, and red for those from the Mid-Atlantic states. Blue coats faced with blue were to be worn by the southern states, with buttonholes bound with white tape. Linings and buttons for all infantry regiments were to be white. Blue coats faced and lined with scarlet and trimmed with narrow yellow tape and buttons were reserved for the artillery corps. White facings, buttons, and linings were to be used by the light dragoons. All woolen small-clothes were to be uniformly white. To varying degrees and with some exceptions, compliance with this regulation was generally achieved during the remainder of the war through the extraordinary efforts of various commanders and the Continental and state clothiers.

Perhaps the most successful at achieving relative uniformity were the regiments of the Mid-Atlantic states, which had already been largely uniformed in blue and red since the arrival of imported French-made clothing during fall 1778. This company officer is dressed in a blue and scarlet uniform of superfine cloth, with white shalloon lining and silvered buttons. His breeches and waistcoats are white, woolen for winter and linen or "janes" for summer. Although the cloth and trimmings were sometimes state-supplied, the uniform was made up at the officer's expense. A single silver epaulette on the left shoulder denotes his rank as a lieutenant, and his spontoon and short saber similarly symbolize his officer's status. He is fortunate in possessing both weapons, as many junior-grade Continental officers were armed solely with the polearm, creating the "unmilitary appearance" commented upon in some inspection returns of the army. His cocked hat is trimmed with the black and white cockade first authorized on July 19, 1780, to be "Emblimatack of the expected Union" of the Continental and French armies. Instead of shoes, he wears the laced half boots favored by European sportsmen and woodsmen, a form commonly known in the eighteenth century as "hi-lows" or "start-ups."

A Powder Horn

This soldier's Powder horn is engraved with artillery themes in addition to his name and date. A resident of Middleborough, Plymouth County, and a member of Capt. Nathaniel Wood's militia company, forty-three-year-old David Shaw was among those who marched in response to the Lexington Alarm of April 19,1775. The following month, Shaw began the first of a series of enlistments, serving in Capt. Joshua Benson's Company of Cotton's Massachusetts Regiment. As part of the army's major reorganization during the spring of 1777, Shaw's company became part of the 5th Massachusetts Battalion, the unit with which he served for the remaining six years of the war. During much of its term of service, the 5th Massachusetts was stationed in the Hudson Highlands, just a few miles north of the village of Peekskill, New York.

BOB MCDONALD COLLECTION

Button Mold

Mold for manufacturing enlisted man's pewter buttons of the 3rd Massachusetts Regiment of the Continental Line, about 1781. A repousse officer's button was set into a pewter block, carved wooden sides added to create the shank, and the casting process was begun. This was found in a Hudson Highlands winter campsite.

TROIANI COLLECTION

Continental Markings

The "United States" brands on the butt face of this American musket indicate this arm was property of the Continental Army at one time. Guns were branded in the stocks "U.S.," "U.States," and "United States." Metal parts (usually the lock or barrel) were often stamped "U.S."

TROIANI COLLECTION

A Refined Button

This beautiful, silver repousse button was from the coat of Col. Joseph Vose of the 1st Massachusetts Regiment, who distinguished himself during the Virginia campaign of 1781 while commanding a provisional battalion of light infantry.

TROIANI COLLECTION

PRIVATE, GASKINS'S DETACHMENT OF THE VIRGINIA LINE, 1781

With the exception of the one regiment on the frontier and some small, scattered detachments, the entire Virginia Line was captured with the surrender of Charleston in May 1780. Attempts to rebuild Virginia's Continental regiments were hampered by the urgent need of reinforcements for Greene's Southern Army, as well as in the defense of the state. The lack of willing recruits induced the state to levy drafts upon the militia and (for the first time) to accept men of color to meet her Continental quotas. Recruits, reenlisted veterans, and levies from the militia were, after rudimentary training and equipping, hurriedly organized into detachments and sent off to respond to the most pressing British threats. Typically, these detachments would be officered by a hodge-podge of Continental officers from various "paper" regiments who had eluded captivity or had been exchanged.

In May 1781, with two invading British armies operating within the state, the only Virginia Continental infantry in the field to oppose them was a small battalion-sized detachment under the command of Lt. Col. Thomas Gaskins. To make matters worse, these half-trained levies were "Neither Cloathed nor Equipped" and were supposed to march to North Carolina. After a series of orders, marches, and countermarches that summer and early fall, the ragged detachment found itself on the siege lines at Yorktown, as part of Anthony Wayne's brigade of Pennsylvanians, with whom they served in the construction and defense of the American siege lines and witnessed Cornwallis's surrender on October 17. In early 1782, the detachment was sent south under Lt. Col. Thomas Posey, where they served with great distinction in the operations against Savannah and, later, Charleston.

Virginia lost a great deal of her stockpiled supplies following the sack of Point of Fork arsenal by a Loyalist and British force on June 5, 1781. Even prior to this, proper linen for hunting frocks was lacking, leading the state clothier to make up "short coats" or jackets of coarse canvas with blue facings as an expedient summer uniform. An insufficient supply of cartridge boxes had been partially alleviated by furnishing many of the troops with japanned tin canisters as a substitute. Keeping the bayonet constantly fixed to the musket obviated the need for bayonet belts and scabbards. Gaskins's detachment received clothing, arms, and equipment in small batches at various intervals. Thus, some men drew the canvas jackets, while others received hunting shirts, along with shirts of brown linen and coarse "osnabrig" overalls. When inspected on June 30, they were described as "literally naked, shirts and blankets excepted . . . [with] not more than 20 prs. of good shoes in the regiment" and were still poorly clothed when reinspected three months later (although sufficient arms "of three different bores" had been issued—this black soldier is seen armed with a captured German musket).

Field Chest

Maj. Caleb Gibbs of the 2nd Massachusetts had his name and unit affiliation boldly carved on the lid of this sturdy field chest following his transfer to that unit on January 1, 1781. Formerly, he had served as captain and major in charge of the Commander-in-Chief's Guard from 1777. He requested transfer to a line unit in order to see combat service before the close of the war; his wish was fulfilled, and he was wounded at Yorktown but recovered and lived until 1818.

ROBERT NITTOLO COLLECTION

TROIANI COLLECTION

French Musket

Detail of markings on a French musket marked to the 2nd New Hampshire Battalion of the Continental Line and the soldier's number. This arm most likely served through the battles of the decisive Saratoga campaign of 1777 and thence throughout the remainder of the war. A true veteran of the Revolution.

TROIANI COLLECTION

French "Charleville" Musket, Model 1766

With the exception of the British Land Pattern muskets, French muskets were the most commonly carried arm of the Revolutionary War. Indeed, by the close of the war, most soldiers in the Continental Army were armed with one of a number of French models imported to America, the most common being the model 1766. By 1775 it was already considered an outdated pattern by the French Army, which had largely reequipped itself with muskets of newer pattern (particularly the model 1774 and, to a lesser degree as the war progressed, the model 1777). Nevertheless, thousands of surplus model 1766 muskets were purchased and shipped for the use of the Continental and state forces, most notably in 1777, when more than 3,000 reached New England in time to be carried into action at the Battles of Hubbardton and Freeman's Farm by New Hampshire and Massachusetts troops.

The model 1766 differs only slightly from its predecessor, the model 1763, primarily in its elongated lock plate, redesigned barrel bands, and lightened stock and barrel, reducing overall weight by nearly two pounds in the later model. These improvements led to its frequently being listed as the "light model 1763 Charleville" on Revolutionary War invoices. The majority of French arms shipped to the United States were from the Charleville manufactory, resulting in the generic application of the term "Charleville" by Americans to all French military muskets. The model 1766 has a 44⅝-inch-long barrel of .69-caliber bore that is band—as opposed to pin—fastened, making it easier to remove and clean than its British counterpart. This factor, plus its light weight (approximately 8½ pounds), made it a popular arm with American soldiers, and it became the pattern for the first postwar American muskets, the model 1795 Springfield and the 1794 U.S. contract muskets.

WILLIAM WASHINGTON'S CHARGE AT EUTAW SPRINGS

Following the relief of the Siege of '96, Lord Rawdon returned to Charleston, leaving his small army of almost 2,000 British and Loyalist regulars under Lt. Col. Alexander Stewart to operate in the South Carolina countryside. Taking position at Eutaw Springs, near Nelson's Ferry on the Santee River, this force is surprised by Maj. Gen. Nathaniel Greene's patriot force of approximately 2,200 Continentals, state troops, and militia on the morning of September 8, 1781. The American advance first encounters a party of unarmed foragers supported by an armed guard, and the fire from the resulting skirmish alerts the British camp. Stewart sends out reinforcements to his outlying pickets to fight a delaying action while he forms a line of battle. The right flank of the British army is anchored to Eutaw Creek by the Flank Battalion, consisting of the light infantry and grenadier companies of the 3rd, 19th, and 30th Regiments of Foot under Maj. John Marjoribanks. The main battle line straddles the road that leads to their encampment and consists of the British and Loyalist infantry, with a few detachments and a small party of mounted infantry left in reserve.

Greene's first line is composed primarily of North and South Carolina militia, which hold their own for some time before being forced back. At this moment, Greene sends forward his second battle line, consisting of Continentals and state regulars. The battle-hardened Maryland Line, on the left flank, in a desperate bayonet charge, drives back the famous "Buffs" of the 3rd Regiment of Foot, and British resistance begins to crumble on the British right—all but the Flank Battalion, which has posted itself behind the thickets of blackjack that line Eutaw Creek. From this vantage point, they pour a devastating fire into the Americans.

Against this threat gallops the gallant Lt. Col. William Washington (a distant cousin of the commander in chief) with his Continental light dragoons, supported by Wade Hampton's Carolina Horse. Washington attempts to charge into what is perceived as an interval between the creek and the right of Marjoribanks' battalion, but he is rebuffed by the thickness of the blackjack and the well-directed fire of the British troops posted therein. Point-blank fire hits the light dragoons in the midst of wheeling by sections across the British front and cuts down men and horses with great effect. Washington, pinned beneath his fallen horse, is wounded and nearly killed at point of bayonet when he is saved at the last minute by a British officer and taken prisoner.

Seen here in the moment before his tragic fall is Colonel Washington. He, like his troopers, wears the white, faced-blue, serge stable jacket favored by the 3rd Light Dragoons for hot weather service. To his front and flank are "light bobs" of the Buffs, dressed in sleeved, light infantry waistcoats or jackets with buff facings, their pouches and belt plates bearing the dragon device of this "ancient" British regiment.

LEE F. MCGEE

NORTH CAROLINA MILITIAMAN, 1780–81

NATIONAL PARK SERVICE

The North Carolina Line ceased to exist with the fall of Charleston in May 1780, its three Continental regiments having been part of that city's defending force. The state, now open to enemy invasion, mobilized its militia and created a state legion composed of cavalry and foot, principally made up of drafts from the militia. The North Carolina militia, like that of Virginia, had a mixed record of service. Posted in the center of the American battle line at Camden, most of the North Carolinians ran without firing a shot after witnessing the Virginia militia to their left flee in a similar manner. However, they fought well as irregulars in numerous small actions and during the pitched battles at Cowpens and Guilford Courthouse.

North Carolina was perhaps the poorest of the thirteen original states, but it did its best to provide for the needs of its own militia and the Continental forces under Gates and Greene during 1780–81. The militia called into service for the 1780 campaign were to be riflemen, clothed in "cloth coloured" hunting shirts with blue capes and overalls of the same materials. Though this attempt at uniformity was not fully achieved, the almost universal use of linen hunting shirts by Carolina militia is well documented. As early as 1777, the Marquis de Lafayette noted that "hunting shirts, loose jackets of gray [natural] linen, [were] very common in Carolina."

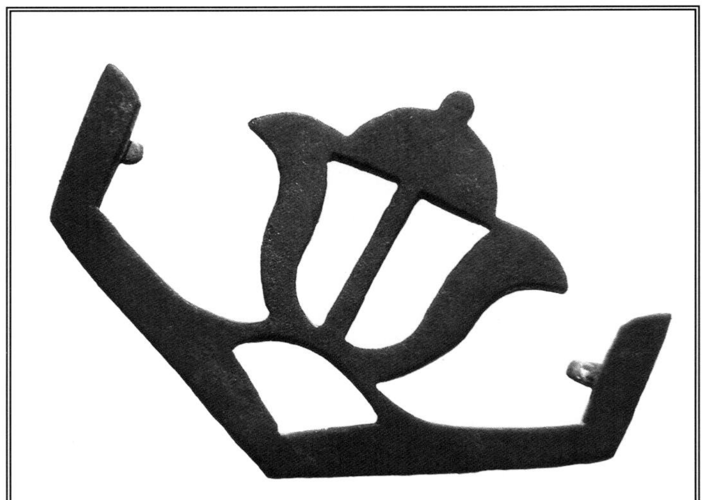

Sword Belt Tip

This brass sword belt tip boldly displays a liberty cap on a pole, a popular patriotic device of the time. It was excavated on a midwar Continental artillery campsite in New Jersey.

BENNINGHOFF COLLECTION

This Carolinian has replaced his rifle (thrown away at the Battle of Camden) with a Long Land musket, although he still employs his rifle pouch and powder horn to carry the ammunition for his smoothbore "firelock." He wears a fringed hunting shirt of natural linen and trousers of cotton "oznabrigs," a coarse material commonly produced by North Carolina weavers during this period. His battered and rustic "flopped" hat protects his head from the sun's brutal rays, while he slakes his thirst with water swigged from an oak "keg" canteen.

Brass-Hilted Swords

The three brass-hilted swords shown here are sturdy fighting weapons as well as fine examples of primitive American folk art. From right to left:

A large dragoon saber with smooth wooden grips and stylized lion's head pommel.

Referred to as "New England Lionheads" by collectors, most specimens of the middle pattern have been discovered in the Massachusetts, Connecticut, and New Hampshire regions. There are many variants, but most appear to be the work of one maker, exhibiting a large, boldly chiseled grinning lion's head with zigzag teeth. Gen. Israel Putnam carried a sword of this very type, which may date several decades before the Revolution.

The heart was a favorite motif of the era, and this more austere saber's guard on the left is decorated with two such cut-out motifs.

TROIANI COLLECTION

VIRGINIA MILITIAMAN, 1780–81

NATIONAL PARK SERVICE

The Old Dominion, having been little troubled by enemy incursions since 1776, became the target of two separate British expeditions that devastated the state, first in 1779 and again in 1780–81. For the next two years, Virginia would repeatedly call up its militia for active service, not only for the protection of its state borders, but also for service in the war-wracked Carolinas. The performance of the Virginia militia was less than stellar during 1780, both in the Battle of Camden and in the defense of their native soil. But well-led and bolstered by the presence of many discharged Continentals in their ranks, they redeemed their flagging reputation during the Battles of Cowpens and Guilford Courthouse, as well as in the Yorktown Campaign.

Virginia militiamen were expected to provide themselves with "a good Rifle, if to be had, or otherwise, with a common Firelock, Bayonet and Cartouch Box, and also with a Tomahawk." This former Continental is armed with a Short Land Pattern musket and wears a green-faced, blue coat drawn from the Virginia Public Store just prior to his discharge from the Continental service. A pair of natural linen breeches, blue stockings, and a flopped hat complete his attire, along with a "spotted" handkerchief of silk knotted around his neck. Shoes are a common civilian form, fastened with ties instead of buckles. A seasoned veteran, he has stowed extra clothing and personal items in his blanket roll, and three days' rations are contained in his haversack.

Ice Creepers

Pair of hand forged ice creepers, which were strapped to the soles of shoes in order to grip on icy ground. These are common finds in winter camps of the Revolution.

TROIANI COLLECTION

A Massachusetts Painted Drum

This boldly painted drum is embellished with a pine tree motif in a cartouche encircled by a gold wreath and an intricate scroll. The Latin motto on one scroll proclaims that "It is sweet and distinguished to die for one's Country." The wooden body is held in shape by iron rose-headed nails typical of the colonial era.

COL. J. CRAIG NANNOS COLLECTION

Waistcoat and Shirt of Col. William Ledyard

Col. William Ledyard was wearing this striped linen waistcoat at the time of his death on September 6, 1781, after the fall of Fort Griswold at New London, Connecticut, to a force under Gen. Benedict Arnold. Surrendering his sword to a Loyalist officer, the recipient immediately ran him through with it. The waistcoat shows clearly the hole made by the fatal thrust and possibly further stabbing by bayonets.

Ledyard's linen shirt also exhibits wound holes similar to those found on his waistcoat. It is a fine example of the typical loose, pullover-style shirt of the second half of the eighteenth century.

COLLECTION OF THE CONNECTICUT HISTORICAL SOCIETY, PHOTOGRAPH BY DON TROIANI

Leather Breeches

Widely used by mounted troops on both sides, leather breeches had the durability and stretch requisite for the rigors of service in the saddle—features lacking in most cloth types. However, they were also widely worn by American militia and regulars, especially during the early part of the war. This pair of the period appears to be of the "tradesman's" form commonly issued to foot troops (although certainly worn by the former when necessity required). Unlike most horsemen's breeches, which had one-piece legs with outseam only, this pair is cut like a pair of cloth breeches with two-piece legs. Thus, the inseam would chafe the soft flesh of a trooper's inner thigh after so many hours in the saddle. Foot troops may have found them hot in the summer, but they were also long-wearing and briar-resistant.

TROIANI COLLECTION

Tin Water Bottle

This American-made, tin-coated sheet-iron "water bottle" differs from its British counterparts in having a flared base, which adds stability when the object is set down. The side loops are for a shoulder string. There are several known variations of this style.

COL. J. CRAIG NANNOS COLLECTION

Washington and Rochambeau before Yorktown, October 1781

Jean Baptiste Donatien de Vimeur, Comte de Rochambeau, was selected to command the French expeditionary force to America in 1780. An experienced, brave, and extremely capable officer, he also proved himself a skilled diplomat in his relations with the American military and political leadership. His ability to exert a joint-command with Washington over the combined armies, yet treat the latter as the senior officer, required a good deal of tact and courtesy, and the two leaders developed great respect and admiration for each other's abilities. Although it was Washington who decided to abandon plans against New York and seize the initiative against Cornwallis in Virginia, it was Rochambeau and his skilled specialist troops—especially the engineers and artillery (experienced as they were in conducting large siege operations)—that ultimately led to a victorious outcome.

Washington, in a later version of his "plain" uniform of blue and buff, is seen in the Allied lines outside of Yorktown, consulting with Rochambeau. Rochambeau wears the royal blue undress uniform of a lieutenant general. It is single-breasted in front, edged with figured gold lace and with twelve gilt buttons down the right side. His pocket flaps and the skirts of his coat are ornamented in a similar manner. On his left breast is worn the embroidered Grand Cross of the Order of St. Louis. His waistcoat and breeches are of scarlet superfine, the breast of the former also trimmed with gilt buttons and gold edging. In the background is a French Engineer officer in the distinctive uniform of that corps: blue coats with black facings, edged and lined with scarlet, and with scarlet smallclothes worn underneath.

"A Toast to His Excellency, General Washington"

A fine pair of silver camp cups carried through the Revolutionary War by Col. Anthony Walton White of New Jersey and bearing his initials in cipher. They are virtually identical to another pair (also by Richard Humphreys, a noted Philadelphia silversmith) made for Gen. George Washington. White served as Washington's aide-de-camp during the siege of Boston and was appointed lieutenant colonel of the 3rd New Jersey Regiment in 1776. After serving with that unit on the Canada expedition, he transferred to the cavalry arm, serving as lieutenant colonel of the 4th Continental Light Dragoons from February 1777 until promoted to colonel-commandant of the 1st Continental Light Dragoons. Captured during the action at Lanneaus's Ferry, South Carolina, on May 6, 1780, he was later exchanged and commanded the Continental horse at the siege of Yorktown and later during Wayne's Georgia campaign in 1782.

JAMES L. KOCHAN COLLECTION

Medicine Chest

This simple medicine chest is typical of the type that would have composed part of the equipage of a regimental surgeon in the army. Filled with an array of hand-blown bottles with pewter tops, some still bear labels with the names of the remedies they once contained. Hand-rolled pills were stored in the small drawers below.

TROIANI COLLECTION

SERGEANT OF LIGHT INFANTRY, NEW JERSEY OR NEW YORK LINE, SPRING–FALL 1782

In December 1780 a British supply fleet carrying clothing for five regiments then serving in the West Indies was captured by a combined Spanish-French fleet under Admiral Cordova. The captured British uniforms were "presented by the Courts of France and Spain to Congress" and shipped to Boston from Cadiz in April 1781, arriving that summer. Earlier in the war, captured red uniforms had been issued out to clothe ragged troops with only minor modifications, which led to mistaken identification—sometimes with disastrous results. Thus, it was decided that these captured uniforms would be dyed brown, after first "taking out the Lining." Afterward, the original linings, buttons, and facings were sewn back onto the coats.

During the winter of 1781–82, the brown coats were issued to the New Jersey, New York, and New Hampshire brigades (including the 10th Massachusetts Regiment) as "the only way of preserving a compleat uniformity in the three Brigades." It is known that an attempt was made to issue the brown coats to each brigade by similar facing colors, and those with green facings went to the New Jersey and New York brigades (deduced from distribution patterns of British regimental buttons excavated from 1782 Continental cantonment sites), including the uniforms originally destined for the British 55th Regiment of Foot. Despite being clothed in the unpopular brown coats, the Jersey and York regiments exceeded all others in their "Elegant Appearance," according to Col. Walter Stewart, inspector of the Northern Army. One French officer who accompanied the Comte de Rochambeau when he reviewed the light infantry on September 22, 1782, noted that they were "dressed in brown coats with green revers and cuffs and white linen pantaloons tucked into black gaiters reaching to the calf."

WILLIAM RODEN COLLECTION

Continental Army Waistbelt Plate, 1780–83

When the French expeditionary force under Rochambeau sailed for North America, it brought the swords, accoutrements, and military trimmings that the Marquis de Lafayette had purchased in France as gifts for the officers and noncommissioned officers of his new command. This command, as he had hoped, turned out to be the Light Infantry Division of the Continental Army. In September the promised gifts arrived. Each noncommissioned officer received, in addition to trimmings for his cap, a short saber complete with scabbard and belt. The French-made saber had a branch on which an interlocked "USA" was engraved, signifying the United States of America. It was carried on a buff leather waistbelt that had a cast brass buckle or belt plate, bearing a similar motif.

The plates are of an open oval form, in which is set a cartouche or rondel bearing "USA" surrounded by a raised rim. Cast in one piece, with two bars set on the back for fastening to belting, it is a form typical of French accoutrement plates of the 1780s and 1790s. Three complete examples, as well as fragments of several others, have been excavated from several post-1780 Continental Army sites in the Hudson Valley, some of which were occupied by Lafayette's light troops.

TROIANI COLLECTION

The Last Shot

Capt. Phineas Meigs, a seventy-four-year-old militia officer who was killed while skirmishing against an attempted British coastal raid on Madison, Connecticut, May 15, 1782, wore this felt round hat. His hat, bearing the hole from his fatal head wound, was recovered from the battlefield and retained by his daughters until donated to the Connecticut Historical Society in 1850. A popular and practical hat form during the eighteenth century, this hat is the only known example to have survived from the Revolutionary War.

CONNECTICUT HISTORICAL SOCIETY MUSEUM, HARTFORD, CONNECTICUT, PHOTOGRAPH BY DON TROIANI

This sergeant is dressed in such a manner, wearing a dyed light infantry sergeant's jacket with the original green facings of the 55th reattached, with the buttons still placed as originally arranged in pairs. The narrow buttonholes and edgings are of white worsted lace, as worn on sergeants' coats in British infantry regiments. His light infantry cap is a form established by long usage in the Continental "Corps of Light Infantry," created by cutting down a felt cap and trimming it with a hair crest and front plate. It is further embellished with lace binding and tassels of silver, along with the characteristic red-over-black plume of the light infantry—all gifts of the Marquis de Lafayette to the noncommissioned officers of his Light Infantry Division in August 1780. His rank as a sergeant is further distinguished by two white worsted epaulettes worn over his wings. Another mark of the Marquis's pride in his light infantry is the French-made, short saber, with scabbard and belt, presented to each sergeant in the corps and bearing an intertwined "USA" engraved on the side branch of the sword guard, with a similar motif cast into the waistbelt plate.

Baron Steuben's Liquor Chest

Most field officers transported a liquor chest with their personal baggage for daily use and entertaining. Friedrich Wilhelm Augustus von Steuben, known as "Baron Steuben," the Inspector General of the Continental Army, was no exception. Von Steuben loved to entertain, and his lavish hospitality and generosity to other officers left him perpetually in debt. His set of gold leaf-embellished bottles and drinking glasses is stoutly housed in a heavy green painted wooden case for the rigors of travel. He was an invaluable asset to Washington and the American cause, instituting a simplified and standardized order and discipline that were codified in his famous "Blue Book," which remained in use by the troops of the United States for more than thirty years.

FRAUNCES TAVERN ® MUSEUM, SONS OF THE REVOLUTION IN THE STATE OF NEW YORK, PHOTOGRAPH BY DON TROIANI

Discharge

Following news of a preliminary treaty of peace in March 1783, Congress authorized conditional discharges for virtually the entirety of the Continental Army. The required certificates were printed at a newspaper printshop in Fishkill and then delivered to General Washington's headquarters in Newburgh. Instead of using a typical pre-printed signature, the commander insisted upon individually signing the more than 8,000 copies needed. When issued his certificate of discharge at New Windsor Cantonment on June 10, Cpl. Lemuel Smith of the 2nd Massachusetts was one of the very few Continentals who had actually served longer than had Washington, a remarkable eight years and one month of repeated enlistments "for the war." Here, indeed, was a veteran of the Revolution.

BY HIS EXCELLENCY
GEORGE WASHINGTON, ESQ;
General and Commander in Chief of the Forces of the
United States of America.

THESE are to CERTIFY that the Bearer hereof Lemuel Smith, Corporal in the Second Massachusetts Regiment, having faithfully ſerved the United States eight years and one month — and being inliſted for the War only, is hereby DISCHARGED from the American Army.

GIVEN at HEAD-QUARTERS the tenth day of June 1783. —

G Washington

By His EXCELLENCY'S
Command,

J Trumbull Jun Sy

REGISTERED in the Books
of the Regiment,

William Torrey Adjutant.

BOB MCDONALD COLLECTION